MULTICULTURAL ASPECTS OF HUMAN BEHAVIOR

ABOUT THE AUTHOR

Willie V. Bryan is Professor Emeritus, Health promotion Sciences, University of Oklahoma, Health Sciences Center. Dr. Bryan was an administrator and professor at the Health Sciences Center for 32 years. In 1985, he received the President's Committee on Employment of the Handicapped Book Award for Psychosocial Aspects of Disabilities, which he co-authored. Before his services at the University of Oklahoma Health Sciences Center he served as a Vocational Rehabilitation Counselor for the state of Oklahoma, and also served as Director of Rehabilitation and Personnel for Goodwill Industries of Oklahoma City. Dr. Bryan has a Master's degree in psychology, emphasis on rehabilitation counseling, another master's degree in education and a doctorate in counseling. He currently is teaching courses on cultural diversity, helping relationships, family counseling and counseling approaches for the Colleges of Liberal Studies and Advanced Programs, University of Oklahoma, Norman Campus.

Third Edition

MULTICULTURAL ASPECTS OF HUMAN BEHAVIOR

A Guide to Understanding Human Cultural Development

By

WILLIE V. BRYAN, ED.D.

C H A R L E S C T H O M A S • PUBLISHER, LTD.
Springfield • Illinois • U.S.A.

Published and Distributed Throughout the World by

CHARLES C THOMAS • PUBLISHER, LTD.
2600 South First Street
Springfield, Illinois 62704

© 2014 by CHARLES C THOMAS • PUBLISHER, LTD.

ISBN 978-0-398-08790-6 (paper)
ISBN 978-0-398-08791-3 (ebook)

First Edition, 1999
Second Edition, 2007
Third Edition, 2014

Library of Congress Catalog Card Number: 2013045956

Printed in the United States of America
MM-R-3

Library of Congress Cataloging-in-Publication Data

Bryan, Willie V.
    [Multicultural aspects of disabilities.]
    Multicultural aspects of human behavior : a guide to understanding
human cultural development / by Willie V. Bryan, Ed.D. -- Third edition.
    Revised edition of the author's Multicultural aspects of disabilities,
2nd ed.
        pages cm
    Includes bibliographical references and index.
    ISBN 978-0-398-08790-6 (pbk.) -- ISBN 978-0-398-08791-3 (ebook)
    1. Minority people with disabilities–Services for–United States. 2.
Minority people with disabilities–Rehabilitation–United States. 3.
Social work with minorities–United States. 4. Social work with people
with disabilities–United States. 5. Multiculturalism–United States. I.
Title.

    HV1569.3.M55B79 2014
    362.4089'00973–dc23

                                                        2013045956

This edition is dedicated to my grandchildren:
Donnita, Joseph, Jayden and Kilah, they are my future.

ABOUT THE THIRD EDITION

This third edition has a title modification, in that the previous two editions were titled *Multicultural Aspects of Disabilities: A Guide to Understanding and Assisting Minorities in the Rehabilitation Process.* This edition is titled *Multicultural Aspects of Human Behavior: A Guide to Understanding Human Cultural Development.* A reason for the title modification is I want to expand and emphasize cultural impacts with regard to human behavior and in doing so my goal has been to identify factors which impact cultural development and cultural perceptions of various groups of people such as persons with disabilities, ethnic/racial minorities, women and the elderly.

In several ways this third edition continues the theme of the first and second editions by providing information with regard to factors that impact the lives of racial/ethnic minorities, persons with disabilities, women and the elderly in America. The information provides information with regard to how culture is defined as well as some factors which help define various impacts on how culture is developed and how culture impacts our daily life activities. Additionally, this edition provides some historical information which has served as a basis for some cultural changes in the United States of America; I refer to this as cultural evolution.

The updates and addition of new chapters will make the text a more complete discussion of cultural information needed by professional helper as they work with their clients and patients.

PREFACE

The often used phrase "the world is getting smaller" is very accurate, not because the earth is getting smaller; however, because of the explosion of technology which provides those that can afford and have access to same, to see, hear and learn about people in distant lands. This access of people about which we have in the past known very little has given us opportunities to expand our knowledge of distant lands, different points of view as well as different beliefs and ways of conducting daily life activities. This access in very simple terminology has given us an opportunity to learn about a variety of cultures that may be foreign to us. What we do with this knowledge will, to a large extent, determine how we as individuals progress mentally, emotionally and humanely. Additionally, as a group of people, from a nationalistically point of view how we react to different points of view will be a significant factor in how we progress or not progress as a nation. Stated in more succinct terms cultural diversity has always existed and today many of us are privileged to have the opportunity to observe and learn about a vast number of diversities that exist. The question is what will we do with this increased knowledge of cultural diversity? Will we value diversity and use this diversity to be inclusive and help build a more humane and tolerant world or will we philosophically bury our heads in sand and preach that our ways of thinking and living is the best and everyone else should conform to our ways of living?

There is ample evidence extracted from throughout the world to point out the fact that cultural diversity has not always been valued. South Africa and its system of apartheid; Australia's treatment of aboriginals; Rwanda, and even the United States' past treatment of some ethnic and racial minorities are only a few examples of devaluing cultural differences. Perhaps, as a human race, we will never completely divest ourselves of prejudice, and hatred but as intelligent beings we have the capabilities of acceptance and tolerance.

W.V.B.

CONTENTS

MULTICULTURAL ASPECTS
OF HUMAN BEHAVIOR

Chapter 1

CULTURE

Chapter Outline
• Introduction
• What is culture?
• Additional evaluation of culture
• Culture or cultures
• The nature of culture
• Disability culture
• Understanding cultural diversity
• Multiculturalism
• Cultural accommodation
• Acculturation
• Conclusion

Introduction

For something that is all around us and for something that is part of us, culture is difficult to define and explain. Perhaps part of the difficulty in explaining culture is the fact there are many dimensions of culture. To the artist culture is in the eyes of the beholder. To be more specific, each person looking at a piece of art will see different things and have a different prospective of what is being displayed and the value of what is displayed. Similarly, with regard to music, the public and music critics as well as musicians themselves also have a variety of opinions with regard to various types of music and its value to the overall culture of music. Behavioral scientist view human behavior and attempt to determine what is influencing the behavior so that appropriate actions can be prescribed and/or taken to modify the behavior, that said behavior is congruent and acceptable to the situation or situations one is encountering.

Culture impacts everyone's lives by influencing how we perceive events that impact us and how we perceive those around us. With regard to how culture impacts our perceptions of others; the values we apply to our fellow human beings are directly related to our views of the person's worth to the societies we consider as being valuable to us. Our prejudices and how we act out those prejudices are directly related to our learned cultural views. Likewise our views of esteem for our friends and others are also directly related to our learned cultural views. Culture is not something with which we are born, thus we humans create culture. As discussed in this chapter, culture is not inherited but is developed through a socialization process; therefore the premise that by classifying persons into ethnic, racial, religious and occupational groups and declaring that they have the same culture, thus we can explain their existence is not only false also this belief is denying the depths of one's human existence. From a behavioral science point of view there are several facts about culture that makes the previously mentioned beliefs of culture untrue. One, **culture is influenced by proximity**; stated in other terms, factors such as where and how we are reared has a major impact upon our cultural development. Two, **culture is not solely determined by ones race and ethnicity**. There can be no question that one's race and ethnicity has a significant influence upon one's cultural development; however they are only two of many factors influencing one's culture. Regardless of ethnicity or racial background, the local social and environmental atmosphere will have an influence on the person's cultural development. This is not to say that racial or ethnic factors do not impact one's cultural development. However what is being stated is that the local culture, in which the person is involved, will have a profound impact upon one's cultural development. Offered as an example is the fact that native New Yorkers, who are African American, have similar mannerism such as speech patterns, as well as some beliefs and attitudes, as native New Yorkers who are Caucasians. Whereas, African Americans in the southwestern part of the United States have similar speech patterns and some attitudes similar to their Caucasian counterparts in the southwest and these cultural differences often are strikingly different than African Americans in the northeast part of the United States. If a person moves, he takes with him many aspects of his current culture; however over time, being influenced by the new cultural environment, he will gradually adopt the new prevailing culture. Thus **culture is mobile**; to be more specific, when we move around and experience new and different things not only do we carry with us cultural components we have obtained through our various contacts and experiences we also add to our cultural repertoire.

In this chapter I will elaborate on culture from a behavioral scientist's standpoint and explain from that standpoint the composition of culture.

Additionally, I will discuss both positive and negative factors which will impact our cultural development.

What Is Culture?

The collective wisdom of anthropologists and others who attempt to explain human behavior and existence have failed to produce a clear-cut definition of culture. In all probability, because of the very subjective nature of what we consider as culture, a definition which is universally accepted will continue to elude its seekers. A comparison of some accepted cultural definitions tends to verify this point. Some behavioral scientist identify culture in the context of being part of the environment which we humans have made and states that it includes our artifacts as well as laws, myths, and the special ways we view our environment. Others who attempt to capture the essence of culture consider it as the things that various people share in common such as religion, language, and economic status, to mention a few. Fairchild (1970) defines culture as all behavior patterns socially acquired and socially transmitted by means of symbols, including customs, techniques, beliefs, institutions, and material objects. In a somewhat different approach, Triandis (1972) does not attempt to define culture but indicates that it is in our heads. He further states that culture is absorbed by individuals in the process of socialization rather than actively taught and acquired.

These various definitions of culture appropriately illustrate that there are numerous variables contributing to the cultural makeup of an individual or group of individuals. Therefore, the primary lesson to extract from this failed exercise in defining culture is to never generalize about culture. It is very tempting to neatly categorize people into specific cultural groups, such as African American culture, American Indian culture, Hispanic/Latino American culture, Asian American culture, and identify characteristics that appear to be shared by members within each group and proclaim to the world that this constitutes the cultural composition of the group. However, despite that there may be some shared characteristics in cultural groups such as skin color, hair texture, and speech patterns, there are also as many, if not more variations within these groups as there are shared traits.

As always, definitions vary according to the definer's point of view. Let us analyze several other definitions to determine if some common view points can be found. Some social scientists defined culture as the "way of life" of a people, including the sum of their learned behavioral patterns, attitudes and collection of material things. Lee (1989) and Axelson (1993) state that culture is the collective reality of a group of people and remind us that it is from this collective reality that attitudes, behaviors and values are formed and become reinforced among a group of people over time. As previously stated, Fairchild (1970) defines culture as behavior patterns which are socially acquired and socially transmitted including customs, techniques, beliefs, institutions, and material objects. And Triandis (1972) argues that culture is in our heads and is composed of the shared experience and knowledge of a self-perpetuating and continuous human group and is part and parcel of our personal reality. His belief is that culture is learned through socialization rather than learned through an active teaching process.

Though these definitions vary, there are, however, some common points one can observe and they are: (1) Culture is a group orientation. Stated another way, culture is common behavior, beliefs, attitudes, and values shared by a group of people; (2) Culture is learned behavior, attitudes, beliefs, and values, not inherited; (3) Culture is learned via socialization rather than through a formal teaching process. Therefore, at the risk of breaking my rule of not generalizing, an operational definition that will be used in this book is as follows: Culture is commonly held characteristics such as attitudes, beliefs, values, customs and patterns of behavior possessed by a group of people, which have been learned and reinforced through a socialization process.

Additional Evaluation of Culture

As one gives casual thought to the topic of culture, we frequently associate culture with racial background. Decades of stereotyping have resulted in linking specific behavior to certain racial groups and this association has become so strong that in part the group as a whole is defined by these characteristics. The association of the behaviors to one's racial background is so interwoven that some regard the "cultural traits" as inherited. In other words, some people view culture and race as inseparable. Ashley Montagu (1997) contradicts this view by informing us that race and culture do not appear to be in any way connected. He further points out that culture is determined by one's experiences rather than anything innate; therefore, culture is the human-made part of the environment. Consequently, what we observe as a common characteristic of a group is a reflection of the similar experiences of its group members, and because these characteristics differ from our own we tend to categorize them as being unique unto that group.

As an example, one of the cultural traits often associated with African Americans is athletic ability. Because of the success that African Americans have experienced in professional athletics such as basketball, football, boxing, and baseball, some non-African Americans believe that African Americans are born with superior athletic abilities and/or they are better physically equipped to excel in athletic endeavors than other racial groups. The truth is instead of innate abilities, the prowess of African Americans in many athletic arenas can be attributed to their life experiences. Countless number of hours of athletic competition among friends and neighbors account for their athletic skills rather than a racial inheritance. Therefore, true to what Montagu postulated, it is one's experiences that determine culture.

Ironically, while Euro-Americans attribute numerous cultural traits to racial minority groups, it is the clustering (living in close proximity) of these racial groups which is stimulated by the dominant Euro-American society that causes similar beliefs, customs, ideas, and values of these minority groups. It is, therefore, quite understandable that a group of individuals who are experiencing similar things will develop similar beliefs, ideas, and other like ways of interacting with their environment. Thus culture must be evaluated with regard to the group's background. The following comment by Montagu (1997) adequately summarizes this point:

> Culture must be evaluated in relation to its own history, and carefully, not by the arbitrary standard of any single culture. Judged in relation to its own history, each culture is seen as the resultant of the responses to the challenges which that history may or may not record. If those challenges have been limited in nature, so will the culture reflecting their effects. If the challenges have been many and complex in character, then the culture will reflect that complexity.

Ashley Montagu's statements clearly indicate that the range and quality of experiences individuals encounter help determine the complexity of one's culture. While this is correct, however, the value which society places on this culture is often determined by the dominant culture. For example, if the dominant culture determines that aggressive behavior is desirable, but subordinate cultures are discouraged or not allowed to be aggressive, their cultural trait of meekness is devalued. If the dominant culture values productivity but places subordinate cultures in positions where their abilities to be productive is limited or the type of productive output of the subordinate cultures is devalued, again the subordinate cultures are placed in a disadvantaged situation. While it is true, that experiences determine the complexity of cultural development, another reality is that the dominant culture determines to a considerable degree the kinds of experiences one encounters. Further, the dominant culture determines the values to be placed upon these cultural traits. It is therefore the devaluing of their culture that minorities including persons with disabilities and other subordinate groups have experienced that causes negative human relations and human interaction.

Culture or Cultures

In previous discussion, reference has been made to inaccurate thoughts of race and culture as inseparable; similarly we tend to group individuals together and associate a particular culture to that group, i.e., Asian American culture, or African American culture. As we give deep and serious thought to the idea of culture, we begin to realize that there is no one culture that fits any group of people. Stated succinctly, there is no one African American culture, nor one American Indian culture. There are numerous cultures associated with any ethnic group. An African American reared in Harlem, New York, will have some experiences similar to an African American reared in rural Oklahoma; however, the two will have many different experiences which will mean their cultural backgrounds will be different. From a cultural standpoint, with the exception of some physical appearances such as skin pigmentation and hair texture, there may be more cultural similarities between the African American reared in rural Oklahoma and a Euro-American reared in rural Oklahoma than between the African American New York native and the African American Oklahoma Native. This is not intended to indicate that the two African Americans, although from different regions of America, will not experience similar acts of discrimination and oppression. This point emphasizes that as a helping professional, one cannot afford to fall into the trap of accepting the conventional view, that there are specific racial cultural characteristics that can be generalized to all members of that racial group.

EACH GROUP DEVELOPS ITS OWN CULTURE. Each individual is part of many cultures and if she intends to be accepted by those cultures, she incorporates many of that group's cultural values. If the group's values are contrary to the person's values, hopefully she removes herself from the group and associates with a group that has values, beliefs, and attitudes that are congruent with her cultural beliefs. Unfortunately, this does not always happen, in too many instances, to be accepted by the majority, some people compromise their standards.

EVERYONE HAS SOME DEGREE OF ETHNOCENTRISM. Ethnocentrism is the belief that one's culture is superior to all other cultures. At first glance, to some, this statement may seem absurd; however, as we give closer and deeper thought to what is being said the truth of this statement is revealed. As Americans, most of us, out of pride in our country and belief in our system of laws and government, think that the American culture is superior to other cultures. Harmful ethnocentrism occurs when a group is told they are better than other groups and this message is constantly reinforced through various forms of propaganda. For example, if the group with which one associates his cultural identity is constantly referred to as being gifted athletically and academically then over a period of time, one begins to believe the message. Pride in one's group is not bad; however, when we act upon our feelings of superiority, then our actions go beyond pride and become prejudice.

BECAUSE WE DECIDE TO IGNORE CULTURAL CONFLICT, THIS DOES NOT MAKE THE SAME DISAPPEAR. Avoidance and burying our heads in the sand does not solve many problems. Confronting and dealing with a problem is usually the best and most appropriate solution. Often conflict and tension are increased when confronting prejudice and bigotry; however, the alternative is usually worse, which is unfair and unjust treatment continues unchecked. In the case of disability discrimination when unproductive beliefs are held, such as persons with disabilities prefer charity rather than employment, if these and other similar beliefs are not challenged, not only does the discrimination continue, also the erroneous belief also continues to be held and perhaps grows stronger in that others adopt similar beliefs.

NO ONE KNOWS ALL THINGS ABOUT ALL CULTURES. In an age where most helping professionals are sincerely concerned about being non offensive to any person or group of people, much concern exists with regard to how much professionals should know about cultures other than their own. Unless a helping professional has a very limited practice, it is impossible to know about every aspect of a person's culture. Honesty is the key word in discussing cultural awareness. Being honest with one's self that one does not know and will not know all aspects of a client/patient's culture and being honest by explaining that he does not know but is willing and interested in learning is not only important but essential.

The Nature of Culture

Cultural Diversity

The often used phrase "the world is getting smaller" is very accurate, not because the earth is getting smaller; however, because of the explosion of technology which provides those that can afford and have access to same, to see, hear and learn about people in distant lands. This access of people about which we have in the past known very little has given us opportunities to expand our knowledge of distant lands, different points of view as well as different beliefs and ways of conducting daily life activities. This access in very simple terminology has given us an opportunity to learn about a variety of cultures that may be foreign to us. What we do with this knowledge will, to a large extent, determine how we as individuals progress mentally, emotionally and humanely. Additionally, as a group of people, from a nationalistically point of view how we react to different points of view will be a significant factor in how we progress or not progress as a nation. Stated in more succinct terms cultural diversity has always existed and today many of us are privileged to have the opportunity to observe and learn about a vast number of diversities that exist. The question is what will we do with this increased knowledge of cultural diversity? Will we value diversity and use this diversity to be inclusive and help build a more humane and tolerant world or will we, as an old saying goes, will we bury our heads in the sand and preach that our ways of thinking and living is the best and everyone else should conform to our ways of living?

There is ample evidence extracted from throughout the world to point out the fact that cultural diversity has not always been valued. South Africa and its system of apartheid; Australia's treatment of aboriginals; Rwanda's treatment of some of its people, and the United States past treatment of some ethnic and racial minorities are only a few examples of devaluing cultural differences. Perhaps, as a human race, we will never completely divest ourselves of prejudice, and hatred but as intelligent beings we have the capabilities of acceptance and tolerance.

As cruel as the following statement may seem, this author believes that all humans are born selfish; self-preservation is the first law of life. When we are born our primary concern is surviving or as the noted psychologist Sigmund Freud has stated a primary goal of humans is to decrease pain and increase pleasure. This self-preservation philosophy is understandable as an early life philosophy and perhaps is the beginning of the idea of self-first and lack of tolerance of other's points of view.

Are We Programmed to Dislike Diversity?

Is it human nature to want to associate with persons of similar beliefs, attitudes, and desires? The probable answer is yes. One experiences a comfort level when interacting with persons of like interests that does not naturally occur when first interacting with persons of differing interests and beliefs. When experiencing a person or persons who appear to be different from us with regard to speech patterns, dress, and mannerisms as well as many other personal differences we tend to avoid contact with them. In this effort to distance ourselves from those that we think are different we too often begin to look for other differences to justify not pursuing a better understanding of those whom we consider different and too often this leads to discrimination. The failure to develop a sense of curiosity with regard to learning about other views and ways of living which can and should lead to eventually accepting different patterns of living and behavior, as long as they are lawful, is the beginning of bigotry and prejudice.

Failure to be accepting of other ways of thinking, living and interacting is the major stumbling blocks to effective cultural diversity. Cultural diversity has always existed. Even in times which we may consider ancient there was some degree of diversity throughout the world. Even in tribes that lived in remote areas there were interactions, although quite often not friendly, with other tribes and the diversity often came in the form of capturing persons of other tribes and relegating them to slavery and in other instances marriage and/or cohabitation would occur. In not so distance past, more "civilized times," the previously mentioned form of diversity occurred with similar results-forced slavery and forced cohabitation. In more recent times the seed of diversity has been planted as a result of the need for industrial and economic progress. To be more specific, as countries and nations have developed economically two things have occurred which has aided diversity; one is the development and expansion of capitalism and two the need for cheap labor to lubricate the wheels of economic progress to support the expansion of capitalism. Stated in other terms, diversity has been aided by the need for "inexpensive" labor and on the other side of this coin, the inexpensive labors' desires and/or need for the resources to help develop a better life for themselves and their families.

Culture is part of every person's physical, mental and emotional composition, thus regardless of how and why persons become or became part of the population of any given society he and she brings with them the culture that they have acquired. Therein appears to be where some of the negative attitudes and hopefully many of the positive attitudes come into play when new persons become part of the established population. The belief of this author is that positive attributes of new comers far outweigh any negative attributes that may occur with the infusion of a new person or group of people into the established population. Therefore stated in positive terms, cultural diversity is good and essential for any society to progress and not become stagnant.

Diversity is Good and Essential

As humans we too often resist embracing diversity because we are resistant to change. Many times we become comfortable with the way things are and have been, thus we cling to the status quo. Fortunately, those that cling to this philosophy are in the minority and eventually have to face and abandon their fears and insecurities of change and become part of the rising tide of progress that accompany diversity. No matter the effort we put into resisting change, this natural force will occur. Change, no matter how much effort we put into resisting, occurs because this is a major way in which life makes progress. Change helps us avoid stagnation. Change is what keeps the human race from becoming obsolete. Life is an experiment, and in reality not all change produces positive and desirable results; however, in the grand picture of life, thus far, we have been able to correct many of our major mistakes, and others that have yet to be corrected remain a "work-in-progress." Offered as examples of work-in-progress are ethnic and racial discrimination, gender discrimination, discrimination of persons with disabilities and age discrimination are but a few that, in this author's opinion will eventually be corrected. The optimism that these and other cultural diversity issues will be corrected is born from the fact that a view of past history has shown we have overcome similar issues and with regard to the issues mentioned we as a society have made significant progress in removing the previously mentioned issues as areas of discrimination.

Diversity Promotes Intellectual Growth

Without intellectual growth from its human inhabitants the human society would digress and become stagnant. One of the things that have enabled humans to progress beyond the other earthly inhabitants is our intellectual abilities. Diversity within the human race has been the catalyst by which we have been able to come forth with significant inventions, intellectual ideas, humanitarian efforts, to mention only a few of the intellectual growth components of life. The positive impact of cultural diversity can be seen in the accomplishments of the following persons whose contributions have impacted in positive ways many people: George Washington Carver, Albert Einstein, Cesar Chavez, Mahatma Gandhi, Marie Tall Chief, Sacajawea, Helen Keller and Clara Barton, Martin Luther King Jr. and Confucius, to mention only a few.

Quite often new ideas and new ways of viewing problems and issues are put forward by persons from diverse backgrounds. Without diversity sometimes persons who have interacted together for considerable periods of time have difficulties in solving some problems and thinking of new ways of dealing with what appears to be difficult and/or unsolvable problems. As an old saying goes "sometimes a fresh set of eyes" is able to see what has been overlooked. This generally speaking occurs because the person or persons with the fresh set of eyes has different experiences and is not constricted by the norms with which the previous groups have been.

Disability Culture

The United States Congress, with the enactment of the Rehabilitation Act of 1973, the Americans With Disabilities Act of 1990, and the Rehabilitation Amendments of 1992, recognized persons with disabilities as a class of people who have been discriminated against similar to some racial minorities.

As previously stated, there is no one culture for any group, i.e., American Indian Culture, African American Culture, or Asian American culture. Likewise, there is no one culture of persons with disabilities. The fact is there are numerous cultures for each group. In fact, each individual belongs to many cultures, rural, southern culture, African American southern culture, African American person with a disability culture, and African American female person with a disability culture, deaf culture and the list could continue.

Each individual moves in and out of various group cultures. When one physically moves from one part of the United States to another, she probably moves into another cultural group and may or may not maintain membership in previous cultural groups. The point of this brief discussion with regard to the sometimes transient nature of culture is to explode the myth that there is a universal culture for African Americans, Asian Americans, American Indians, Hispanic/Latino Americans, and yes, persons with disabilities. There are African American cultures and Native American cultures, etc.

Despite the reality that there are multiple cultures for each group, the perception remains that there is a universal culture particularly with respect to racial minority groups. Consequently, a set of characteristics are ascribed to the group and all that belong to the group are generally considered to possess these characteristics. In some instances, these characteristics are positive, but in most cases they represent a less than complimentary opinion of the group. Regardless of whether they are positive or negative, applied universally, they are a gross misrepresentation of a group of people. Because these characteristics often become the benchmark by which individuals within that group are judged, they create obstacles of stereotypes and prejudice through which the individual is unable to navigate and set himself free.

Tainter (1995) identifies what he considers cultural experiences of persons with disabilities which fit the universally-applied characteristics category. One cultural experience is the view of persons with disabilities as "damaged goods." Tainter points out that to overcome this image, the person feels he must strive to get rid of the differences. Perhaps this impact explains why some persons with disabilities deny their disability and engage in unwise behavior, attempting to be "normal." Another common cultural experience of persons with disabilities which is shared with racial minority groups is the belief that people within these groups who succeed are extraordinary. As Tainter reminds us, this is a patronizing concept which implies if persons with disabilities try hard enough they can succeed. Henderson and Bryan (1997) add to the list of universally-held common cultural experiences by identifying the following common perceptions of persons with disabilities:

people with disabilities are inferior, are less intelligent, totally impaired, dependent and need charity, and prefer the company of others with disabilities.

Persons with disabilities who are members of a racial minority group also have the added cultural experience of their minority group. In universally-held cultural misperceptions, the person can be placed in a situation of double jeopardy in that he must navigate his way through the mazes of misconceptions of both cultural groups. Because of the misconceptions of cultural experiences of racial minority persons with disabilities and the peril at which they are often placed because of this inaccurate understanding, there is a tremendous need for more study and better understanding of the cultures of racial minorities and persons with disability and the impact of the intersection of the two cultures, especially by those who are helping professionals.

Understanding Cultural Diversity

In expressing his influential opinion with regard to how the newly formed government's education system should be developed, Thomas Jefferson emphasized the point that persons should be educated to manners, morals and habits that were congruent with those of the country. The manners, morals and habits to which President Jefferson referred were Euro-American cultural values which had been established as the dominant cultural views of the new nation. This point of view coupled with the melting pot theory, which promoted the blending of all cultures in the United States into one culture, a unique American culture, entrenched the idea that Euro-American lifestyles, morals, values, attitudes, and beliefs were the standards by which all Americans should both live and be judged. To restate a previous point, there always have been and probably always will be a "dominant" culture. This is a reality of life; however, the extent to which other groups' cultures are subordinated and the negative or positive evaluations the group members experience as a result of being judged by the dominant culture's standards determines the impact the dominant culture has upon subordinate cultures.

For decades Euro-American culture has been the dominant culture in America and has had a major influence on virtually every aspect of life including how helping professionals interact with their clients. Recently, helping professionals have begun to question the appropriateness of using one standard to evaluate diverse groups of people who have many life experiences which are considerably different than the dominant cultural standards. Helping professional educators have begun to review their training standards and ask some probing questions about the validity of teaching and training counselors, social workers, rehabilitation counselors, psychologists, psychotherapists, and other helping professionals to evaluate all of their clients and patients with one measuring stick, especially the evaluation of racial minority and persons with disability group members. Both the helping professional educators and the helping professionals themselves have begun to review past as well as present experiences of not taking appropriate consideration of their client's/patient's own cultural background in the helping process. They have begun to question whether the fact that over 50 percent of racial minority persons do not return for counseling after the first session may be attributed in part to the helping professional demonstrating a lack of understanding of the person's cultural standards. Likewise, the low percentage of minority clients/patients following through with treatment plans is also added to the list of things to consider with regard to inadequate understanding of diverse cultures.

The "assumption of universality" is how Keisier (1966) refers to the belief that helping professional practices formulated on the basis of Euro-American cultural standards could be applied uniformly to all clients. Keisier and a growing number of authors (Bryan, 1996; Henderson and Bryan, 1997; Ridley, 1995; Sue, 1990; Atkinson, Morton and Sue, 1993) have taken exception to this approach which has been widely used in the helping professions. These authors as well as others argue that most traditional theories and practices are biased in favor of white middle-class males. Concurrent with this opposition, numerous books, articles, monographs, and results of proceedings have been published with the expressed purpose of sensitizing helping professionals to the cultural diversity within their client/patient population. Additional discussion of these and other relevant points are put forth in the chapters which discuss ethnic minorities, women and the elderly.

Multiculturalism

At first glance, the term "multiculturalism" appears to be a safe and non-offensive word meaning many cultures. Proponents of multiculturalism view it as a concept of giving recognition to the viewpoints of all cultures which contribute to American society. They further think of multiculturalism as understanding, giving value to and accepting the contribution made by the various cultural groups in America. The concept of many cultures tends to be in conflict with the idea of the melting pot theory which promotes the idea of one culture made from many cultures. The multiculturalists' view the idea of promoting a one-culture or blending various cultures in one "American Culture" as being detrimental to the cultures being blended. In fact, the multicultural view is that it is not a blending but a forced acculturation into the dominant culture. In other words, it is not a melding of cultures into a unique culture which fairly and accurately represents all cultures (if this is possible) but an acceptance of the dominant culture's viewpoint, thus relegating other cultures to a position of lesser importance. The multiculturalists do not necessarily fault the dominant culture's values as being evil or wrong, but find fault that the views, attitudes, and ideas of the dominant culture have become the benchmark for American society and oppose the degree to which attempts are made to impose its will and standards upon the subordinate cultures. From the multiculturalist's viewpoint, too often in an attempt to impose its will, the dominant culture degrades the subordinate cultures for not "attaining" the standards of the dominant culture. In the view of multiculturalists, many, if not most, of the dominant culture's standards are good but not exclusive.

In America, Euro-Americans are the dominant culture and there are some specific characteristics and standards that are highly respected by this group which serve as the benchmark by which other groups tend to be judged. A brief review of four of these characteristics illustrates the absence of a multicultural approach:

1. *Individualism*–Many Euro-Americans value independence. From elementary schooling through high school, rugged individualism is emphasized. The pioneering efforts of early Euro-American settlers are romanticized in textbooks, television, movies, etc. This results in early identification with the idea that independence is valued and dependency is less valued. This sends the message that every individual should be as independent and self-reliant as possible and individualism is more important than a group. If one is reared and educated to believe in this philosophy it is difficult to find any fault with this belief; however, from the viewpoint of those who subscribe to multiculturalism, the idea that the individual is more important than the group and independence is valued more than a collective effort does not provide sufficient value to some Asian or Pacific American cultures which emphasize sublimating individual efforts for the good of the group. Perhaps not to the extent some Asian and Pacific Americans emphasize group efforts over individual ventures, some America Indian tribes view the tribal agenda as more important than individual achievement. There has been negative impact on persons with disabilities with regard to the emphasis placed upon independence and individualism, particularly those persons by virtue of their disability having a need for assistance. The multiculturalist would propose that the devaluing of dependency may cause some persons with disabilities as well as others to feel inadequate and be treated in a like manner.

2. *Achievement*–Within America's dominant culture, individual achievement is equated with success and in an economically-based society, success

is equated with the accumulation of goods and property. The idea of achievement, from the multiculturalist standpoint, is not wrong. America would not be and could not continue to be a world leader if it did not value achievements. The multiculturalist may take issue with overwhelming emphasis on accumulation of material goods. This emphasis does not allow room for valuing those cultures which deemphasize the collection of individual wealth. The implication for some persons relates to the emphasis on individual achievement and more important is how success is determined. Using persons with disabilities as an example, both individual achievement and accumulation of goods are difficult.

3. *Verbal Expression*–Euro-Americans place more value on verbal communication than interpreting nonverbal communication; therefore, those individuals who can eloquently express themselves verbally are perceived to be more intelligent than the shy quiet person. Multiculturalists would remind us that some Asian and Pacific American cultures and American Indian cultures place considerable value upon silence and/or nonverbal communication.

4. *Nuclear Family Structure*–The nuclear family is considered to be the father, mother, and unmarried children. The influence and contributions of relatives and close friends are minimized. Children within the nuclear family concept are considered equal to the parents, in that their ideas and expressions are to be given as much consideration as adults. As will be discussed in other chapters of this book, the extended family which encourages the input of other relatives such as grandparents, uncles, aunts, and cousins is an integral part of some minority cultures.

These are a few of the cultural values many Euro-Americans hold in high esteem and by which subordinate cultures are judged. Those who subscribe to multiculturalism would argue that all of these values are good as well as beneficial in some settings; however, they would remind us that their objections revolve around the idea that there are other viewpoints which exist and when appropriate, need to be given equal consideration instead of being sublimated to the dominant culture's points of view.

Opponents of multiculturalism view the concept as a part of Affirmative Action and they further view it as a way of condoning preferential treatment for minority groups. Those opposed to multiculturalism make reference to the areas of education and employment especially hiring priorities as examples of what they consider as its undesirable effects.

Opponents of multiculturalism appear not to have strong opposition to making the educational curriculum more culturally representative by including the accomplishments of various racial and ethnic groups in history texts. However, they have taken exception to making what they consider fundamental changes in curriculum such as was proposed in including Ebonics as a form of English. The strongest opposition in the area of education targets what they believe to be preferential admission of minority students. To be more specific, they contend that lesser academically qualified minority applicants are being admitted to colleges and universities than nonminority applicants. They further identify the practice of designating specific scholarships for racial minorities as further evidence of multiculturalism advocating preferential treatment. Therefore, from their perspective, multiculturalism is synonymous with discrimination.

Bradford Wilson, executive director of the National Association of Scholars (1998) articulates that group's opposition to Affirmative Action and multiculturalism with the following remarks:

> The focus on race-conscious affirmative action policies fit naturally into a discussion of multiculturalism because such policies substitute nonintellectual criteria—race and ethnicity—for intellectual criteria—standardized test scores, grades, and scholarships—in the way that multiculturalism uses group identify to justify curriculum upheaval and faculty hiring.

Part of what multiculturalism is concerned is the focus on racial and ethnic identity as the defining characteristic of an individual. Racial preferences or race conscious affirmative action policies are rooted in the idea that a person's race or ethnicity is sufficient reason to take them seriously or not take them seriously.

Some opponents of multiculturalism make the point that the proponents of this concept support it on the basis that it helps minorities overcome the effects of past discrimination; however, in their opinions, multiculturalism actually does more harm than good in the educational arena in that persons who are poorly prepared academically are admitted, thus experiencing failure and lowering of their self-esteem.

Similar arguments are presented as opponents attack the concept of multiculturalism with regard to employment. Those that support the multicultural concept point out that access to quality education and technological training which would prepare racial minorities and persons with disabilities for career status jobs have traditionally not been available; therefore, to require them to compete for jobs with those who have had access to appropriate education and training is ridiculous. The opponents counter with the argument that employers should not be forced to hire less qualified individuals. They suggest that an answer is to develop the needed training and make the training available to everyone.

The unanswered question in this debate revolves around "prejudice." If those that have been excluded are trained and brought to the knowledge level of those who have not been excluded, will employers hire minorities and persons with disabilities at the same rate they hire others or will past prejudices and preconceived stereotypes enter into and hamper the hiring decision? For those who contend that prejudice will be a factor in hiring decisions, they contend outside intervention will be required. Multicultural opponents counter by saying that in this scenario, any time a minority or person with a disability is not hired, the employer will be accused of being prejudiced.

Cultural Accommodation

What does "understanding diverse cultures" mean? With regard to the helping professions, does this mean developing a theory and practice for each of the racial minority groups as well as persons with disabilities, women, and the elderly? Do culturally sensitive helping techniques imply the opposite of the assumption of universality to which Keisier referred? These are valid and important questions. These and other relevant questions will be addressed in subsequent chapters.

Acculturation

Within a given society, of all the cultural groups which exist, in most cases one will become the dominant culture and as previously stated, many of that society's activities, belief systems, values, and standards are determined by the dominant culture. In an attempt to be accepted by and be considered part of the society, subordinate cultures attempt to emulate the dominant culture. This is a form of acculturation. Some social scientists say that acculturation, within the context of American society, refers to the degree to which an individual identifies with the attitudes, lifestyles, and values of the predominant culture. In American society, there are numerous dominant cultural characteristics and the extent to which individuals and groups of individuals deviate from those characteristics and standards determine how much they are devalued. Likewise, the closer they mimic and/or incorporate them in their lifestyles, the more they are valued. Many of Euro-American cultural standards are so well woven into the fabric of American society that not only do members of the dominant culture accept them as the correct standards by which to live, but in many instances the subordinate culture also makes this same judgment. Unless carried to an extreme, there is, generally speaking, nothing wrong with Euro-American standards. The major problem in American society has been the extent to which the dominant culture has suppressed the subordinate cultures. The lack of consideration given to other points of view and ways of doing things as well as lifestyles is what has been questioned, not the right or wrong of Euro-American cultural standards. One might correctly observe and point out Chinese culture in China is dominant and serves as a benchmark by which societal standards are judged in that country. Also in some countries, societal standards are based upon a religious orientation and one religious sect dominates all other groups, religious and nonreligious oriented. Appropriate responses to these observations are: (1) The fact that one culture completely dominates another in any part of the world is no justification for such occurrences in other parts. This would be similar to justifying oppression by pointing to country X and saying that it has a high standard of living for the majority of its people despite a restrictive society. (2) America is composed of many different groups of people who have worked together to develop the country and society into a world leader; therefore, each cultural group should be valued. (3) The uniqueness and greatness of America has, to a large extent, been based upon the diversity of ideas. The freedom to think, dream, and work toward moving those dreams into realities has been a hallmark of American society. Therefore, one fact that has distinguished America from many other societies has been its diversity.

As diversity is considered in America, it is unfortunate but not surprising that persons with disabilities are often overlooked. Zawaiza (1995) feels that diverse, underserved and/or special populations are usually euphemisms for persons from minority groups. As a society, what we often fail to realize is that persons with disabilities are the most diverse group of people in America, both numerically and in composition. First, they are the largest minority group, and second, they are composed of every segment of American society, represented by all age groups, all racial groups, both genders, and all economic strata. Few groups in America can claim this level of diversity. Despite the diversity, persons with disabilities are too often viewed as one-dimensional. For example, in the helping relationship, the professional helper will too frequently consider only the person's disability or her racial background. When more than one factor is considered, it most often is gender and racial background rather than gender, race, and disability.

The following comments by Tainter, Compisi, and Richards (1995) provide insight into why persons with disabilities must be considered as an integral part of the diversity of America.

Developing strategies to include people with disabilities in our communities, including the workplace, this is a view that considers disability as part of the fabric of diversity. It must embrace the diversity of all persons with disabilities and consider as members of the disability community. This community in itself is a cultural group that has come to be identified as a civil rights minority group that requires the same strategies and remedies for inclusion as other minority groups. For persons with disabilities from ethnic minority back-grounds, we must acknowledge and respect all aspects of their diversity. Ig-noring any one aspect of a person's background, be it ethnicity, gender, or dis-ability does not benefit the person or the society as a whole. It is a view that asks for the presentation of persons with disabilities in a context of dignity and quality, not pity and patronization.

Davila (1995) recognizes that in the past, persons with disabilities have been viewed one-dimensionally and the result has been a disregard of the needs of this significant group of people. To avoid this deletion of needs in the future, Davila tells us that it is incumbent upon us to recognize persons with disabilities from all backgrounds to ensure that their concerns are placed on the national agenda, and that persons with disabilities receive their share of resources, moreover persons with disabilities must demand that they receive the skills and knowledge needed to succeed in life.

Many of the characteristics of the disability culture have negative conno-tation such as persons with disabilities are often considered inferior to the person without a disability. Persons with disabilities are often thought to be less intelligent. In some instances, persons with disabilities are considered docile and in other cases, they are considered aggressive. In the instances when they are thought of as aggressive, it is often associated with rebelling against one's condition or status in life, again a negative connotation to being a person with a disability. When these cultural characteristics and values are placed beside and compared to the following dominant culture's values of perfectionism, independence, aggressiveness, self-expressiveness, autonomy, self-determination, accumulation of goods, task-oriented, materialistic, achieve-ment, control, and competitiveness, one not only obtains a view of the level to which persons with disabilities must become acculturated as well as the difficulty they may experience in attaining these levels.

Conclusion

Cultural diversity in America is inevitable; cultural diversity in America is good and desirable, and because of cultural diversity many aspects of Ameri-can society will experience change. Other groups in addition to ethnic/racial minorities, women and the elderly have to be considered as integral parts of America's cultural composition and one of those is persons with disabilities. The group which we call persons with disabilities consist of every component of any diversity group in America, thus they are the most diversified group in the United States and the world. Another fact about cultural diversity is that persons with disabilities, including persons with disabilities from ethnic/ racial minority backgrounds as well as women and the elderly, are part of this diversity; thus a relevant question is, "What are some of the changes that will have to occur to accommodate persons with disabilities and what will be some of the effects of more and more persons with disabilities becoming part of the American mainstream?" Books are written on changes that will take place in the twenty-first century as a result of America becoming more diverse; therefore, this conclusion cannot adequately address the many changes. However, major changes must occur for all persons to feel welcome and as integral parts of the overall American society.

Review Questions

1. Why is defining culture difficult?
2. Do you believe there is a disability culture? Defend your position.
3. Explain what the "assumption of universality" means.
4. What does multiculturalism mean to you?
5. What does acculturation mean?
6. How would a person with a disability attempt to become acculturated?

Suggested Activities

1. Interview someone from a cultural background different from your own to learn about his/her customs, beliefs, rituals, etc.
2. Interview a person with a disability with the goal of determining how he/she feels with regard to being a person with a disability.
3. Research the concept of multiculturalism and identify both the pros and cons of the concept.
4. Contact your state's Vocational Rehabilitation Office to determine how many persons with disabilities reside in your state, and of them, how many are from racial/ethnic minority groups and how many are male and female.

References

Atkinson, D. R., Morton, G., & Sue, D. W. (Eds.). (1993). *Counseling American minorities: Cross cultural perspective* (4th ed.). Madison, WI: William C. Brown.

Axelson, J. A. (1993). *Counseling and development in a multicultural society* (2nd ed.). Pacific Grove, CA: Brooks/Cole.

Bryan, W. V. (2001). *In search of freedom* (2nd ed.). Springfield, IL: Charles C Thomas.

Davila, R. R. (1995). *Leadership for a new era. Disability and diversity: New leadership for a new era.* President's Committee on Employment of People With Disabilities, Jan., 24–27.

Fairchild, H. P. (Ed.). (1970). *Dictionary of sociology and related sciences.* Totowa, NJ: Rowan and Attanheid.

Henderson, G., & Bryan, W. V. (1984). *Psychosocial aspects of disability.* Springfield, IL: Charles C Thomas.

Keisier, D. (1966). Some myths of psychotherapy research and the search for a paradigm. *Psychological Bulletin, 65.*

Lee, C. C. (1989). Multicultural counseling: New directions for counseling professionals. *Virginia Counselors Journal, 17,* 3–8.

Montagu, A. (1997). *Man's most dangerous myth: The fallacy of race.* Walnut Creek, CA: Alta Mira.

Ridley, C. R. (1995). *Overcoming unintentional racism in counseling and therapy: A practitioner's guide to intentional intervention.* Thousand Oaks, CA: Sage.

Sue, D. W., & Sue, D. (1990). *Counseling the culturally different: Theory and practice* (2nd ed.). New York: John Wiley and Sons.

Tainter, B., Compisi, G., & Richards, C. (1995). Embracing cultural diversity in the rehabilitation system. *Disability and diversity: New leadership for a new era.* President's Committee on Employment of People with Disabilities, Jan., 28–32. Triandis, H. C. (1972). *The analysis of subjective culture.* New York: John Wiley. United States Bureau of the Census. (1990). Washington, DC.

Zawiza, T. W. (1995). Stand and deliver: Multiculturalism and special education reform in the early twenty-first century. President's committee on Employment of People With Disabilities and Howard University.

Suggested Readings

Betancourt, H., & López, S. R. (1993). The study of culture, ethnicity and race in American psychology. *American Psychologist,* June, 629–636.

Carkhuff, R. R. (1986). *The art of helping.* Amhurst, MA: Human Resource Development Press.

Carney, C. B., & Kahn, K. B. (1984). Building competencies for effective cross-cultural counseling: A developmental view. *The Counseling Psychologist, 12,* 111–119.

Davenport, D. S., & Yurich, J. M. (1991). Multicultural gender issues. *Journal of Counseling and Development, 70,* 64–71, September-October.

Jahoda, G. (1984). Do we need a concept of culture? *Journal of Cross Cultural Psychology, 15,* 139–151.

Thurer, S., & Rogers, E. S. (1984). The mental needs of physically disabled persons: Their perspectives. *Rehabilitation Psychology, 29,* 239–249.

Walker, S., Orange, C., & Rackley, R. (1993). A formidable challenge: The preparation of minority personnel. *Journal of Vocational Rehabilitation, 2*(1), 46–53.

Wilson, B. (1998). Seeing no evil. *Black Issues in Higher Education, 14*(23), 18–20, January.

Chapter 2

UNDERSTANDING HUMAN BEHAVIOR

Chapter Outline
• Introduction
• Understanding Self
• Tips for Increasing Cultural Sensitivity
• Psychological Theorists' Views
• Assessing Behavior
• Summary

Chapter Objectives
• Present Some Theorists' Views of Human Behavior
• Present a Method of Assessing Human Behavior

Introduction

In any helping profession which involves assisting humans to be successful one must develop basic understandings of human behavior. In this chapter we will approach this understanding by viewing our reactions with regard to acceptance and rejection of others and explain our behavior from the standpoint of some of the leading psychological theorist which represent psychoanalytical, person centered, Adlerian, gestalt, existential and behavioral. It is imperative that we understand our feelings, attitudes and behaviors with regard to cultures which represent different belief systems and attitudes other than our own. Positive personal and psychological growth will only occur when we develop an understanding of **our personal** beliefs, attitudes and reactions to persons who represent and express, through words and actions, different beliefs and actions than our own and beliefs and actions which are outside of our comfort zones. This does not mean that we have to totally accept those actions and viewpoints; however it does mean we should learn to develop an understanding that our way or ways are not the only way of

24

doing things and there are different ways of accomplishing goals which can help enrich our lives.

These and many other issues with regard to understanding human behavior will be addressed in this chapter. However, first we must understand ourselves with regard to our beliefs and attitudes which will come into play as we as helping professionals attempt to assess persons we are attempting to help.

Understanding Self

Understanding self in the context of this chapter is referring to things one should do to become culturally sensitive. The reader should notice that the author is not saying become totally culturally competent. Being culturally competent implies one is knowledgeable of the various cultures he encounters and competent to deal with various cultural issues that may arise. It is the author's opinion that no one can become totally culturally competent. There are too many aspects of culture for anyone to become competent in all aspects of culture. The best one can expect with regard to cultural competence is to become aware of one's own attitudes regarding various cultures which he/she encounters, either directly or indirectly, and try to ensure that the foundation of these attitudes is not prejudice, bigotry, myths, and irrational thinking. Given the variety and complexity of cultures, the helping professional striving to become culturally sensitive must be aware of the fact that he/she will eventually make mistakes in interacting with persons of different cultural persuasions. As long as they are honest mistakes not intended to be malicious, they should be treated as learning experiences, mistakes not to be repeated.

Personal Inventory

Unless we are specifically challenged to do so, rarely do we question our belief system. Questions such as what are some of my basic beliefs and what is the foundation of those beliefs are rarely confronted. Although this type of self-examination would help us to become more sensitive with regard to our interactions with others, it is understandable that this kind of self-soul searching does not occur on a routine basis. However, as a helping professional, this type of self-examination is essential, because one's views with regard to human nature influence how one interacts with clients/patients. The following exercise is designed to prompt the reader to examine his/her beliefs with regard to human nature. The reader is asked to write on a piece of paper his/her response to each question. Do not simply answer the question yes or no; defend your answer. The implications for the helping professionals are

(1) a better understanding of what the reader believes causes humans to react as they do and (2) an awareness of one's beliefs and how they affect interaction with others. The questions of this self-inventory to be addressed are:

- What is the nature of humans?
- Do individuals have innate drives to do good deeds?
- Are individuals evil and have to be guided toward appropriate behavior?
- Are humans selfish, primarily concerned with their own survival?
- Do individuals strive to create a balance in their lives (in this context balance means striving to be of benefit and comfort to others as well as striving for self-satisfaction)?
- What is your view of human development? (What has the greatest influence on human personality development?)
  1. Nature
  2. Nurture
  3. Combination
- What roles does past behavior play with regard to human personality development?
- Do past events affect present behavior?
- Do you believe that humans repress certain events and feelings associated with those events? If the answer is yes, how do these repressed feeling affect present and future behavior?
- What are the basic goals of humans?
  1. Survival
  2. Happiness
  3. Service to humanity
  4. Ecological balance (harmony between self and environment)
  5. Greed (accumulation of personal wealth)
  6. Spiritual
- In your opinion, what should the basic goals of humans be?
- Based upon your cultural background, what constitutes normal and socially acceptable human behavior?
- How is the previously mentioned normal and socially acceptable human behavior fostered?
- Based upon your cultural background, what constitutes abnormal or socially unacceptable human behavior?
- What are some of the reasons people develop unacceptable human behavior?
- In situations where the environment (prejudice, oppression, paternalism, etc.) contributes to abnormal and/or socially unacceptable behavior, what responsibility, if any, does the individual with the problem bear?

- How is behavior changed?
- What are some of the techniques you would use to aid in behavioral change?

Tips for Increasing Cultural Sensitivity

Accept Others as Equals

There has been considerable commentary on the destructive nature of ethnocentrism. As previously stated, there is nothing wrong with having pride in one's culture; however, problems arise when we view our cultures as being superior to others. When we view things that are different as being inferior and worthy of either elimination or not the same courtesy and considerations as our cultures, then we cross the line from being proud and patriotic to being bigots and suppressors of human rights. Mature individuals not only accept differences, they also celebrate the opportunities that accrue from learning about something new. Personal growth occurs when we open our minds and hearts to accepting and learning from new experiences. If we view new and different experiences from this view point, we will have accepted others and their differences as equal to our own cultures.

Expand Comfort Zones

Most people prefer to think of themselves as open-minded and recognize that, generally speaking, there are various points of view to virtually all issues. Despite their declaration of accepting differences, the real truth is that most people blanket themselves with beliefs, attitudes, and opinions which they rarely change; thus the aggregate of these personal views become their comfort zone. All humans have comfort zones and we rarely like to venture beyond them. When we are faced with new experiences, too often, we subconsciously view them as a threat to our emotional equilibrium and reject the differences, because to consider them presents the possibility of having to change or move beyond our comfort zone. To be culturally sensitive, one must learn to expand the comfort zone and take in new information, ideas, and ways of viewing life.

Recognize That There are Only a Few Absolute Truths

Change is the first law of the universe. To live means things are constantly changing. As the decades and millenniums pass, we gain new information about our surroundings and this information help explode long-held erroneous beliefs. At one time in human history, we accepted as absolute truth that the world was flat, and that the sun revolved around the earth. Even today we accept irrational views with regard to our fellow human beings as being absolute truths. Women are the weaker sex; certain minorities are evil, lazy, and dishonest; and persons with disabilities need protecting are only a few of these views. To be culturally sensitive, one has to recognize that stereotyping of individuals, and stereotyping of beliefs are some of the most debilitating things we can do to another human being. One must recognize that there are few absolute truths in this world. If one is religious, the fact that there is a God perhaps is the only absolute truth, and for those who do not believe in a supreme being, perhaps change is the only absolute truth.

In the helping profession, truth is an elusive concept. Truth in this context is not whether the client or patient is being honest; rather, it means what is right or correct. For an individual, there can be several truths. Likewise, what is good for one individual is not always correct for someone else with a similar cultural background. Some may say that this is stating the obvious, but is the obvious really being stated? Unfortunately, don't we tend to group people together, and based upon what is believed to be common characteristics, we treat them the same?

Next we will look at how some of the pioneering behavioral psychologists explain human behavior.

Theorists' Views

Sigmund Freud

As psychological theorist developed their therapies, one of the major components with which they engaged time and effort is to enunciate their understanding of human behavior. As have or will be stated several times in various chapters concepts of human behavior are critical to the development of a helping relationship therapy. It is almost impossible to assist a helpee with an effective helping plan without having some concepts of why the helpee behaves the way he does.

Psychological therapy and any other helping approach would be much simpler if there was one, or perhaps two, correct ways to view and understand human behavior. The reality is that there are many ways to view human behavior and many of the views have some degree of validity. Some of the varieties of viewing human behavior are evident in the concepts which some of the leading psychological therapist have used in developing their psychological approaches to helping.

Arguably, the most influential theorist of the twentieth and thus far in the twentieth first century is Sigmund Freud. The reason I contend he is the most influential is not because he is the most accurate, or the most popular psychological theorist, but because his views have influenced most modern psychological theories, therapies and helping professionals. In some cases other therapist and theorist have used various components of his theories and therapies to develop their therapies, while in other cases some therapist have disagreed significantly with Freud and developed their therapies in opposition to some of his precepts. Either way Freud, directly or indirectly have influenced most modern day therapies and helping approaches.

With regard to Freud and human behavior, in his development of psychoanalytical therapy, Freud contends that human behavior is predicated upon information that is stored in the subconscious mind. Freud contends that material that is stored in our unconscious memory influences our current behavior. Therefore, to understand current behavior one needs to have an understanding of what is stored away from our conscious memory and to have an understanding of why that information is not readily available to our immediate recall. Some may view human behavior in this context as predeterministic behavior; behavior that the person has little or no control over its release, since the person is reacting to information and feelings which have been stored away in the subconscious. The reality is that the person does have control. Perhaps the subconscious does have some control over the thoughts and feeling the person has; however the release of the energy, in the form of reaction, can be controlled by the person. By thinking before acting, the person can control and direct the release of energy. Assisting the client to think before acting can be a major goal of the helping professional in working with clients with regard to controlling behavior.

Freud seems to have been implying that the irrational forces, unconscious motivations, and biological and instinctual drives determine our behavior. Freud's concept of the unconscious influencing current behavior, from a psychoanalytical therapeutic standpoint, can be considered as holding the key to understanding problematic behavior. This understanding is developed because Freud discussed the fact that one of the reasons we store information in our subconscious is that the information is too troublesome to psychologically handle thus to protect our mental state we, in a sense, forget the action or significant portions of the action. Also in understanding Freud's concept of the unconscious one must remember the basic element of psychoanalytical theory is that as humans our basic instinct is to prevent pain and increase pleasure; therefore hurtful information or memories are relegated to the unconscious to avoid pain. Thus, from a psychoanalytical theory standpoint a goal with regard to assisting a client is to bring the unconscious to the conscious level so the client will understand why she behaves in certain ways.

An additional goal is to strengthen the client's ego so that her behavior coincides with reality.

A compact summary of psychoanalytical view of human behavior is: (1) human behavior is driven by instinctual urges; (2) the unconscious repressed material provides a major influence on current behavior; and (3) defense mechanisms are developed to compensate for the repressed material and to avoid psychological pain. Psychological and other theorists may disagree with Freud with regard to the importance of the unconscious; however, most do not disagree with the concept that the unconscious exist and does influence behavior. Therefore, a major contribution Sigmund Freud made to psychological theories and the understanding of behavior has been the fact that he has brought to awareness the fact that the unconscious exist and has an impact upon behavior. Where other psychological theorist disagrees with Freud is the extent that the professional helper should devote to working with the client regarding understanding information held in the unconscious.

Alfred Adler

In contrast to Freud's concentration on the unconscious as holding the key to why we behave the way we do, a former colleague of Freud, Alfred Adler developed his individual psychology or Adlerian therapy as almost the opposite of Freud's contentions. Adler did not believe that the professional helper had to concentrate on the unconscious to understand the motivation for human behavior. Adler contended that at an early age, around six years of age, we begin to think about what we would like to be in life. Adler says that we begin to develop a concept of our **ideal self**, and in this process we begin to realize that we are not where we should be with regard to being that ideal self. He called this feeling or realization a state of **inferiority**. In this case inferiority does not mean we are less than others, but we are not what we should be. It is at this point that we begin to work toward our ideal self and to use an Adlerian phrase trying to reach a state of **superiority**. Again the term superiority does not imply what we normally think when we hear the word, again in Adlerian terms it means being the best we can be.

As we begin to develop our long range life goals, to move from the state of inferiority toward the state of superiority, we begin to develop our patterns of behavior that leads toward these life goals. Therefore, based upon Adlerian theory, our behavior is predicated upon two things, our environment or social setting and our perception of that setting. Adler's theory views human behavior as having a linear progression moving from the previously mention state of inferiority toward a state of superiority. In this progression, all behavior should be considered from a social context. Adler believed that humans strive to be part of a social order, thus their behavior should be judged from the social environment within which the person is involved and the contribution or lack thereof that the person makes to that social environment.

Adler posits that behavior is influenced by events. He further promoted the idea that behavior occurs in a social context; therefore for the helper to more accurately understand a person's behavior the helper must become aware of the helpee's perception or phenomenological perspective. Adlerian theory concentrates on three areas of motivation: (1) people are motivated by their setting of goals, (2) people are motivated by the way they deal with the tasks they face in life, and (3) people are motivated by their social interests. Thus as a person makes positive contributions to his social environment the behavior is considered normal or appropriate. Conversely, negative contributions to the social environment means the behavior can be considered as not living to his potential of positively contributing to the society in which he lives.

Adlerian theory of human behavior differs significantly from the Freudian theory in that Adlerian theory promotes the idea that behavior is rooted in a conscious awareness as opposed to the Freudian view of behavior being unconsciously motivated. Adler believed that it is our present perceptions that form our reality and influence our behavior, not past experiences. As previously stated Adlerian theorists posits the idea that behavior is to be viewed in a social context. To be more specific they believe the individuals who express social interest usually focus their social inclinations toward positive and healthy activities. Socially active, mentally healthy people show an interest in activities that benefit society. Individuals who have poor mental health are more likely to be selfish and direct their interaction in ways that primarily benefit themselves. According to Adler, our success and happiness are directly correlated to social connectedness. Individuals who lack social connection are often discouraged and can lead unproductive lives. (Corey, 2005)

From the Adlerian prospective, to assist those clients who have lost their social connection, thus are in need of a psychological helping relationship, the professional helper must work with the client with regard to reeducating him back on a healthy and socially connected pathway. During reeducation, the helper will assist the client to better understand his ideal self; reeducating the client to his original goals. According to Corey (2005) and Bitter (2007) individuals with social interests strive towards healthy and socially useful aspects of life, whereas neurosis, psychosis and criminal behavior can be understood as a retreat from these tasks.

Carl Rogers

Person centered therapy which was developed by psychologist Carl Rogers has at least six basic concepts that he believed were central to human development and they are: (1) The client is fundamentally the center of his world. (2) Since a client is the center of his world his perception is reality and therefore to what the individual will react. (3) A client's behavioral goals are to meet her needs as she perceives them. (4) Portions of a client's perceptions are then incorporated into one's self. (5) One's perceptual field and interaction with the environment combine to develop the self. (6) Human beings behave in ways that are consistent with their personal concept of self.

Although Carl Rogers through his person centered therapy does not specifically address what constitutes normal or abnormal behavior, one can deduce from the basic philosophy of the theory some concepts of human behavior. Person centered therapy belongs to the humanistic school of psychological thought and as such believes in the growth potential of humans. Growth potential in this case means the ability to understand ones' life situation and within the appropriate setting can find appropriate solutions to ones' problems.

What does the previous information tell us about Carl Rogers' unspoken beliefs with regard to human behavior? One, we have the ability to recognize appropriate or correct behavior versus inappropriate behavior. Two, we are part of a social environment, thus we have the ability to understand the social norms of our environment. Three, while we may be the center of our own world we have the ability to recognize that we must interact in socially acceptable ways. Four, since we have the ability to recognize the previously mentioned social norms, we have the ability to correct maladaptive behavior and conform to prevailing societal standards.

One important concept of person centered therapy which relates to behavior is the idea that as humans we react to our perception of reality. This perception of reality is what helps determine our behavior in a given situation. However, unless the person has severely impaired cognitive abilities, she knows right from wrong, appropriate from inappropriate behavior; therefore one of the goals of person centered therapy is to assist the helpee by establishing a therapeutic environment conducive to correcting her perceptions.

A key to person centered therapy is that the professional helper does not have to tell the person what is the correct behavior or course of action, she, as previously stated, has the ability to find the right course of action. Again, the role of the professional helper is to help establish the right therapeutic environment for the client to correct her perceptions.

Fredrick (Fritz) Perls and Laura Perls

Gestalt therapy which was developed in the 1940s by Fredrick (Fritz) Perls and his wife Laura is also part of the humanistic school of psychotherapy. The Perls through their gestalt therapy differs from Sigmund Freud and psychoanalytical therapy in that it concentrates on the present rather than placing an emphasis on past events and the unconscious. It also differs from its fellow humanistic therapy stable mate Adlerian therapy from the standpoint of its emphasis on present behavior rather than the future which is a component of Adlerian therapy. Although Adlerian therapy can be interpreted as being both present and future oriented.

The key word in gestalt therapy is **awareness** of how one is feeling and perceiving events at that particular moment in time; therefore gestalt therapy is a present rather than past or future oriented therapy. Gestalt therapist emphasizes that understanding behavior in the present moment is key to understanding "why a person behaves as he does." Focusing on the past can be a way to avoid coming to terms with the present (Corey, 2005, P. 195). Although gestalt is present oriented some therapist recognize that past events or perceptions of past events do affect current perceptions and they call this **unfinished business**. Remaining true to the foundation philosophy of present orientation, the therapists assist the client in working through these feeling by having him concentrate on how this situation is making him feel in the here-and-now. Therefore, the helpee's phenomenological view point is critical to understanding motivation of human behavior.

Existential Theorists

There is not one person who developed existentialism; the philosophy of existentialism has existed since humans developed reasoning abilities. As will be discussed, the philosophy of existentialism is an integral part of many psychological therapies, particularly humanistic therapies.

Existentialism is a philosophy more than it is a therapy. The essence of existentialism is that as humans we are in a constant state of change and evolving; additionally we have the capability to have the ultimate control of our lives. The ultimate control of our lives is how we think about our self and our life situations. Existentialism teaches us that as human being we will have suffering in our lives; however, the important control is how we deal with life events; how we, within our mind, think about and handle these events. Existentialism teaches us not only about suffering but about all aspects of our lives and again how we think and react to whatever events, at least from a cerebral standpoint, determine our behavior. Thus this is our ultimate life control. Therefore, existentialisms contribution to our understanding of human behavior relates to our perception of events and how this perception impacts our life situation. Stated in other terms, as humans we have the ultimate control of our lives, which is how we perceive our life situations and this perception or feelings with regard to our situations determine our behavior. A paraphrasing of the ninetieth century European born philosopher Friedrich Nietzche may best illustrate existentialism and human behavior. "If one has the why to live he can withstand almost any how."

From a psychological therapeutic standpoint, existentialism is considered as part of the humanistic school. It is my opinion that humanism should be part of what should be considered the existentialism school. Stated another way, because existentialism philosophy is part of each humanistic therapy it appears that existentialism is the underpinning of these therapies; therefore instead of the humanistic school of psychological thought therapies such as Adlerian, person centered, gestalt, etc. they should be part of the existentialism psychological school of thought.

As previously stated no human being invented, founded, or constructed existentialism; it is, in my opinion, part of the human spirit. The philosophy of existentialism has existed ever since humans began to think about their worlds and their lives beyond self-preservation. For thousands of years humans have contemplated their existence and what their lives mean. Corey (2005) captures the essence of existentialism with the following words "being a person implies that we are discovering and making sense of our existence" (p. 136). The philosophy of existentialism can be found in the teaching of all major religions that promote peace, love, self-sacrifice and making choices.

Three basic principles characterize existentialism's view of human behavior: one, humans have choices; two, humans are responsible for their behavior; and three, humans have the freedom to change. There are two basic roles the helping professional should assume with regard to existentialism philosophy and human behavior when working with a client who is experiencing life situations and is seeking professional help; one, work with the client to help him understand where he is not living a fully authentic life and is not utilizing his options with regard to making appropriate life choices. Two, assist the client in taking responsibility for his behavior and not blaming other for his life situations. The professional helper may have to point out to the client that others may have contributed to his life situations and may have limited his choices; however, choices do remain and using those options may mean some hardship and/or suffering, however, that is part of life and he will be stronger for having taken control of his life.

Abraham Maslow

Doctor Maslow's humanistic approach to human motivation posits that human behavior is predicated upon satisfying needs. In this regard he put forth his famous hierarchy of needs, where he proposed that as humans we have certain needs which occur in a progression fashion that must be met. Stated in other terms, there are basic or lower level needs which must be met before higher level needs can be met; therefore, our behavior is based upon meeting the required needs. The needs and their levels of importance to humans are: the lowest and most basic needs that motivate human behavior are physiological needs: food and other life sustaining elements, shelter and at least minimum levels of comfort. The second level of needs according to Maslow's hierarchy of needs is safety and security needs. While this level appears to be a straight forward set of needs, one must also remember safety and security is relative to one's life situation and environment. The third level, love and belonging needs indicates that once levels one and two have been met our behavior is motivated by trying to seek the companionship of friends, coworkers and other acquaint as well as develop close and devoted relationships with family. Additionally, at this level our behavior seeks intimate and loving relationships with sweethearts. The fourth level is self-esteem needs, where our behavior motivation relates to receiving the respect of others and self-respect. The highest human need which impacts our behavior is self-actualization which means we are attempting to fulfill our human potentials. Other theorists have referred to this as meeting our fullest potential and being fully authentic.

Behavioral Theorists

The foundation for behavior therapy is classical conditioning and operant conditioning. Russian physiologist Ivan Pavlov is considered to be the first to demonstrate classical conditioning. Pavlov demonstrated when an unconditioned stimulus such as food produces an unconditioned response such as salivation and is associated with a conditioned stimulus such as the ring of a bell, if the paring is repeated often enough the conditioned stimulus will alone produce the unconditioned response. This established the relationship of stimulus and response (behavior).

B. F. Skinner expanded the knowledge of behavior with the concept of operant conditioning. Skinner postulated that behavior that is positively reinforced will be repeated; conversely, behavior, which is punished or ignored, will be eliminated. Skinner's contribution established the concept that the quality and/or type of reaction to the stimulus determine what will happen to the behavior.

Other behaviorists such as Arnold Lazarus, Albert Bandura, Albert Ellis, Aaron Beck and Joseph Wolpe as well as others have made significant contributions to the understanding of human behavior. Aaron Beck introduced principles of learning theory to behavioral therapy which has led to the development of cognitive behavior therapy. Albert Bandura also have made significant contributions to the concept of what affects human behavior as he also utilized principles of learning theory to help explain how behavior is changed. According to Gerald Corey (2005), Bandura posited that "behavior is influenced by stimulus events, by external reinforcement and by cognitive mediation experiences" (p. 230). Albert Ellis introduced the concept of human's irrational thinking as a major factor affecting how humans behave, thus creating rational emotive behavior therapy.

As one may observe, the original function of behaviorism (classical and operant conditioning) treated human behavior as significantly devoid of the influence of the process of thought (Bryan 2007). However, with the previously mentioned contributions, of introducing, cognition and learning theory to behavior therapy, human behavior therapy has shifted, now recognizing that we have the capability to impact our environment, which in turn will have significant impacts upon our behavior.

The Author's Views of Behavior

ALL BEHAVIOR HAS PURPOSE. To be an effective helping professional one has to become adept at observing and making assessments with regard to behavior of the helpee. Regardless of whether you believe that behavior is a result of attempts to satisfy instinctual urges, or the result of our ego attempting to control those instinctual urges, or perhaps some other view such as behavior is reacting to perceptions of social and/or environmental events, you have to recognize that all behavior has purpose. It is a necessary requirement that you develop a reasonable and logical understanding of the client's behavior. Alfred Adler in his theoretical foundation of individual psychology emphasized that behavior is purposeful, goal directed and conscious. Too often as helping professional we become aware of clients' behaviors and make judgments, such as the behavior is good or bad, appropriate, or inappropriate, rational or irrational. These types of judgments may be necessary; however, they do not answer the major questions that must be answered; what is motivating this behavior; why is this behavior occurring; what is the purpose of this behavior? Without reasonable answers to these and other questions with regard to the purpose of the behavior, the helper basically is groping in psychological darkness trying to understand the helpee and his life situation. Also without an understanding of the purpose of the behavior, many times the solutions that the helper and the helpee develops becomes at best a temporary solution, because without knowing the purpose of the behavior and more specifically which needs are being met by the behavior, the behavior and problems it creates will reoccur.

BEHAVIOR IS LEARNED. With the exception of the instinctual urges of an infant to meet primal survival needs, most other behavior is learned. Behavior is learned from significant others. In this case significant others mean more than family, and includes close friends and peers and persons for whom one has considerable respect. Significant others can mean persons with whom one does not have a relationship, but the person has acquired status that one would like to have. This status can be, from societal standpoint, either positive or negative. To be more specific, the status could be having considerable material possessions, such as occupational position, money, cars, clothing and jewelry that have been obtained through dubious and/or illegal means. The helpee may not admire the person, but have some admiration for his accomplishments and possessions; thus this person's behavior may serve as motivation for the helpee.

The professional should review the helpee's past to discover what the client learned, how the facts were learned, and under which conditions they were learned to understand what is considered, in his, the helpee's mind as acceptable and unacceptable behavior. Additionally the helper should determine what are the consequences or benefits of the behavior and finally the helper should determine which changes the helpee would like to occur with regard to the behavior.

HUMAN BEHAVIOR IS AFFECTED BY PERCEPTION. One of the most common beliefs of humanistic therapies is that our beliefs and attitudes of our surroundings affect the way we behave. Our perceptions are our realities. The fact that one's perception is inaccurate does not change the behavior what does impact change in the behavior is a new perception, hopefully a more accurate one. A significant concept of cognitive behavior therapy is that our thoughts impact our behavior; thus cognitive behavioral therapist help clients develop goals and work with the client to change perceptions; therefore changing behavior.

BEHAVIOR IS AFFECTED BY SOCIAL NORMS AND ENVIRONMENTAL FACTORS. All societies establish both formal and informal rules by which its inhabitants are expected to conform. Likewise, to be considered good citizens most people conform to the rules established by its society; therefore, their behaviors are influenced by these formally stated or implied rules of conduct. Some people however choose not to conform and their behavior is often judged to be abnormal or maladaptive. In some cases this is a correct and appropriate evaluation, but in some instances, societal rules are unfair and/or applied unequally, thus defiant behavior, while against societal standards is warranted. Regardless of compliance or noncompliance, the social norms and environmental factors, impact human behavior.

To be effective, the helping professional must be aware of the social norms and environmental factors that surround the helpee. Understanding social norms is more than having an understanding of the federal, state, and local laws. The understanding must extend to community and family standards. The helper must also develop and understanding of the client's perceptions of these various formal and informal standards of conducts and an understanding of the benefits and disadvantages of conformity or nonconformity.

BEHAVIOR IS A RELATIONSHIP BETWEEN COGNITIVE PROCESSES AND ENVIRONMENTAL FACTORS. Very similar to the discussion regarding behavior being affected by environmental factors and social norms, one's behavior is a response to how the individual conceptualizes his surroundings. This means that most behavior is not spontaneous and instinctual. Most behavior is a product of some thought, albeit sometimes hurried and perhaps irrational, being given to the rewards and possible punishment of the act. This also means that most behavior changes as a result of ones surroundings. To elaborate, most people will assess their immediate environment to determine the rewards or punishment of behavior within that environment; consequently, behavior is adjusted based upon the perceptions of the immediate environment.

As is indicated by the various views of theorists with regard to what motivates human behavior, there are a number of thoughts concerning what and how human behavior is motivated. It is imperative that the professional helper develop his/her theory of human behavior. Additionally, the professional helper must formulate ideas with regard to assessing behavior.

Assessing Behavior

An important part of understanding human behavior and effectively helping a helpee is to be able to make assessments of the person's motives, reactions, actions and feelings with regard to her life situations. The helper should not think that his initial assessment is chiseled in stone; the reality is that as the helper and helpee moves through the helping process and the helpee becomes more comfortable with the helper, new information is released by the helpee thus additional feelings of the helpee are revealed. Therefore, the initial assessment must be revised. Because the initial assessment may not be totally accurate should not be an inhibiting factor in making needed assessments. There are two types of assessment which must be made. One assessment is assessing the motivations for the current behavior. The second type of assessment relates to assessing the variables which are impacting the life situation(s) being encountered by the helpee, as well as resources which the helpee currently possess which can be used to help resolve the life situation(s).

With regard to assessing factors motivating behavior, the helper must determine the following: (1) what the helpee has learned with regard to consequences of his behavior; (2) what is normal behavior in the helpee's environment; and what is abnormal behavior in the helpee's environment and if the helpee is engaging in abnormal behavior, what is the basis for this behavior?

Assessing the helpee's concept of the consequences of his behavior, as previously stated, is very important because if the helpee has either been rewarded for his behavior or not received any significant negative consequences of the behavior there has been little to no incentives to change the behavior assuming the behavior is inappropriate. The knowledge obtained from this assessment will give the helpee a window into the mindset of the helpee. The helper's assessment of what is considered normal and abnormal behavior within the helpee's environment is critical. The helper will make a mistake of significant magnitude if he judges the helpee's perception of right and wrong, normal and abnormal behavior based upon his, the helper's standard. Even, making a judgment based upon prevailing societal standards is not sufficient to determine the helpee's perception of what is normal or abnormal within his personal life. The helpee may have been reared within a family, either nuclear or extended, which either promotes or condones some behavior which is in opposition of societal standards. Offered as examples, a helpee may have been reared in a family environment where excessive alcohol consumption and or use of illegal substances are accepted. The helpee will recognize that this type of behavior is not condoned by the general society; however this type behavior is both accepted and condoned within his immediate environment. Other scenario could be developed, however I think the point has been made.

With regard to assessing life situation variables some of the initial assessment items should be: (1) Identifying major issues facing the helpee. (2) Identifying any cultural, ethnic and/or racial issues impacting behavior. (3) Determining if there are any acculturation issues to be considered. (4) Identify family dynamics. (5) Identify the person and/or family crisis meeting resources. (6) And identify the person and/or family's definition of the issues.

Joseph Ponterotto and his associates (1995) with the following comments provide and appropriate summary of the importance of assessment. Although their comments are referencing the helping profession of counseling they can apply to many if not all helping professions.

Successful counseling requires an accurate assessment of the client's concerns, which includes an in-depth understanding of the factors that influence the client's experience, perception, and presentation of her or his problems. Furthermore, comprehensive assessment entails viewing the client as a unique individual, as a social unit within a family and as a member of a cultural group (p. 357).

Identifying Major Issues

When working with a client, as much as possible, the client should be the one that determines the life issues that he feels are the most relevant, at that time, and the ones which should be the first to receive attention. Although this is the ideal, the helper should develop ideas with regard to significant issues affecting the helpee's life. The issues developed from discussion and observation with the helpee should be used by the helper to help guide the helpee and his development of goals for the helping relationship

Identifying Cultural Factors

The helping professions have begun to recognize that racial, ethnic and gender issues can have a significant impact upon the behavior of clients. As discussed in Chapter 1, "Culture," client's cultures have a tremendous impact upon how they view their life situations. The client's perception of how fair or unfair society is to him and others, which he consider to be similar to himself, impacts his view of many aspects of his world. Clients who believe they are oppressed or have been oppressed, quite often will have a significantly different view of society than someone who has been privileged to have been dealt with fairly by society. Euro-American culture has been the dominant culture in America for several hundred years and its domination has been so encompassing that virtually all other cultures have either been suppressed, assimilated, or eliminated. Critics of the domination of Euro-American standards would argue that other cultures have had to conform to the Euro-American culture's standards or risk being significantly diminished. Euro-American culture has been the benchmark by which most everything in America is judged (Bryan, 2007, P. 28). To the extent cultural groups feel displaced from the mainstream society, their feelings of loyalty to the norms of the society may equally be displaced.

When one speaks of cultural diversity, often issues of discrimination of various groups become part of the discussion. Most of the time issues of racial and ethnic discrimination take center stage; however, women of all ethnic and racial groups arguably have been the recipient of discrimination as much if not more than some other ethnic and racial groups. Women clients may feel when they are being seen by a male helper, they are not going to be taken as seriously as a male client and that their issues are going to be minimized.

The United States of America attempts to keep political issues and government separate from religion and many religious issues. However, from a personal standpoint for those persons who participate in or adhere to some organized religion, their faith means a great deal to their ever day life. In fact for some their religious faith has more relevance to them than perhaps any other cultural component of their lives. Considering the importance that religious faith play in some client's lives the helping professional must develop an understanding of the impact that religion may have upon the client and his/her life issues. In fact the helper may find that the client's religious faith may serve as a valuable resource in resolution of some of the client's life issues.

Identifying Acculturation Issues

Related to ethnic/racial considerations is level of acculturation. This can be of particular concern when working with clients who were not born and reared in the United States or lived a significant number of their formative years in a foreign country. As previously stated everyone and their behavior to some extent are impacted by the environment in which they have lived. Customs, traditions, and belief systems supported by the social environment play a role in determining how clients behave. Persons coming from such environments relocating to the United States, generally have two major choices. One, they can isolate themselves with others that share the same or similar cultural traits, or they can immerse themselves into American ways of thinking and acting. With regard to the later, some immigrants choose to involve themselves into American ways of living and also attempt to maintain some of their original homeland cultural ways. When this occur the parts of American ways they adopt is called acculturation. Helping professionals working with immigrants must be aware of the level of acculturation of their clients. Important questions to be considered are: (1) what are the behavioral values the client(s) are holding onto from their original homeland? (2) How do these differ from the local social values? (3) How much of the local values do the client(s) understand and accept as appropriate behavior?

Helping professionals assisting families who are immigrants or some of its members are immigrants, must be cognizant of the fact that within the family there may be several levels of acculturations. Some immigrant families, based upon tradition and/or economic survival, may have several generations living within the same household. Therefore, there may be some in the family that are totally traditional home country with regard to their cultures; also within the same household may be members who have been exposed to both the original country's traditions and American ways of life. Additionally, some families will have a third level of acculturation of children that either were born or reared during their formative years in the United States. This type family can present unique situations for the professional helper. The helper must determine the various levels of acculturation that exist within the household; also he must determine if the various levels of acculturation are presenting any conflict with regard to the issue(s) being discussed and finally he must assist with solutions which firmly addresses the issue(s) and respects the other levels of acculturation.

Identifying Crisis Meeting Resources

Once we settle into routines we become comfortable with them and/ or accept them as part of our lives. Once these routines have become embedded into our daily existence too often we become reluctant to change. The point being made is that for most people change is difficult; therefore the fewer new things that the professional helper has to introduce into the person's life the less chance of rejection occurring. Given this fact the helper must work with the client to determine the resources she has to use in dealing with the life issue. In many instances, the old proverb that one cannot see the forest for the trees is appropriate when working with some clients. Helpees may become so engrossed in what they consider problems and this level of involvement too often creates in their minds feelings of hopelessness, consequently they may overlook possible solutions to the problems. Stated in other terms because of this feeling of being overwhelmed by the situation, clients often overlook resources with which they have to apply to the situation. Wise helpers will first look to the client for resources he has and encourage the client to use them.

Determining Definition of the Issue

The helper must determine how the client defines the problem(s). Does he view the problem as the worst thing that could have happened to him or does he view the problem as indeed a problem, but he has faced problems before and he will have to work at resolving these issues. Determining how the client defines the problem(s) will give the helper clues with regard to the frame of mind of the client and will also provide the helper with information about how to assist the client.

The helper must not fall into the trap of assuming how the client will react to a situation. Also the helper must not compare this client's situation with other similar situations and evaluate the current client's response to previous client's responses. There are numerous factors that make each situation unique. It is sufficient to say that the helper does not have to mentally run through a list of variables such as race, ethnicity, gender, and socio-economic status to remind him of differences to consider; he simply has to remind himself that each client is a unique individual.

Summary

In summary, as previously stated, understanding human behavior is an essential requirement for a helping professional to be successful in assisting a helpee. Several theorists' perceptions of what motivates human behavior have been provided to give the helper a glimpse of how they evaluate their helpee's behavior. The point being made is that there is no one right answer to understanding the motivations of human behavior, rather there are numerous ways of viewing human behavior. The helper is encouraged to borrow from any of the theorist discussed as well as those not discussed and add to his/her perceptions and beliefs with regard to human behavior. It is certainly acceptable for the helper to utilize theorist's perceptions as his/her basis for handling behavioral issues until he/she has enough practical and professional experience to develop a theory of human behavior that is unique to his/her perceptions.

Also the professional helper must learn to assess behavior. Understanding what motivates human behavior is very important; likewise, being able to assess helpee's current situation in which the behavior is occurring is equally important.

Review Questions

1. What were some of Sigmund Freud's views with regard to what motivates human behavior?
2. What were some of Alfred Adler's views with regard to what motivates human behavior?
3. What were some of Fredrick and Laura Perls' views with regard to what motivates human behavior?
4. What were some of Carl Rogers' views with regard to what motivates human behavior?
5. What were some of the existentialists' views with regard to what motivates human behavior?
6. What were some of B. F. Skinners' views with regard to what motivates human behavior?

7. What were some of Albert Ellis' views with regard to what motivates human behavior?

Mental Exercise

1. Describe your views with regard to what motivates human behavior.

References

Bryan, W. V. (2007). *Multicultural aspects of disabilities* (2nd ed.). Springfield, IL: Charles C Thomas Publisher, Ltd.

Bitter, J. R. (2007). Ansbacher memorial address: Am I an Adlerian? *Journal of Individual Psychology, 63*(1), 1–31.

Corey, G. (2005). *Theory and practice of counseling & psychotherapy* (7th ed.). United States: Brooks/Cole.

Ponterotto, J. G., Casas, J. M., Suzuki, L. A., & Alexander, C. M. (Eds.) (1995). *Handbook of multicultural counseling.* Thousand Oaks, CA: Sage.

Suggested Readings

Blumberg, M. S. (2005) *Basic instinct: The genesis of behavior.* New York. Thunder Mouth Press.

Crook, L., Chagnon, N., & Iorns, W. (Eds.). (2000). *Adaptation and human behavior: An anthropological perspective.* New York: Aldine deGruyter.

Edgeton, R. B. (2005). *The balance of human kindness and cruelty: Why we are the way we are.* Lewiston, NY: Edwin Mellen Press.

Greene, R. R., (editor) (2008) *Human behavior: theory and social work practice* (3rd ed.). New Brunswick, NJ: Aldine Transaction.

Hall, J. C., & Bowie, S. L. (Eds.). (2007). *African American behavior in the social environment: New perspectives.* New York: Haworth Press.

Kainz, H. P. (2008) *The philosophy of human nature.* Chicago, IL. Open Court.

Robbins, S. P., Chatterjee, P., & Canda, E. R. (1998). *Contemporary human behavior theory: A critical perspective for social work.* Boston: Allyn & Bacon.

Smith, J. L. (2000). *The psychology of action.* New York: St. Martin's Press.

Van Wormer, K., Besthorn, F. H., & Keefe, T. (Eds.). (2007). *Human behavior and the social environment: Micro level: Individuals and families.* Oxford. Oxford University Press.

Chapter 3

DISCRIMINATION

Chapter Outline
• Introduction
• What is discrimination?
• Brief history of discrimination
• Legacy of discrimination
• Prejudice
• Conclusion–The ISMs

Chapter Objectives
• Provide a brief description of what constitutes discrimination
• Provide a brief description of some impacts of discrimination
• Provide a brief description of various forms of prejudice
• Provide a brief description of some impacts of prejudice

Introduction

Discrimination has existed as long as humans have existed. There are a number of reasons why discrimination of humans exist and continue to exist, very few of these reasons are good and valid. Discrimination, in its various forms, has been the cause of cruel and inhumane treatment, which has not only been the reasons for human loss of life, also has resulted in a waste of human resources in the form of decreased productivity, stagnation of creativity, denial of spiritual rights, stagnation of psychological, sociological and emotional growth.

In most cases discrimination divide people rather than bring different groups of people together to better utilize the God given talents each has which can be used to help build societies that encourage and value human differences. Differences such as opinions and ways of approaching issues can be utilized as valuable ways of solving problems rather than viewing with

45

suspicion persons with different points of view and devising ways of eliminating and/or neutralizing those persons. There is no question that there are people who have radical views of how life should be thus there has to be some constraints on their actions.

What Is Discrimination?

According to Ritzer, Kammeyer, and Yetman (1982), discrimination is the behavioral expression of prejudice. Gordon Allport (1979), in his seminal work on prejudice, presented a model of acting out prejudice which consists of five phases: antilocution, avoidance, exclusion, physical attack, and extermination. His model ranges from a mild form of discrimination to the ultimate act of discrimination. Understanding these forms of discrimination provides us with a prospective on prejudice and how one form of prejudice without being controlled may progress to more severe forms of discrimination. The model also provides us with knowledge of how prejudice impacts the victim. The interpretation of the stages draws considerably upon the writing of Ponterotto and Pedersen (1993).

Antilocution is perhaps the least aggressive form of prejudice and is represented by prejudicial conversation conducted by individuals sharing similar opinions. Most individuals engaged in this type of behavior will vehemently deny their behavior is prejudicial in any way. Rather, they indicate this is simply a matter of expressing their opinions. Although this form of prejudice is nonaggressive, it can be very dangerous in that it can have both a multiplying and inciting affect. An opinion may multiply when an opinion is shared with another person; he then shares it with someone else and so on until a much larger group is expressing this viewpoint. Additionally, in the process of multiplying the opinion, individuals may become incited to take aggressive action.

An example of this level of prejudice is two or more persons expressing their opinions that an independent living center for persons with severe mental disabilities proposed for their neighborhood is going to create a safety risk for their families. At this level of prejudice, the discrimination is only talk and in most instances the information discussed is based upon hearsay, rumors, and stereotype rather than fact. However, as previously implied, without facts that contradict misinformation, the next level of discrimination (avoidance) occurs.

Avoidance goes beyond talk and places into action efforts to avoid individuals and/or groups declared unwanted. The persons engaged in conducting the avoidance generally are willing to accept some inconveniences to eliminate interaction with those being avoided. As an example, a family moving their children from public neighborhood schools and sending them several miles away to an expensive private school to avoid having their children interact with children of different cultures and/or racial backgrounds.

During the integration period, mid-1950s and the decades of the 1960s and 1970s, the avoidance behavior was common as racial minority students were given their rights to an equal education and began to attend formerly nonminority schools. At considerable expense, some parents either moved to areas where there were no minorities or placed their children in expensive, private schools. This was repeated when neighborhood covenants were declared illegal. This was the practice where homeowners would either sign an agreement or it was placed on their title to their property that they would not sell their property to persons of certain races. Again, when this was declared to be illegal, some owners, rather than live next to or in the neighborhood with those they had attempted to exclude, often would sell their homes, sometimes taking a loss. Today we continue to hear of similar behavior. In some cases, families have elected to move when the decision is made to locate a facility for persons who have a mental disability or a halfway house for former substance abusers in or near their neighborhood.

Exclusion is the third level of discrimination which may take the form of getting a petition signed to exclude an individual or group, for example, from membership in a social club or organization. An appropriate example is when homeowners in a neighborhood circulate a petition to block the development of an independent living center in their area. Additionally, the neighborhood covenants discussed in avoidance is also an excellent example of exclusion.

Physical Attack is the fourth level of discrimination which becomes much more serious than those already mentioned. This stage requires heated and often irrational emotional reactions which lead to physical violence. Physically abusing the occupants of the mythical independent living center or breaking the windows in the center are examples of a physical attack. Numerous examples from the American Civil Rights Movement could be cited; however, the author believes that the reader recognizes the point.

Extermination is the final stage of discrimination which is the ultimate act of discrimination represented by taking the life of a person from another culture or racial background. This was illustrated in the bombing of African American churches in the southern United States during the Civil Rights era of the 1960s. Also, the elimination of thousands of Jewish people by the Nazi forces is a constant reminder of the extremity of extermination.

The last two stages, physical attack and extermination, indicates that prejudice has reached the stage of hatred and the victim of the discriminatory act is thought to represent some type of threat to the perpetrator.

Brief History of Discrimination

Survival Techniques

Undoubtedly prejudice and discrimination have existed in some form as long as there have been groups of people. As previously stated, it is not uncommon for people to elect to associate with others who share similar interests, beliefs, and values. This form of natural selection is normal. During the earliest history of human existence, individuals grouped together for survival; they assisted each other with their safety and sustenance needs. Undoubtedly, selection into these ancient groups was not only based upon one's ability to contribute to the group's well-being but was also based upon attributes that were familiar and nonthreatening to the group. Persons who looked different, acted different, communicated different, walked different, and perhaps smelled different than what the group was accustomed were rejected for inclusion into the group. This was perhaps one of the first forms of human discrimination. Those who were rejected as members of one group probably banded together with others who had similar characteristics, thus forming another group which perhaps rejected others who did not look, act, communicate, walk, or smell as they. This natural selection continued and many groups came into existence. Each one of these groups not only rejected "abnormal" would-be members, but in the process became suspicious of the person and the groups the "rejects" eventually formed. Because these people were "different," contact with them was deliberately avoided. Due to the lack of contact, suspicions developed in their curious minds which led to preconceived ideas about the group and its behavior. Active minds sometimes invented behavior for the group and these preconceived ideas and prejudgments were told around campfires with the young listening at a distance, absorbing many of the interesting details and these stories were repeated around their campfires when they became adults with their young attentively listening. Each group was equally guilty of creating fictional stories about the other groups. As groups engaged in battle against each other, their distrust, dislike, and discrimination became more ingrained into their interaction patterns.

Tool of Power

Over the centuries, discrimination has evolved from a survival technique into a "tool of power." The "in"-group characterizes the "out"-group as inferior and bestows many negative connotations to the attributes of the out-group and its members. By lowering the status of the out-group the in group's status is increased and a feeling of superiority is embedded in the members' minds. For "keeping the out-group members in their places," in-group members are rewarded with privileges such as better paying jobs, higher quality of education, etc. In summary, the in-group obtains a position of power over the out-group and consistently uses this to keep the out-group in subordinate positions.

The purpose of this brief historical time travel along the road of discrimination is to illustrate that discrimination probably began as a survival technique and discrimination of one group against another has been passed down for several hundred generations with each generation believing it has both the right and the reason to behave in the manner they do. As times have changed and humanity has progressed, likewise discrimination has made changes. No longer is our survival dependent upon discrimination, if in fact it ever was, but we persist in finding ways to exclude, avoid, and attack others and, yes, occasionally even exterminate people we consider different and inferior to ourselves. The additional point to be made is currently that there is neither justification nor valid reason for discriminating against each other. Natural group selection is normal and is likely to continue as long as humans exist; however, the viciousness of discrimination is not normal and does not have to be perpetuated generation after generation.

Legacy of Discrimination

One of the physical laws of nature is that for every action there is a reaction. With regard to discrimination and disabilities there have been numerous reactions such as low self-esteem and a dependency on others for resolution of some of their problems, just to mention two. Perhaps the major impact or legacy of discrimination can best be seen in the areas of education, employment, economics, housing, communication, and transportation. The impact of discrimination of persons with disabilities in an economically-driven society is that poor educational attainment serves to limit one's employment potential which in turn impacts one's earning ability. The lack of adequate financial resources severely limits one's ability to purchase necessary goods and services, not to speak of items that go beyond the necessities of life which makes for a more comfortable existence and can improve one's position on life's status totem pole. Too frequently, the result of this chain of events set into motion by discrimination is a dependency upon local, state, and/or federal public assistance, thus continuing some of the negative feelings about persons with disabilities and ethnic/racial minorities. At this point the legacy of discrimination will be viewed as it relates to education, employment, and the economic condition of persons with disabilities.

***Education*–**A dissertation does not have to be written to explain the educational status of a large segment of the population of persons with disabilities. The following statement taken from the National Organization on Disability/Louis Harris Survey of Americans With Disabilities (1994), while dated provides a convincing summary. Based upon a comparison of the survey of a national cross-section of adults eighteen years of age and older who did not have disabilities, the conclusion is "it is clear that adults with disabilities are less educated than those without disabilities." The results from a similar survey conducted by the same organizations in 1998 indicate that this statement remained true. A closer analysis of this survey reveals: adults with disabilities are twice as likely as adults without disabilities to have less than a high school education (22% vs. 9%).

Without question, the previously stated facts demonstrate that discrimination has placed some persons with disabilities in a disadvantaged position with respect to educational attainment; despite this information, a comparison of this survey (1998) with a similar survey conducted in 1986 provides hope in that there has been some improvement of the educational level of persons with disabilities. The comparison provided the following results: (1) in 1986, forty percent (40%) of adults with disabilities had not completed high school, whereas in the 1998 survey, the percentage had decreased to 22 percent. (2) Approximately three in four adults with disabilities have at least a high school education, whereas in 1986, three in five had a high school education. Perhaps the trend toward improved educational status of persons with disabilities, especially those requiring special education, can be attributed in part to legislative action such as the Individuals With Disabilities Education Act (IDEA) which, according to Zawaiza (1995), is the primary source of federal aid to state and local school systems for instructional support services to children with disabilities. Through the passage of this act, Congress attempts to insure that all children with disabilities are provided a free, appropriate education in the least restrictive environment. The Act also gives the parents of children with disabilities the right to be involved in the process of determining the type and nature of their child's education through an individualized plan (Bryan, 1996).

***Economics*–**In 1994, a Harris survey compared the economic situation of persons with disabilities in that year with persons with disabilities in 1986 and the survey results indicated that Americans with disabilities may have been better educated than their counterparts of 1986; however, their income or earnings had not kept pace with their educational attainments. The 2002 U.S. Census Bureau report shows that in the first decade of the twenty-first century, people with disabilities economically lag behind nondisabled persons. Of persons age 25 to 64 with no disability, 39.3 percent had personal income of less than $20,000 and 12.3 percent lived in households with total household income below $20,000. In comparison, among persons with non-severe disabilities, 47.6 percent had personal income less than $20,000 and 18.3 percent lived in households with total household income below $20,000. Among persons with a severe disability, the gap widens considerably in that 76.6 percent had personal income below $20,000, and 37.8 percent lived in households with total household income below $20,000.

Employment–Perhaps no one feature defines an American more than the type of work he/she performs. We frequently identify persons by their job. Pete, the janitor; Fred, the plumber; Mary, the attorney; and Sarah, the dentist; the job attached to their names tells us a great deal about them. One, we are able to judge their level of education; two, we get some idea of their economic status; and three, we are able to judge a little about their working environment. In short, a person's line of work defines a large number of things about the person. Likewise, to be unemployed and/or not able to work defines things about the person also. Unfortunately, much of how we think of an unemployed person (unless they are retired) is negative. True, persons who are unemployed by virtue of a disability are often not painted with the same negative brush stroke as a person who does not have a disability and is unemployed; nevertheless, there is a specter of devaluation. While a major reason for employment difficulties of persons with disabilities is attitudinal barriers of employers and other nondisabled persons, the author is not implying that every person with a disability who is unemployed is so because of discrimination.

The discrimination that persons with disabilities encounter is one of the most difficult forms of discrimination to eradicate. First, the discriminator is often unaware that his behavior toward persons with disabilities constitutes discrimination. From a point of view of ignorance, we act in a patronizing manner; we may speak for, think for, and act in behalf of persons with disabilities, thinking that we are sparing them the trouble or embarrassment of failing. Second, persons without disabilities will strongly deny their prejudices. As previously indicated, it generally is not socially acceptable to express negative feelings with regard to persons with disabilities. Despite our denial of prejudice, our actions often reveal our inner feelings. Third, the discriminator, through various acts of charity and avoidance of personal contact, cleanses his conscious from feelings of guilt. Today most discriminatory acts are not blatant and are nonviolent and often issued without malicious intent; therefore, convincing oneself that no discrimination has occurred becomes much easier. Without recognizing that a problem exists, extermination of the problems becomes extremely difficult.

Prejudice

A simplified explanation of prejudice is "prejudging" or making decisions about someone or a situation before obtaining sufficient facts necessary to make an informed decision. Given this definition, prejudice can be either positive or negative; however, in most instances when we speak of or think about prejudicial action or statements, it is usually within a negative connotation. Likewise, when we consider the meaning of prejudice, it is often associated negatively with a racial situation. Persons with disabilities in the past as well as presently have been prejudged. First, we will look at why we are prejudiced then view prejudices with regard to disability and next we will look at prejudice associated with race and finally we will intersect the two factors of disability and race.

Why Are We Prejudiced?

According to Allport (1979) and Ponterotto and Pedersen (1993), three factors contribute significantly to the development of prejudicial views: (1) ethnocentrism, (2) lack of significant intergroup contact, and (3) preference for categorization.

Ethnocentrism–The American Heritage Dictionary defines ethnocentrism as the belief in the superiority of one's own ethnic group. Without doubt, everyone should have pride in their cultural background; therefore, there is nothing wrong with being proud of one's heritage. Group identity is strengthened when one has reasons to speak proudly of his group's standards and accomplishments. Being proud is not the problem, but the feeling of superiority and the extent to which group members will express this superior feeling create the problem and set the wheels of discrimination in motion. Ethnocentrism can lead to racism in that as group members began to "buy into" the belief that their ethnic group is superior to all other ethnic groups, they often will confer benefits to its members to the exclusion, and in some cases at the expense, of other groups. These benefits may take the form of political, social, economic, and educational advantages to mention a few. Except for the most blatant racist, the awarding and receiving of favorite individual or group status is often unintentional or covert prejudice rather than openly overt prejudice. For some ethnic groups, ethnocentrism is so deeply ingrained in their daily lives that most members of the group do not give much thought to the favorite or superior status which they enjoy. Perhaps the following illustration will provide an example: When one has been awarded a job for which she competed against a person from another ethnic and/or cultural group who had comparable skills and credentials, it is ego satisfying and psychologically safer to think that the job was awarded based upon one's superior skills and credentials rather than preference being given because of one's group membership. Another example of not being aware of receiving benefits based upon one's group membership is one ethnic and/or cultural group receiving lower bank loan interest rates because of a perceived better credit risk status of the ethnic group over other groups. Perhaps Lee (1989) summarizes the issue of ethnocentrism with his comments that the manner in which group members view themselves in relation to others can shape attitudes, behaviors, and values.

***Lack of Significant Intergroup Contacts*–**Ponterotto and Pedersen (1993) provide the essence of this problem with their comments that separation between human groups is common-people often prefer the company of their own kind as a matter of convenience. However, despite the fact this behavior is accepted as natural, this preference to associate primarily with like-minded individuals leads to a form of cultural ignorance. The lack of contact with persons from different racial and cultural backgrounds from one's own is often a major reason for the development of stereotypes, prejudice as well as other misperceptions. This certainly is the situation with regard to racial minority groups and persons with disabilities. With regard to racial minorities, many erroneous ideas, attitudes, and beliefs were developed about them as being inferior mentally and morally bankrupt to justify the treatment to which they were subjected. As a result, many racial minority groups have been shunned and the result is a poor and inaccurate understanding by the dominant culture.

Spicer (1989) offers the following remarks which add emphasis to the negative impact of the lack of intergroup contact:

> Throughout the world, many people tend to value their way of life and reject other lifestyles. Our sense of belonging and social harmony can be disrupted when we encounter other cultures and we often seek to maintain our equilibrium by viewing these other people as inferior and even dangerous. Because our prejudices are largely unconscious these negative stereotypes can persist and, without our knowing it, have an impact on our interaction with other people.

Ironically, minority groups have a better understanding of the dominant culture than the reverse. The major reason for this is the subordinate cultures have to understand and correctly interpret the actions of the dominant culture to survive in the society dominated by them. For most people dealing with the "unknown" is difficult, resulting in our tendency to avoid same. As a society, we have experienced considerable difficulty in understanding disabilities because we have had a tendency to limit our contact with those who possess them. Although considerable medical advances have occurred over the past fifty years which have provided us with much information with regard to the causes of disabilities, the fact remains that we continue to struggle with our lack of understanding of why two persons may have similar medical conditions and one makes a complete recovery while the other experiences a disability. Throughout the ages, the collective wisdom of humans pondering this and other situations associated with disabilities have often ended in frustration realizing that there are probably some things associated with human existence we will never completely understand.

Preference for Categorization–we are a society of categorizers. We classify people by race, gender, economic status, physical condition, height, weight, hair color, religious preference, and so on. We categorize because it is convenient to do so and in reality in some instances, it is helpful to do so. Classifying these attributes provides us with a quick and convenient way of identification. During the process of classifying individuals and/or groups, we attach labels to them and unfortunately sometimes those labels are less than complimentary and the description of those labeled are too often based upon false information and equally false perceptions. Regardless of the inaccuracy, once applied, these labels stick and generation after generation of group members suffer the consequences. After generations of these prejudiced labels have been perpetuated, they become accepted as truth. Forgotten is the fact that these labels were based upon our need to categorize people and the assigning of attributes without having sufficient intergroup contact.

Conclusion–The Ism's

I have established that discrimination is the behavioral or acting-out of one's prejudice; therefore, racism, sexism, and handicapism or disablism are forms of discrimination. Charles V. Willie (1984) correctly argues that racism and sexism are forms of institutional oppression. This author would add to the list–handicapism. United States Supreme Court Justice Thurgood Marshall described racism as demeaning to individuals and the nadir of social responsibility and further stated that it condones oppression and tramples on fundamental rights. Pierce (1969) relates racism to a disease that consists of an attitude, ideation, and behavior based upon the assumption of the superiority of the dominant culture's skin color. Pettigrew (1973), in describing racism, viewed it as the acting out of intergroup prejudice against a race other than one's own in a way that limits the opportunity and choices open to the victimized group. Ridley (1989) described racism as "any behavior or pattern of behavior that tends to systematically deny access to opportunities or privileges to members of one racial group while perpetuating access to opportunities and privileges to members of another racial group."

Although the preceding discussion and descriptions relate mainly to discrimination based upon one's race, sexism and handicapism are similar except in sexism the group that is victimized is either male or female, but in the situation of handicapism, the victims are both male and female and the discriminating factor is the person's physical, mental, and/or emotional condition.

The acts of discrimination which most often receive publicity are related to one's race. An individual or group of individuals being insulted by the issuance of racial epithet often followed by violence against one's person because of his/her skin color and/or racial group affiliation is an example of what is often associated with racism. While these acts actually happen and one is too many, the reality is that this form of racism occurs the least in number within America. A minority person is far more likely to be passed over for promotion on her job, or be ignored in a work conference conversation, or simply be excluded from meetings that involve the making of policy than she is to be physically and/or visibly abused. Likewise, discrimination based upon one's gender or physical, mental, and/or emotional condition is more likely to be in the form of exclusion, ignoring, and patronizing than elimination by physical means. The overt forms of discrimination of physical and/or verbal abuse have receded and given rise to what many human and civil rights specialists feel is as destructive, if not more so, especially to the human spirit, that being covert discrimination which is represented by exclusion, ignoring, and other subtle forms of denial of rights. Overt discrimination, which often is illegal, generally can be dealt with better because the action and its perpetrators' intentions are obvious. One does not have to expend time and energy attempting to convince the perpetrator and others that a problem exists. Even though the creator of the act may believe he is justified in his actions and beliefs, the inappropriateness of same is readily observable to most objective-minded persons. Therefore, actions to correct the problem can begin. Conversely, covert discrimination is subtle and difficult to detect and more difficult to prove. The persons involved in covert discrimination will vehemently deny that they are prejudiced and offer strong objections to the suggestion that they discriminate. When confronted with the reality that he has failed to hire an African American female who has a disability, supervisor "A" denies that his decision was based on either her race, gender, or disability. When provided with additional facts that the person he failed to hire had more experience and generally was better qualified than the person hired, his answer probably will continue to be one of denial. Several reasons will be offered, such as "I did not think she could physically handle the job," or "I hire the best qualified person regardless of race, sex, or disability and it was my opinion that the person I hired was the best qualified." A difficulty with covert discrimination is the denial. Until the persons are convinced that their actions represent a stumbling block to others, corrective action is difficult. The person who is guilty of covert discrimination not only denies discrimination but often truly believes his actions are nondiscriminatory. This is a good indicator that he subconsciously has accepted many of the stereotypes and prejudgments that surround minorities, women and persons with disabilities and have accepted them as fact and are acting upon these misconceptions. If one thinks of the many stereotypes and misconceptions associated with a minority group, then women, and next, persons with disabilities, and finally combine all within one person (an African American female with a mental disability), one can easily imagine a very difficult set of circumstances that individual has to overcome.

The result of racism, sexism, and handicapism is the disenfranchisement of a group of people. They are often denied through discrimination their rights promised to them by the laws of America, and to add insult to injury, they are frequently blocked in their attempts to better their conditions.

There will be additional discussion of racism, sexism, and handicapism and its impact upon the helping relation in future chapters. Additional tips on how the helping professional can overcome these effects and keep this type of discrimination out of the helping relationship will also be discussed in future chapters.

Review Questions

1. List the five phases of prejudices and give an example of each.
2. What have been some of the impacts of discrimination against persons with disabilities, ethnic minorities and women?
3. What are the three factors listed in this chapter that contribute to the development of prejudicial views?
4. What is the foundation of race-based prejudice in America?
5. What are some ways attitudes are formed?
6. What are some of the ways one can eliminate stereotypical thoughts and ideas with regard to persons of different cultures?
7. How can discrimination be used as a "tool of power?"
8. What is meant by discrimination as a "survival technique?"

Suggested Activities

1. List ten (10) stereotypes you have with regard to persons with disabilities. How many are negative?
2. Interview a person with a disability who is also a member of a racial minority group; ask the person if he/she has experienced discrimina-

tion as both a racial minority and as a person with a disability. If he/she indicates having experienced discrimination, ask which was the most difficult to handle–racial discrimination or discrimination on the basis of his/her physical, mental, and/or emotional status.

3. Think about the origin of your beliefs and attitudes about both racial minorities and persons with disabilities.

4. Imagine that a transitional house for persons with a mental and/or emotional disability is being planned for your community and you are hired by the city government to work with the community in an effort to get the community to accept the facility and its occupants. Develop your strategy to combat stereotypical attitudes and avoid possible discrimination of the future occupants of the proposed transition house.

5. Research your state's governmental structure to determine which agency(ies) handles discrimination complaints and how they are handled. Also, determine if the agency has had complaints of discrimination based upon disability.

References

Allport, G. (1958). *The nature of prejudice.* New York: Doubleday, Anchor Books.

American Heritage Dictionary (3rd ed.). (1992). Boston: Houghton Mifflin.

Bryan, W. V. (1996). *In search of freedom.* Springfield, IL: Charles C Thomas.

Gellman, W. (1959). Roots of prejudice against the handicapped. *Journal of Rehabilitation, 40,* 4–6.

Lee, C. C. (1989). Multicultural counseling: New directions for counseling professionals. *Virginia Counselors Journal, 17,* 3–8.

N.O.D. (1994). *Harris survey of Americans with disabilities.* New York: Louis Harris and Associates.

Pettigrew, T. F. (1984). Racism and mental health of white Americans. Quoted in *Racism, sexism and elitism.* Willie, C. V. Institute for Responsible Education, Boston.

Pierce, C. M. (1994). Is bigotry the basis of the medical problems of the ghetto? Quoted in Carter, J. H. *Journal of the National Medical Association, 86*(7), 543–547.

Ponterotto, J. G., & Pedersen, P. B. (1993). *Preventing prejudice: A guide for counselors and educators.* Newbury Park, CA: Sage.

Ridley, C. R. (1995). *Overcoming unintentional racism in counseling and therapy.* Thousand Oaks, CA: Sage.

Spicer, J. (1989). *Counseling ethnic minorities.* Minnesota: Hazeiden.

Willie, C. V. (1984). *Racism, sexism and elitism equity and choice: Institute for responsible education.* Boston.

Zawaiza, T. W. (1995). Stand and deliver: Multiculturalism and special education reform in the early twenty-first century. In *Disability and diversity: New leadership for a new era.* Washington, DC: President's Committee on Employment of People With Disabilities and Howard University.

Suggested Readings

Abramowitz, S. S., & Murray, J. (1991). Race effects in psychology. In R. M. Crystal & R. J. Alston, Ethnicity and culture in rehabilitation counseling: The perspective of three prominent counselor educators. *Rehabilitation Education, 5*(3), 209–214.

Brodwin, M. G., Hong, G. K., & Sorian, M. (1992). Discrimination, disability and cultural considerations; Implications for counselors. *California Association of Counseling and Development Journal, 12,* 9–14.

Eisenberg, M. G., Giggers, C., & Duval, R. J. (Eds.). (1982). *Disabled people as second-class citizens.* New York: Springer.

Fine, M., & Asch, A. (1988). Disabilities beyond stigma: Social interaction, discrimination and activism. *Journal of Social Issues, 44,* 3–21.

Funk, R. (1987). From caste to class in the context of civil rights. In A. Gartner & T. Joe (Eds.), *Images of the disabled.* New York: Praeger.

Graham, S. (Ed.). (1992). Most of the subjects were white and middle-class. *American Psychologist, 47,* 629–639.

Hahn, H. The politics of physical differences: Disability and discrimination. *Journal of Social Issues, 44,* 39–47.

Chapter 4

RELIGION

Chapter Outline
• Introduction
• What is Religion?
• What is Atheism?
• What is Agnosticism?
• How and why religion began
• What is the purpose of religion?
• Why are there many different religions and religious views?
• Religion and culture
• Overview of the five major religions
• Some commonalities and differences of the five major religions
• Implications for helping professionals and others
• Conclusion

Chapter Objectives
• Provide an overview of the five largest religions
• Provide an understanding of religion as culture
• Provide information with regard to commonalities and differences of the five largest religions
• Provide information about religion that helping professionals and others should know

Introduction

Perhaps as long as human kind has existed on earth, we have in some was paid homage to a supreme power or powers. The deities to which we have expressed humbleness sometime were called God or gods and in some instance they were called spirits. In antiquity, humans attempted to explain frightful events by assigning a supreme power or powers as the controlling being responsible for the action. Thunder and lighting, floods, fires, destructive winds, plagues, and famine are but a few of the extraordinary events that early humans attempted to explain and justify by indicating that the gods or spirits were angry. Not only were they attempting to explain the cause of supernatural events, they were also acknowledging that there was a power or powers greater than they as individuals and collectively as a group. They also were acknowledging that this power or powers had the potential to significantly influence their lives and they needed to, in some ways, humble themselves to them, or perhaps suffer disastrous consequences.

In the areas of cultural diversity and multiculturalism, when attempting to understand variables impacting the life of an individual, we ascribe considerable importance to one's ethnicity, race, and or gender as though they are the most important variables to consider. However, for those who believe in a supreme being, their **faith** is as important as ethnicity, race, and gender, and perhaps influences their actions and beliefs more than these previously mentioned variables. In America, we attempt to separate church and state and perhaps this is the reason, when we discuss cultural impact, faith or religion is secondary to ethnicity, race, and gender, when in reality, for many people, faith/religion is **dominant**.

It has been said that the question is not whether we worship God, but the real question is which god. There is considerable truth in this statement; because everyone worships some god. For some, it is a spiritual being; for others, it may be the worship of a material god—money, clothes, automobile, etc.

Religion or the expression of faith goes beyond attending religious services. The expression of faith includes adhering to some, if not all, of the basic principles and beliefs that serve as the foundation of the faith. Additionally, the expression of faith also includes recognition and at least occasional celebration of important historical events of the faith. Similar to ethnic/racial groups who celebrate or recognize significant events related to that part of their culture, individuals of a religious persuasion also place great importance in significant events related to their faith. Therefore, for some people, their religious faith transcends all the other variables of their cultural composition.

The need for helping professionals to understand the impact faith may have in the helping process is very important. For those persons who believe in a supreme being, if they practice their faith, they will in all probability rely on the same in stressful situations or times of crisis, and for those who believe in a supreme being but may not be actively practicing their faith, in stressful situations many will seek help from a higher power than mortal humans.

Throughout recorded history and perhaps before, individuals and groups have engaged in conflicts where lives and property were destroyed in the name of religion or something akin to religion. The basis of these conflicts often were set around philosophical beliefs of what their Supreme Being or beings had established as the way life should be conducted.

What is Religion?

Some people define religion according to their spiritual belief preferences such as Christianity, Islam, and Judaism to mention three. An obvious fault of this type of definition is the definition basically declares the other religions as inaccurate representations of religion without providing an accurate operative definition of religion. Others may define religion by identifying, traditions, practices, and beliefs which constitute a specific religion or several religions. Again those that do not follow the specified traditions, practices and beliefs are in effect declared as non-religions. Others simply describe religion as "a belief system." This has an obvious flaw of not describing a belief in what; if one says a belief in religion, then one is not describing what religion is. Tylor (1871) defined religion as "the belief in spiritual beings." Geetrz (1973) identifies religion as a cultural system and Asal (1982) defined religion as "an organized collection of belief systems, cultural systems and world views that relate humanity to spirituality and sometimes to moral values." Makinde (2013) points out that religion is envisioned to give meaning to life and clarify the source of life and the origin of the world. He further points out that in all societies around the world, the belief in supernatural power exists, therefore, what influences human beings influences society. Asal (1982) in earlier comments serve as a foundation for Makinde's position when he stated "in most cases, humans develop morality, ethics, laws, and way of life from religion." Although more of a fact than a definition, religion has for many people the impact of motivating and inspiring people to do good things and achieve things that goes beyond benefiting oneself but inspires and motivate others to do honorable things. According to Geertz (1973), "Whether anyone likes it or not, religious beliefs are unavoidable aspects of life with respect to cultural values, politics, even finances. These relationships between religion and society are visible in Islamic religion and Muslims social cultures. The relationship between religion and society is also obvious in Christian social cultures, morality, ethics and governance. It is reflected in Buddhism social cultures and governance in society." There is no definitions of religion know to this author that does not have some flaws; therefore I shall not attempt to provide a definition. However I will point out that defining religion is somewhat like trying to define the wind. One cannot see the wind; however, one can feel and see the impact of the wind. Similarly, religion is not something one can visually see; however for persons who consider themselves religious they can feel and see the impact of religion. Continuing with the analogy of wind and religion, similar to each person's personal preference with regard to experiencing wind, some people like a very calm and quite day, others may like the wind blowing vigorously against their bodies. Likewise with regard to experiencing religion, some like a very smooth and sedate flow of religious services, while other like loud, animated religious services. While religion tends to escape an accurate or definitive definition, the effects of religion are a powerful force in many people's lives.

For many people who consider themselves religious or have some religious faith it is very difficult to imagine human life without some connection to a supernatural faith. For those persons they perhaps have difficulties comprehending the development of the universe and its continual existence without their being superhuman involvement. Likewise, they may have difficulty believing that their lives, to some extent, are not guided by a power or powers greater than their own. Also, for some, having a faith in powers beyond their own adds additional meaning and comfort to their lives, as they encounter difficult times. Additionally, the belief in an afterlife for some gives additional meaning to their relatively short existence.

Other than Religion

Although, it may be difficult for many to believe what we see and experience in life is all that exists of our being occupants of this planet, there are those that either do not subscribe to religion and an afterlife, or have serious questions with regard to the existence of religion and a supernatural force or forces. Some of these non-believers and doubters are called either Atheists or Agnostics.

Atheism

Atheism is not a religion, because persons who consider themselves as atheist do not believe in a god or gods or supernatural beings; however they have a belief system which makes them unique from a cultural standpoint. As previously stated they do not believe in a supreme being. For those who believe in a supreme being or beings it perhaps is difficult to comprehend the thinking of atheists particularly from the standpoint of how life events beyond human control occur. How did the universe form? Why did the universe form? Do life events occur randomly? What controls do humans have over their destiny? Those and many other questions are the essences of the thinking of those that do not understand atheism.

What is Atheism?

A simplified definition of an atheist is one that does not believe in the existence of a god or gods and a lack of belief in an afterlife. A major reason for this lack of belief in a god or gods from the atheist's viewpoint there is no evidence that such Supreme Being or beings exist. One common factor in many religions is the belief in some type of life after physical death; however with regard to the belief of atheists there is no life after death. Stated in other terms the atheist's point of view is once a person dies that is the end of his/her existence. This viewpoint appears to be based upon their belief that there is no proof that life exists or will exist after death. Persons of various religious faiths may argue this from the standpoint of their religious documents which specifically discuss life after death. An atheist's response may be this is a belief without concrete documentation of such existence. The end result of this argument relies on one's belief system.

As one reviews his/her beliefs of right or wrong, acceptable or non-acceptable behavior in a given society one will find that what is deemed acceptable or non-acceptable is based upon a given societies rules of appropriate behavior. One may argue that many of these rules have been extracted and perhaps modified from religious precepts; however an atheist's viewpoint with regard to how right and wrong are developed is that each society develops it's views of what is acceptable regardless of from where they are based, thus this is what helps govern the behavior of all people.

Some atheist's viewpoint with regard to how the world began is very straight forward—"they do not know." Although some if not many religious persons believe in the "big bang" theory, others believe in the "creation theory." The bottom line with regard to this controversy is no one at this point in history really knows the answer. The question of how the world began presents an interesting balancing act for some religious people, on the one hand they are professing their beliefs with regard to creation of the world brought forth by a supreme being and on the other hand they are accepting scientific information that moves one to believe that there is scientific evidence that supports an enormous event that set the world on track to develop life as we currently experience life. Given this possible contradiction, the atheist's answer "they do not know how the world began" appears to be a reasonable answer.

What is Agnosticism?

While some people may think of agnosticism and atheism as being the same philosophy, however there is a significant difference between the two concepts. Whereas, as previously stated, atheists do not believe in God/ Supreme being whereas agnostics simply say they do not know whether there is a Supreme Being. Agnostics without totally rejecting the existence of a Supreme Being and concepts such as afterlife, they basically state that they do not know whether such exist. From this statement there is an appearance that Agnosticism holds out some hope that some religious precepts are true to mention only one, life after death which would allow the possibility of experiencing past love ones.

Both agnostics and atheists sometime suffer similar discrimination by being labeled as "God Haters," which appear to be an incorrect evaluation of their beliefs. Both appear to be saying that there is not sufficient evidence for them to accept concepts and beliefs of traditional religious beliefs.

How and Why Religions Began

Perhaps as long as human kind has existed on earth, we have in some way paid homage to a supreme power or powers. The deities to which we have expressed humbleness sometime were called God or gods and in some instance they were called spirits. As previously stated, in antiquity humans attempted to explain frightful events by assigning a supreme power or powers as the controlling being responsible for the action. Thunder and lighting, floods, fires, destructive winds, plagues, and famine are but a few of the extraordinary events that early humans attempted to explain and justify by indicating that the gods or spirits were angry. Not only were they attempting to explain the cause of supernatural events, they were also acknowledging that there was a power or powers greater than they as individuals and collectively as a group. They also were acknowledging that this power or powers had the potential to significantly influence their lives and they needed to, in some ways, humble themselves to them, or perhaps suffer disastrous consequences.

From the beginning of time on earth humans have recognized their power paled in comparison to events such as the ones previously mentioned. Perhaps because of this acknowledgment of physical inferiority humans began to develop a belief in power or powers beyond their control. Perhaps, in addition to the fear of the unknown powers, and the reality of the unpredictability of these powers early humans began to mentally invent reasons for the existence of these uncontrollable events. Along with these mental inventions came the creation of supreme or supreme beings that not only had the power to create these events, but also had the power to control such events. Paying homage and worshiping the supreme power and/or powers is perhaps the beginning of religion.

In addition to early humans seeking something and/or someone greater than themselves to hopefully control things which they were unable to control, they perhaps began to question their own existence. Stated in other terms, questions such as why we are here and what happens once we no longer have physical existence began to germinate in their minds? This type of thinking probably led to them questioning why they existed and what was the meaning of life, which led to a connecting question, what happens after death? At some point in early human history the brain power of humans reached a point where the thinking beyond the day-to-day grind lead them to believe that their existence meant more than what happens on a day-to-day basis. They perhaps began to question whether life had meaning beyond the short period of time they existed. Stated in other terms was there life after death? Along with this type of thinking and questioning came the development of the belief that there has to be more. Additionally, the thinking may have followed the following line of thought, what is there after death and what are the conditions for achieving the afterlife? Does everyone achieve the same afterlife? If there are different afterlife events, what are they and what determines who obtains which afterlife event? With this type of thinking religion began to expand and take on additional meaning; meanings beyond giving meaning to and protection from events beyond their control.

The incorporation of religion in our lives is perhaps an acknowledgment that, as human beings, we are not all powerful. Events such as ones which have been previously mentioned as well as invisible things such as diseases and deaths were unquestionable evidence to early humans that there were powers beyond human control. As humans we recognized that something's or someone existed that are more powerful than we humans. Thus, the spirit or spirits that possessed these powerful forces had to have extraordinary powers and in the minds of early humans, rituals were developed to pay homage to this power as well as decrease the chances of the powerful spirits becoming angry and releasing more destruction. Perhaps this is what has led to many of the beliefs and rituals of many religions of today including the five major religions which will be discuss later in this chapter.

What is the Purpose of Religion?

As human understanding of nature has increased we have, to a great degree, moved away from some of our unfounded beliefs; thus many religions have evolved into codes of conduct which allow us to have a somewhat sane, rewarding and hopefully orderly life as well as preparation for an afterlife. Although, as humans we are, metaphorically speaking, at the top of the food chain we as our distance relatives recognized there are forces in nature such as tornadoes, hurricane, lightning strikes, to mention only three over which we have very little control. Religion or faith, whichever we choose to call our higher order beliefs, tend to give us some comfort when we are confronted with things over which we have no or very little control. Robinson (2004) believes that religion has established social structures that give meaning to its inhabitants. He cites aspects of morality and virtuous living as originating from religion. While difficult or impossible to explain or give a sensible reason for its existence or happening we take solace in thinking and believing that there is a higher power that causes or allows these thing to happen and that power has a reason for allowing such to happen and one day in this life or another life we will understand the reasoning for such actions. Therefore, religion/faith provides us humans a reason to continue our lives and believe that there are reasons for living. Stated in other terms, things for which we do not understand and/or have no explanation for their existence we attribute their existence to the will of a power or powers greater than our own. To experience life's events over which we have little or no control without faith that there are reasons for their existence would be overwhelmingly demoralizing. Without the previously mentioned faith, life would have very little meaning. Denison, Kvisto, McClenon, and Swatos (1998) believe religion is one of the tools that have explained the meaning of life in the world.

It is a truism that there are numerous views of what religion is and religion's cultural impact upon various societies. As previously stated Tylor (1871) defined religion as the belief in spiritual beings. Geertz (1973) and Asal (1982) defined religion as "an organized collection of belief systems, cultural systems, and world views that related humanity to spirituality and sometimes to moral values." The authors continue by reminding us that religion is envisioned to give meaning to life and clarify the source of life and the origin of the world. They continue by saying that even if someone decides not to be part of any religious group, he or she is still shaped by the society and religion. Their final comments assert that in most cases, humans develop morality, ethics, laws, and way of life from religion; therefore religion is an integral aspect of any society.

However, Johnstone (2007) reminds us that religion is not in full support of facts as established by scientific innovations. In many cases, facts and policies of life have conflicted with religious beliefs and dogma. He further points out that during such instances, religion has been branded as a thwart of growth and development in the modern life style. Eric Morrison (2013) in the following comments lends some support to Johnstone's assertions:

> Religion through its influences with regard to those who practice religion, from a cultural standpoint impacts society in both positive and negative ways. In some societies, religion has acted as an obstacle to the adoption of modernistic

facets of living and interaction of human life. As far as it has influenced morality and equitable living of the past ages, religion does not support scientific and
other innovative features that propel the societies to embrace new challenges
and approaches of living. For instance religion is skewed towards aspects of
church doctrines, beliefs and perception, in most cases, it neglects the necked
reality expressed through science in the world.

Religion Sets Standards for an Orderly Society

Other than natural disasters more wars and major destruction of human
life and property has occurred as a result of religious beliefs than any other
events. Despite this fact, arguably no other doctrine has had a greater influence upon developing an orderly world society than religion and some of its
major precepts. As we look at the five major religions we see that each one
promotes, among other things, love, harmony, peace and respect for other
humans. Some may take exception to this statement; however it is this auth-
or's assertion that it is the various egotistical and selfish viewpoint interpretations that humans have made of the precepts that have created conflict, not
the religious doctrines. Offered as examples, the Ten Commandments in the
Torah and the Holy Bible and the Eight Fold Path of the Buddhist religion
each promotes living together in peaceful harmony.

One may question the impact religion has on world events when we view
destruction and upheaval that too often exist in today's world; however, one
must also consider how much worse world affairs would be without the calm-
ing effects of rational individuals influenced by their religious beliefs. If one
considers a basic nature of humans to be selfish and too often greedy, the impact of persons under the influence of their religious beliefs often is the calm-
ing effect of bringing rational thinking to dangerous and selfish situations.
Additionally, often it is the influence of religious beliefs that brings sanity to
situations after both human made and natural disasters occur. Yet an additional view point with regard to religion is it helps human kind define what
is good and bad and gives guidelines with regard to how to live one's life.

Religion Gives Meaning to Suffering and Sacrifice

Undoubtedly, throughout the history of human kind we have given thought
to many questions of human existence, one such question relates to human
suffering and sacrifices. To be more specific, questions such as why do we suffer, what is the purpose of suffering and what is the relevance of sacrificing?
One of the major mysteries of the world in which we humans live is the question of why we suffer. In some instances suffering is a result of our own actions or in many cases lack of action and in other instances events beyond

our control causes us to suffer. The old axiom of suffering causes us to become stronger persons may be true in some cases, however the fact remains that few people enjoy the emotional and physical strains caused by suffering. In some religions the issue of suffering is addressed in a manner that let us know that suffering is part of life and the fact we endure emotional and physical pain is part of life, thus enduring such suffering can be and is good for our souls. In the Christian religion we are reminded that the leader of this religion suffered and his disciples suffered. This implies that suffering is part of the human existence and that as humans we will suffer. The Hindu religion also recognize suffering as a part of the composition of human existence and points out that by living a moral, just and honorable life he/she in the afterlife will escape suffering. Similarly, the Buddhist religion through its Four Noble Truths explains that life is suffering and identifies what causes suffering as well as offer a remedy for eliminating suffering through an Eight-Fold Path which is discussed in more detail in this chapter under Five Major Religions heading.

Religion Defines Life After Physical Death

As we review the five major religions, it will be noted that each makes references to some form of life after death. Questions that can be raised with regard to these references are does life continue in some form after physical death; and is the reference to heaven and hell designed to promote a civil society?

Is Everything Discussed in Religious Documents, Such as the Holy Bible, to be Taken Literally?

Viewing religion from a cultural perspective, one has to raise the question of should everything in the various religions and their holy books be taken literally? Additionally and perhaps more importantly is the question, was the statements included in the previously mentioned documents meant to be taken literally or were they included to emphasize certain points? Raising these questions is not intended, by this author, to question the validity and/or the accuracy of the content authors of the Holy Scriptures rather they are raised to stimulate thinking.

If Religion No Longer Existed Would We as Humans Develop Something Similar to Religion to Explain Our Existence?

Two of the great areas of debate with regard to human existences continue to be why are we here and how did we get here? With regard to how did we get here, science through the concept of evolution offer an answer by emphasizing humans evolved over millions of years from lower forms of animals. In opposition to the evolution theory various religious views provide an explanation of human existences as occurring from supernatural intervention, to be more specific, humans did not evolve from lower forms of animals, some supernatural being created and willed what we know today as humans into existence. It is amazing that despite magnitude of the gap between these two viewpoints modern society has allowed these two views to continue to exist in the human domain.

One of the things that separate humans from many forms of animal life is the vast curiosity of us humans. Despite some of the commonalities between some animals, such as primates and humans, religion provides humans with what we humans like to think of as moral dignity and responsibility. Moral dignity and responsibility means the ability to consider and care for the well-being of others beyond our own skin and kind.

Why Are There Many Different Religions and Religious Views?

It is virtually impossible to accurately identify and list all of the world religions because there are many different religions and many branches of those base religions. The fact that there are many philosophies and beliefs that are considered a religion is testimony regarding the importance an enormous number of people place on the precepts and beliefs which govern. direct and impact their lives. Additionally, there is a significant number of people in the world, if not, a majority of persons who believe in a power or powers greater than themselves which have a significant impact upon their day-to-day lives as well as their future on earth and perhaps beyond.

As is discussed in this text, many, if not all, of the cultural views one develops is a result of environment. As humans we develop many of our beliefs and attitudes from our contact and interaction with significant others and those with whom we respect. Ironically, some of our attitudes and beliefs which help form our cultural views are the result of interacting with person whom we significantly disagree. In this case, our cultural views are in opposition to those with whom we disagree. Given the fact that religion is to a large degree culture; therefore religion is significantly influenced by the regions in which we live and interact. As we review the five major religions we will see that each of these religions follows this concept of being developed in response to certain cultural situations prevalent at the time of the religions conception. A similar situation occurs with regard to religions which separate from the base religion and develop either a new religion or a denomination of the base religion. This is generally the way that religions have multiplied and expanded across the world.

Religion and Culture

Religion or the expression of faith in something or someone greater than one's self goes beyond attending religious services. The expression of faith includes adhering to some, if not all, of the basic principles and beliefs that serve as the foundation of the faith. Additionally, the expression of faith also includes recognition and at least occasional celebration of important histori-cal events of the faith. Similar to ethnic/racial groups who celebrate or rec-ognize significant events related to that part of their culture, individuals of a religious persuasion also place great importance in significant events related to their faith. Therefore, for some people, their religious faith transcends all the other variables of their cultural composition.

It has been stated that religion unite humans, which is partially true, and this would be a completely great act if everyone agreed upon what is the best interest of human kind. Unfortunately, there is no oneness and never will be, with regard to this issue. A religion's views will set standards of decorum however true to the mental makeup of humans some of those views will be questioned which will lead to a break away from some of the precepts of those views thus a new group of religious concepts will be formed. Many times this type of action is berated by those that do not agree with the newly formed religious concepts; however, this is how cultures are established, like-wise this is how various religious views and concepts are formed.

Another fact that perhaps explains a reason there are numerous different religions is testament to the mental versatility of humans. Stated in other terms, humans are endowed with the ability to process information.

One may ask the question how relevant is religion in today's society? An answer can be found in the fact that there are a large number of beliefs and philosophies which are tagged as religions. Thus if religion is not relevant in today's society, then religion would disappear; instead more and more reli-gions appear almost yearly if not more often.

OVERVIEW OF THE FIVE MAJOR RELIGIONS

This part of the chapter will provide a brief overview of the following faiths/religions: **Christianity, Judaism, Islam, Hinduism, and Buddhism**.

This author is very much aware that scores of books have been written about each of the faith/religions mentioned in this chapter, which indicates that there is a tremendous amount of information on each subject; therefore, no attempt is being made to give detailed coverage of any of the previously mentioned faith/religions. It is hoped that the reader will be inspired to do additional research to increase his/her knowledge.

Christianity

Brief History of Christianity

Jesus of Nazareth was born and reared a Jew and when he began his ministry he differed with the Jewish religion when he proclaimed himself as the Son of God. His preaching of salvation upset the Jewish religious structure of that time. Jesus of Nazareth had disciples who assisted him with his ministry as they began to convert followers from the traditional Jewish religion of that time. Some of the differences in the teaching of Jesus Christ brought him into conflict with many in the Jewish establishment as well as the Roman Empire. According to Blainey, (2012).

> Palestine at that time was on the outpost of the Roman Empire which was ruled by leaders that preached that man should obey the gods of the Roman Empire. Blainey continues by stating that the start of Christianity was very turbulent for the first Christians when they began to shun the gods of the Roman Empire. He further contends that the division between the first Christians and the Roman Empire is what led to the death of Jesus of Nazareth. After the death of Jesus it was His disciples who continued to spread the word of God. In 313 AD the Edict of Milan was signed between Constantine, the Roman emperor in the west and Licinius the emperor in the east which allowed Christians to openly practice Christianity without the fear of persecution. Later Constantine embraced Christianity and the Christian religion became the preferred religion of the west. Blainey, in his time frame of the development of Christianity moves forward by pointing out that during the Reformation of the 1600s the Christian church with regard to some of its doctrines were challenged by Martin Luther, and John Calvin as a result the Protestant church of the Christian religion was formed by Martin Luther.

According to Bryan (2007) Martin Luther viewed salvation as a gift from God through the forgiveness of sin and this should not be dictated by the Pope and the Bishops of the Roman Catholic Church. Nail, (2013), makes us aware that these basic beliefs gave everyone, no matter their social class or gender the right to practice religion. This split which is referred to as the Protestant Reformation was the first major spilt of the Roman Catholic Church. Rome and the Roman Empire's army during the time of Jesus Christ's physical appearance on earth were the military and political rulers of the region in which Christianity developed. Christianity and its influence spread throughout the Roman Empire and later throughout the rest of Europe; as we know today, Christianity has also spread throughout the rest of the world. Christianity, which is one of the most influential of the major world religions, is also one of the youngest religions.

There are three main divisions of Christianity: (1) Roman Catholic, (2) Eastern Orthodox, and (3) Protestant. The first of the three divisions that existed was Roman Catholicism. Many of the first churches were established by the Apostle Paul, but were persecuted and even considered by some to be illegal. However in the fourth century, Constantine won his place as Roman emperor and gave praise to the Christian God for his victory, in battle, by proclaiming his conversion to Christianity thus its status as a major religion in the Roman Empire. This gave Christianity a strong footing and ensured its survival. The Roman Empire fell in 476 A.D. and the Eastern and Western Christians were no longer unified by the centrally located Rome and the differences in their beliefs and practices began to create even more divisions between them. After many years of debate between the two regional groups, in 1054 AD a split occurred between the Roman Catholic and the newly formed Eastern Orthodox religions, which did not recognize the authority of the Roman Catholic Church. The differences in doctrine lead to the creation of the second major division.

The third division came about in Europe. As previously mentioned a German Monk named Martin Luther posted what later came to be called "95 Theses," which called out any who wished to debate on certain doctrines and practices of the Roman Catholic Church. The movement that occurred as a result of Martin Luther's actions is referred to as the Protestant Reformation, which has led to the development of what is termed Protestant churches.

As previously mentioned currently there are three major divisions within the Christian faith: Roman Catholic, Eastern Orthodox, and Protestant. Within the Protestant group are numerous denominations such as Baptist, Methodist, and Church of Christ, to mention only three. Within the various branches of these denominations are further divisions such as the Southern Baptist and Free Will Baptist to mention only two. Further division can also be seen along ethnic/racial lines. While most Protestant denominations have become open to persons of all ethnic/racial groups, most, however, remain segregated, perhaps not by edict, but by tradition. This is especially true in the case of African Americans. During the period of slavery and reconstruction, primarily in southern American states, although not exclusively in those areas, African Americans were not welcome in churches where the congregations were predominately Caucasians. Denied access to their home countries' religions, many African Americans adopted and developed branches of the Caucasian-dominated churches, to help serve their religious inclinations. Thus the separation of religious congregations along racial lines in America continues today. Regardless of the division or denomination of the church, the Holy Bible is the scared text of all groups.

As previously stated there are three major divisions of the Christian religion. The Eastern Orthodox formed the second division when it broke away from what some consider the original Christian church, the Roman Catholic Church in 1054 A.D.; the division occurred as a result of disagreement over doctrine and ecclesiastical authority. Even though most Eastern Orthodox churches have common beliefs, principles, and doctrines, each tends to be oriented toward the nation in which it resides, Russian Orthodoxy, Romanian Orthodox, and Bulgarian Orthodox to name only three as examples.

Some Basic Beliefs of Christians

Although there are three divisions and numerous denominations within the Christian religion, there are some beliefs that are held in common by all. Some of them are:

- All Christians believe in one God, who is the Father and Creator of all human kind.
- All Christians belied in the Trinity: the Father, the Son and the Holy Spirit.
- All Christians believe that Jesus of Nazareth is the Christ and is the Son of God, born of a Virgin and was sent to Earth to live a sinless life, thus setting an example for earthly faithful to follow.
- All Christians believe in the Virgin birth.
- All Christians believe that Jesus was crucified for human kind's sins and was buried and resurrected in three days and later ascended to Heaven.
- All Christians believe the Bible is the Holy Scripture provided as encouragement and guidance by which they are to live.

Significant Events of Christianity

There are numerous events and significant dates that are important to Christians; however, not all Christians observe each of them. Despite this, the two most important events in Christianity and, generally speaking, observed by all Christians are Christmas Day, which represents Jesus Christ's birthday, and Easter, which represents the resurrection of Jesus Christ.

Summary

One of the major precepts in which most if not all Christians and Jews believe is the Ten Commandments.

1. You shall not have other gods beside me
2. You shall not carve idols for yourselves in the shape of anything in the sky above or on the earth below or in the water beneath the earth; you shall not bow down before them or worship them.
3. You shall not take the Lord's name in vain.
4. You shall keep holy the Sabbath day.
5. You shall honor your father and mother.
6. You shall not murder.
7. You shall not commit adultery
8. You shall not steal.
9. You shall not bear false witness against your neighbor.
10. You shall not covet your neighbor's house. You shall not covet your neighbor's wife.

Commandments one through four are guides with regard to love and worship of God. The last six are guidelines for loving and caring for others. All of the commandments can be considered culturally based.

Judaism

Brief History of Judaism

It is impossible to understand the history of Judaism without discussing the history of the Jewish people. Much of the early history of Judaism is told in the first five chapters of the Old Testament of the Bible (Torah). Abraham is considered the founder of the faith, which is called Judaism. When one traces the lineage of Abraham, it is recognized that some of the best known persons of the **Torah** are of the seed of Abraham. Isaac, and Jacob, also known as Israel, whose decedents were called Israelites, all are of the lineage of Abraham. According to Scripture, descendants of Jacob migrated to Egypt where they were enslaved and Moses received the Law from God and lead them from bondage.

The word Jew can refer to any person of Jewish parentage; thus this means any one born of those descendants of the group described in biblical and post biblical sources. Jew is also used to refer to an ethnic, cultural, and religious group who adhere to a body of beliefs known as Judaism.

The history of the Jews is replete with conflicts, victories, and defeats as they struggled to attain and retain the "promise land." Today, the Nation of Israel, which was established in 1948, is recognized by Jews as their homeland. The word homeland is somewhat misleading in that not all Jews originate from the current State of Israel. To better understand what a Jew is, one needs to understand that from a cultural standpoint, the term Jewish is not a designation of a race of people. Anyone through the process of conversion can become a Jew; therefore, a Jew can be of any race or ethnicity. Additionally, one does not have to be born in Israel to be a Jew. Also one does not have to be born a Jew, as previously stated, he/she can become a Jew by going through the process of converting to Judaism. Given this information, to a large extent, being a Jew is a way of life and perhaps a state of mind. Furthermore, one does not have to be religious to be a Jew.

To further understand Judaism, one must understand that currently there are three major sects or versions of Judaism: **Orthodox, Reform,** and **Conservative**. Orthodox Judaism believes in the teachings of the concepts in the Torah and further believes that they are unchanging and should be followed unaltered as outlined in the Scripture. Reform Judaism does not strictly adhere to all Jewish traditions as do the Orthodox Jews. Conservative Judaism believes in the scholarly study and interpretation of the Torah. Stated another way, followers of the Conservative philosophy believe that the beliefs of Judaism should be open to evaluation and interpretation and be changeable based upon contemporary scholarly findings, study, and interpretation.

One can see that defining Judaism is both complex and a multifaceted endeavor and as previously stated is almost impossible to define without defining what a Jew is. For Orthodox and Conservative Jews, a Jew is defined as any person whose mother was or is a Jew or any person who has completed the process of conversion to Judaism; whereas, for the Reform Jews, children whose mother or father was or is a Jew is Jewish as long as they were reared as a Jew.

Some Basic Beliefs of Judaism

In listing some of the beliefs of Judaism, only some of the beliefs held by the three major sects of Judaism have been listed. There are other beliefs held by Orthodox Jews that Conservative and/or Reform Jews may view in different ways.

The basic theological premise of the Jewish faith is namely that God exists, that He created the world by His will, and that He revealed His will to Israel and mankind at Sinai (Donin, 1972). Jews believe in one God. As previously stated, the Torah, or the first five books of the Hebrew Bible (Old Testament), is the foundation of doctrine, customs, and observances. The Oral Torah served to provide clarification for many of the commandments; this served as the cornerstone for what was to become the Talmud.

The bond between the Jewish people and the land of Israel began during the time of Abraham. When the children of Israel fled oppression and slavery in Egypt, they sought the land that had been promised them in Deuteronomy 34:4 (Trepp, 1980).

In summary some of the basic beliefs of Judaism are:

- God exists.
- God is the Creator of all that exist.
- God is incorporeal (without a body)
- God has communicated through prophets.
- The Torah was revealed by God to Moses.

Significant Events of Judaism

Halackhah: The system of Jewish law is Halackhah; its major emphasis is on deeds as it asks for a commitment in behavior. The law also deals with ethical obligations and religious duties.

Sabbath: Day of rest, starting at sundown on Friday evening and lasting through sundown Saturday.

Kosher: Kashrut, more commonly known as keeping kosher, sets forth what Jews may eat, the acceptable method of slaughter of animals, and the cooking utensils and cleaning methods that may be used. With regard to acceptable foods to eat, generally speaking, the rule is that Jews may eat any land mammal that has cloven hooves and chews its cud; this includes sheep, cattle, goats, and deer. From the water, they may eat anything that has fins and scales. Shellfish such as lobsters, oysters, shrimp, clams, and crabs are excluded. With regard to fowl, birds of prey may not be eaten; however, fowl such as chicken, geese, ducks, and turkeys are permitted. Rodents, reptiles, amphibians, and insects are forbidden (Rich, 2005).

There are restrictions with regard to combining foods. One may not eat meat and dairy together; however, eating fish and dairy, or dairy and eggs is acceptable. These are a few of the rules and/or restriction; for more information, one should consult a Jewish dietician or Rabbi. Also one must be aware that not all Jews adhere to all of these practices.

Jewish Festivals: Some of the festivals observed by Jewish people are **Rosh Hashanah, Yom Kippur, Sukkoth, Hanukkah, Passover** and **Shavuot**.

Rosh Hashanah is the Jewish New Year, which occurs in the fall.

Yom Kippur, the Day of Atonement, is the climax of the High Holy Day season. It is considered a day of spiritual reckoning where Jews spend the entire day in the synagogue in prayer, meditation, and fasting.

Sukkoths is a thanksgiving festival. This is a time of rejoicing, engaging in hearty meals which symbolize a bountiful harvest.

Hanukkah is perhaps the second most observed Jewish holiday. This holiday is based on a historical story of a miracle. The story relates that the Greeks had entered the temple and desecrated all of the holy oil except for one flask. Based upon volume, this oil should have lasted only one day, instead it lasted eight day. Thus the tradition of lighting candles for eight days.

Passover is the most observed holiday for the Jewish people (Rich 2005). Passover celebrates the Jewish peoples' exodus from Egypt and their bondage in that area. On the eve of the exodus, the Jews marked their doorpost with lambs' blood, and the angel of death which killed all Egyptian firstborn children passed over the houses marked with the blood. As a result of this event, it is written that Pharaoh released the slaves and allowed them to leave Egypt.

Shavuot celebrates the giving of the Torah to the Jewish people (Rich, 2005).

Summary

As previously stated the Ten Commandments which are in the Torah is a guide for all Jews.

Islam

Brief History of Islam

Islam is the youngest of the major religions of Christianity, Judaism, Hinduism, and Buddhism The faith that we know as Islam began in Mecca during the Seventh Century A. D. The city of Mecca is situated close to the Red Sea, which in earlier times this location made travel to Mecca easier for persons of the Islamic faith. This is where many of the early Muslims lived and where Islamic culture began.

The Islamic Prophet Muhammad was born around 570 A. D. in Mecca Arabia and is said to have had a revelation from the Archangel Gabriel which lead to the establishment of the religion Islam. According to Berry (2007) in 610 C.E., Muhammad visited the caves outside Mecca to meditate. The angel Gabriel appeared and spoke the word "Iqraa: which means recite or read. Also according to Berry this was the first revelation within the series of revelations given by Allah (God). Allen and Toorawa (2011) also inform us that these revelations lasted for the next twenty-three years. The revelation among other things revealed to Muhammad that there was only one God, **Allah**, and He is the Creator of the world. It should be noted that during that period of time in the Arabic region of the world, as well as other part of the world, belief in and worship of more than one god was common.

After the initial revelations, the Prophet Muhammad was able to convert some of his relatives, including some in-laws and his wife Khadija, to Islam. The Arabic word Islam means the submission or surrender of one's will to the only true God worthy of worshiping, Allah, and anyone who worships Allah is called a **Muslim**. Additionally, the word Islam means peace, which is a natural consequence of total submission to the will of Allah.

According to the Islamic religion, Adam was the first prophet sent by Allah. It is noted that Muhammad is a prophet, not a god nor considered the Son of God. Additionally, the Islamic religion considers Jesus and Abraham as prophets; however Muhammad is considered to be the greatest and major prophet.

After the death of Muhammad in 632 A. D., Abu-Bakr became the leader; some Muslims did not accept him as the successor thus there was an ideological split in the Muslim world; the division produced two major groups: the Sunni and the Shi'a. The division appears to have been primarily over earthly leadership of the Muslim faith. Today there are a number of Muslim sects around the world. In the United States, within the past century there has been a development among African Americans groups, commonly referred to as **Black Muslims or Nation of Islam**. Regardless of the sect, all follow many of the teachings of the Prophet Muhammad and acknowledge Allah as the one and only God.

Basic Beliefs and Traditions of Islam

The **Qur'an** is the holy scripture of Islam which was revealed to the Prophet Muhammad by Allah. The Qur'an contains valuable information, practices and scriptures for practicing Muslims. To Muslims, the Qur'an is the word of God and these words express to them His will. The relevance of the Qur'an to Muslims can be compared to the relevance of the Torah to Jews and the Holy Bible to Christians. The Qur'an is divided into 114 chapters and the chapters are divided into verses.

According to John Sabini (1994), there are **Five Pillars of Islam** and the foundation of the Islamic religion is based upon these five pillars and these actions are ones that all Muslims must perform, if possible, to remain on the correct path. These pillars are giving testimony to: **faith, prayer, almsgiving, fasting,** and **pilgrimage**. The following explanation of the five pillars is based upon the writings of John Sabini.

Testimony: (Shahada) This is the profession of **faith**. "There is no god but God; and Muhammad is the messenger of God."

Prayer: (Salah) Every adult Muslim, male or female, of sound mind and body, is required to pray five times a day: at sunset (beginning of the Muslim day), in the evening, at dawn, at noon, and in mid-afternoon. The Qur'an promises that those who pray and perform good deeds will enter Paradise, and tradition also states that each prayer absolves one of minor sins. An important fact that helping professions should know is that a Muslim at prayer should not be interrupted, stared at, or photographed and a person should not walk in front of the praying person (Sabini, 1994).

Almsgiving: (Zakat) Benevolence and giving to the less fortunate is highly valued. Not only is it valued, it is mandated by the Qur'an.

Fasting: (Sawm) According to Sabini, fasting is meant to test the self-denial and submission of the faithful Muslims and permit those that have abundant resources to experience the deprivations of the poor. Both men and women and all but the youngest children are required to fast. Once a year for a period of one month, Muslims are required to abstain from food, drink, smoking, and sexual relation during the hours of daylight. This occurs during **Ramadan**, the ninth month of the Islamic calendar. It is noted that the Islamic calendar is based on the Lunar months which have twelve months in a year; however, the Lunar year is shorter than the solar year by about ten days.

Pilgrimage: The major pilgrimage is called the **Hajj**. The Qur'an requires that every adult Muslim of either gender and in sound body and mind make a pilgrimage to Mecca at least once in a lifetime, if possible. The destination is the Holy Mosque in Mecca.

Significant Events of Islam

There are a number of celebrations and events associated with Islam, and as is the situation with the other major religions, not all Muslims fully participate. Also, some events are celebrated more fully within one Muslim country and not so in another. Most of the major events have been outlined in the belief section.

Summary

In recent years, for a variety of reasons, persons of Muslim faith have received considerable negative press; however, it is important to separate the religious faith of this religion from actions by persons and/or governments which interpret and use violent acts as part of the requirement to be a Muslim. We should recognize that this religion is based upon peace and recognize other religious leaders such as Jesus Christ and Abraham, to mention only two, as holy persons. While some may debate the action of some persons considered a Muslim as defining the religion, again the fact is the religion is based upon peace.

Buddhism

Brief History of Buddhism

The founder of Buddhism, or as he referred to himself, **way-shower**, was **Siddhartha Gautama**. He was born in approximately 560 B. C. in the area that is present-day Nepal, India. Gautama's father was a local ruler who practiced Hinduism; therefore Siddhartha Gautama was reared in the ancient Hinduism religion. Much of the narrative of Gautama's life is weaved with legends in that most of his history was written long after his death. By way of legend, it is said that a white elephant touched the side of Gautama's mother and by this action she knew she was with child. The white elephant was considered a divine animal, and its action of touching the side of his mother became evidence of the divine destiny of the coming child. Legend also records that his mother gave birth to him in a standing position while holding on to a branch that had miraculously lowered itself to assist her. With regard to his birth, it is also reported that he did not emerge through the womb, but emerged painlessly from the side of his mother, thus saving him the trauma of a vaginal birth. This method of birth is important in that it is believed that a vaginal birth wipes out the memory of past lives and is further believed by Buddhists that Siddhartha Gautama retained memory of all of his previous lives. It should be further explained that Buddhists believe that one is born, dies, and reborn until he/she attains **Nirvana**. Nirvana is considered to be a state of existence where suffering no longer exists.

As previously stated, Siddhartha Gautama was born into royalty, privilege, and affluence, but at approximately age twenty-nine, he had a life changing experience that provided direction to the rest of his life. While out riding, he encountered four sights that would change his life and began his quest for enlightenment, or Buddha (the term Buddha means enlightenment). The sights he saw were: an old man, a sick man, a dead man, and a holy man (Ganeri, p. 10). Since he had led a sheltered life, he had not experienced many of the realities of life: infirmity, death, and illness. These sights gave him cause to contemplate the many aspects of life. Due to this contemplation, Gautama decided to leave the comfortable life he had known in search of answers to the question of how to find the positive counterparts of the suffering states of birth, aging, illness, death, sorrow, and corruption (Armstrong, p. 5). He then began to devote his life to extreme asceticism, which he later abandon because he was not finding the answers to the perplexing questions thus he began to devote his life to meditation.

While meditating under a tree, Siddhartha Gautama found the answer. This discovery became known as **the middle way**. The middle way is the principle that between extreme asceticism or depravity and indulgence is a rationed life in which the body is given what it needs to function optimally, but no more (Novak & Smith, 2004). A result of his meditation, and what contemporaries call revelations, there have developed within the Buddhist tradition **Four Nobel Truths** and an **Eight-Fold Path**, which will be explained in the next section basic beliefs.

Some Basic Beliefs of Buddhism

As have previously been mentioned, Siddhartha Gautama was reared in the Hindu religion, but he did not think that some of the precepts of the religion answered some of the basic questions of life, such as why do humans suffer? Although he did not find the answer to this and other questions of life through Hinduism, he retained one of the basic Hindu beliefs, that being reincarnation after death. Gautama believed, and this became a major part of Buddhist belief, that one is born, dies, and is reborn again and again until one attains the state of Nirvana. As previously mentioned, Nirvana is considered to be a state of existence where suffering no longer exists and the causes of suffering have been removed.

Also as previously mentioned, Buddhists believe there are Four Nobel Truths and these truths explain suffering. They are (1) life is suffering. This basic truth is saying that suffering is part of living and being human. (2) Cravings cause suffering. (3) To end suffering, one must end cravings. (4) The means to end cravings can be found by following the Eight-Fold Path. If one follows the Eight-Fold Path, it will lead him/her to **Enlightenment** (Buddha). The steps along this path are (1) Right Views, (2) Right Intentions, (3) Right Speech, (4) Right Action, (5) Right Livelihood (occupation), (6) Right Effort, (7) Right Contemplation, and (8) Right Meditation. As one can extract from these steps to Enlightenment, they deal with morality. If one has the correct morality and intentions, he/she is on the correct path to Enlightenment.

There are a number of versions or sects of Buddhism and some appear to have elevated Gautama to the status of deity; however, he did not proclaim himself a deity. He said he was a way-shower.

Significant Events of Buddhism

As is the case with the other major religions, there are a number of celebrations; however, the two most important festivals for most Buddhists are **Wesak** and **Dharma Day**. **Wesak** is the celebration of the Buddha's enlightenment, and is considered the most important celebration in the Buddhist year. Buddhists plan most things around a lunar calendar; therefore, this festival is held on the full moon of May/June. **Dharma Day** celebrates the day in which the Buddha arose from his session of enlightenment.

Summary

The person who many refer to as Buddha, however he considered himself as "the way shower," saw several forms of life which distressed him and he dedicate his life to finding ways of living which counteracted suffering. In this process he developed Four Nobel Truths and the Eight-Fold Path. Some may consider this similar to the Ten Commandments of Christianity and Judaism and Five Pillars of the Muslim faith.

Hinduism

Brief History of Hinduism

Identifying the history of Hinduism is more difficult than identifying the history for the other major religions because there is no one central individual or figure to which one can associate its development. Some Hindu individuals say the religion has existed forever. Hinduism is **henotheistic** with regard to its identification of deities. Stated another way, Hindus believe in a central deity, called **Brahman**, which is a pervading spirit or oneness of the universe, present in all things considered sacred and honored. In addition to Brahman, some may also worship what is considered minor deities.

The few historical things that are known about Hinduism indicate that the basis of the religion is a mixture of an ancient civilization of people, and their religious beliefs, who lived over 5000 years ago in the Indus Valley region of the Indian continent and the religious beliefs of Aryan people who invaded the Indus Valley region approximately 3000 years ago. Although the history of Hinduism is difficult to identify, what is known is Hinduism is the oldest religion of the major religions, Christianity, Judaism, Islam, and Buddhism, and perhaps the oldest religion in the world. Hinduism is the dominate religion of India.

Hinduism differs somewhat from the other major religions discussed in this text in that there is no one defined founder, no single scripture and no universal set of teachings. Many of the teaching of the religion throughout its history have differing philosophies and there have been many different holy books written. Some Hindus do not consider Hinduism to be a religion but a way of life. However, the followers of Hinduism follow a basic set of principles and concepts and believe in Brahman, whom they consider to be the Supreme Being.

While Hinduism recognizes only one Supreme Being, there is a triad, to be more accurate, one God with three persons: Brahma, who is considered the creator of the world and all creatures; Vishnu is considered the preserver of the universe; and Shiva is considered the destroyer to assure that re-creation can be achieved. It has been said that Hindus worship multiple forms of the one God but there are several other secondary gods or deities that Hindus may or may not worship because of the differing teachings. One thing that separates Hinduism from other religions is that there are many different practices and beliefs within the religion itself. Some of the deities that may be worshiped are:

Surya–God of the Sun
Kali–Goddess of time and death
Bhuvaneshwri–Queen of the phenomenal world
Indra–god of thunder, rain as well as other events. (Hardon, 2013)

There are four sacred Hindu Vedas texts and they are: Rig Veda, Sama Veda, Yajur Veda and Atharva Veda. Veda means wisdom, knowledge or vision. The laws of the Vedas regulate social, legal, domestic and religious customs. The Vedas are the most sacred books of India and are the original scriptures of Hindus teachings. Each Veda contains four separate parts, which include hymns, rituals, theologies, and philosophies. These Scriptures are the doctrines that encompass all facets of Hindu life. Dharma is considered the divine power that makes things possible and is regarded as the morality that steers humans to act ethnically and in service to humanity and to God.

According to Hardon (2013) the Rig Veda is the oldest Hindu literature and contains hymns. The earlier writings in the Rig Veda spoke of gods of the earth, god of the air, and gods of the bright heaven. By the end of the Rig Veda writing it began to speak of and worship of unknown gods. The Sama Veda was written to compliment the Rig Veda and provided four chants and tunes for some of the hymnal prayers. The Yajur Veda addressed not only the gods but also to the cultic objects that acquired sacred character by reason of invocation. The final book in the Veda is the Atharva Veda which is considered to be very similar to the Rig Veda, but incorporate magical spells or witchcraft.

Again, using Hardon's information base with regard to Hindu religion Karma is generally thought to govern the cycles of reincarnation. Karma is a Sanskrit word whose literal meaning is "action" and refers to the law that every action has an equal reaction, either immediately or at some point in the future. Hindus believe that human beings can create good or bad repercussions for their actions and Karma determines how they live their next life- good karma results in rebirth to a higher level while bad karma can cause a person to be reborn at a lower level or even as an animal.

Some Basic Beliefs of Hinduism

Perhaps the best understanding of the Hindu religion does not come from its history, but from its basic beliefs and goals. A major goal of people who are Hindu is to attain **moksa**, or **enlightened liberation** of the **Atman** or **self** from the wheel of rebirth or the cycles of birth and death. **Reincarnation**, or **samsara**, is the belief that one is reborn after death. The physical form of rebirth is determined by the level of spiritual purity that the person has achieved by the time of his or her death.

The belief in **Karma** is a major aspect of the Hindu religion. Karma is the law of action and reaction. For every action taken, we face a reaction in the future. Therefore, chance and luck, from the Hindu perspective, does not exist. Consequently, everything happens according to the positive or negative energy stored from our actions in the Karma. In coordination with Karma, the **Dharma** is used to assure spiritual growth toward moksa. Dharma is a set of moral codes and correct behaviors that are taught in ancient texts and rituals. Hinduism promotes the belief in meditation and rejection of the material world as the final step to **Nirvana** where the Atman (self) and Brahman (absolute spirit) are reunited resulting in the individual attaining moksa (enlighten liberation).

As previously stated, the Hindu religion is a henotheistic religion which believes in the oneness of spirit (Brahman) but may worship that spirit by way of a multitude of gods who are seen as coming from a divine source. The sacred texts of the Hindu religion are the **Vedas** (wisdom). The Vedas are four collections of religious writings, believed by Hindu followers to be inspired, composed approximately 3000 years ago. Vedas are considered the oldest and most profound source of Hindu wisdom available to study. Vedic chants are used in modern worship ceremonies. The **Brahmans** and **Upanishads** are texts that seek to explain the Veda and are often used as reference material and are the basis of specialized branches of Hinduism. The religion does not have explicit doctrine or institutional forms of worship; therefore, the practices have become regional in expression. Stated in other terms, in different areas and regions of the world where the Hindu religion is practiced, each has developed its own expression of the faith.

Considering the fact that expression of the Hindu faith is regionalized, one source of identity is which creator god they choose to follow. The three major figures of the modern creation gods are **Brahma** (the creator), **Vishnu** (the preserver), and **Shiva** (the destroyer). These three represent a **Trimurti** (trinity) of perspectives about the universe. Vishnu is the generative and positive force. Shiva is a destructive force which is necessary in the creative process. Brahma balances these two opposing forces. The three are not separate beings but different aspects of the one universal spirit.

Significant Events of Hinduism

Because Hindu religion is regionalized, it is virtually impossible to list all of the significant events and festivals.

Summary

The Hindu religion is the oldest of the five major religions and in some way the most difficult to explain to persons not of the Hindu faith. As is the case with the other four major religions the Hindu faith promotes peace and harmony in life.

SOME COMMONALITIES AND DIFFERENCES OF THE FIVE MAJOR RELIGIONS

Commonalities

Codes of conduct: All of the five major religions have codes of conduct.

Restrictions on consumptions of certain foods: Muslims abstain from eating pork; this is also true of some persons of the Jewish religion. Other religions avoid eating the flesh of animals for various reasons. Hindus avoid eating beef because they view cattle as sacred. Buddhists avoid eating the flesh of some animals because they believe the killing of animals is a cruel practice.

Belief in an afterlife: Christians believe in heaven and hell; they believe the direction of one's afterlife depends on how one lives his/her life on earth. Islam and Judaism have similar beliefs although they may have a different name for heaven and hell. Hindus and Buddhists believe in reincarnation.

The Buddhist believe that one is reincarnated until he/she has lived a life of Nirvana where reincarnation ceases.

End of time: Islam, Judaism, and Christianity believe that a savior will come when the world ends. It should be noted that Christians believe that a savior, Jesus, has come and will return at the end of time.

Holidays: All of the five major religions have holidays/special days and or occasions set aside to honor or emphasize specific past events that are considered central to their religion. Provided as examples: Christians celebrate the birth of Jesus, Muslims celebrate the birth of their major prophet Mohammad and Buddhist celebrate the birthday of Buddha, Siddhartha. Jews celebrate Hanukkah and Hindu celebrate Bikrami Samuat (Hindu New Year).

Differences: Each of the five major religions has different holy guidelines to which they adhere. Jewish faith has the Tanakh and the Talmud. Christianity has the Holy Bible. Islam has the Qur'an. Hindu has several books including Vedas, and Upanishads and Buddhism also has many books including the Tripitaka and the Mahayana.

Similar Teachings Found in Christianity and Hinduism

The following information was extracted from *Parallel Teachings in Hinduism and Christianity,* Wolfe, G. (1995):

(Christian) Acts 17:27, 28: Yet [God] is not far from each of us, for in Him we live and move and have our being. (Hinduism) Upanishad: The whole universe came forth from Brahman and moves in Brahman. . . . In Brahman it lives and has its being.

(Christian) John 8: 12: I am the light of the world; he who follows me will not walk in darkness but have the light of life. (Hinduism) Bhagavad Gita, chapter 10 verse 11: I destroy the darkness born of ignorance with the shining light of wisdom.

(Christian) Revelation 22: 13: I am the Alpha and the Omega, the first and the last, the beginning and the end. (Hinduism) Bhagavad Gita, chapter 7 verse 6, and Chapter 10 verse 20: I am the origin of the whole world and also its dissolution. . . . I am the beginning, the middle, and the end of all things.

Implications for Helping Professionals and Others

What does religion have to do with the helping process? What does religion have to do with cultural diversity? As helping professionals, when we delve into religious background or lack of same, aren't we getting into a sensitive area? As helping professionals, don't we have enough to consider when analyzing clients without involving ourselves in perhaps a controversial area such as religion? These are perhaps similar questions that were either asked or crossed the minds of professional helpers when the issue of considering race and ethnicity as variables in the helping process emerged.

As a helping professional, involving one's self into a client's religious beliefs can be risky. However, what is being proposed is not trying to change a client's religious beliefs but understanding those beliefs and their impact upon the client's behavior. This understanding is necessary when attempting to develop a reasonable helping plan. This understanding is similar to considering one's race and/or ethnicity and the experiences associated with these variables as well as some of the beliefs and values to which the person's cultures expose him/her. Likewise, beliefs and values learned from religious association provide powerful influences on a person's belief systems.

This author contends that if a client/patient believes in a power or powers greater than oneself, this devotion and the beliefs and rules associated with this devotion are a stronger force upon one's behaviors than racial and ethnic influences. For persons who have some devotion to religious beliefs, these beliefs have an impact upon their health belief system. Some clients/patients, if they are influenced by religious beliefs, may feel that their illness and/or disability are the will of God; therefore, their recovery and/or rehabilitation is determined by His will. Similarly, where the person's religious doctrine promotes cause and effect, the person may believe that past behavior is the reason for his current situation. Do these predestination beliefs mean there can be no helpful intervention? The answer to this question is intervention is possible. One goal should be to help them (the helpees) understand that intervention is not meant to change their beliefs, but the fact that there are numerous dimensions to human life should be pointed out to them and that spirituality is a very important dimension that can be used to aid in the healing, recovery, and helping process. The approach a helper should take will be determined by the type of help that is being offered. If the helper does not feel comfortable involving himself in the client/patient's religious life, he should seek the assistance, with the permission of the client/patient, of a helper who is trained in this area.

An important fact the helper should remember is that he does not have to become an expert on religion and religious beliefs. However, as it is important to understand some things with regard to a client's racial and ethnic cultural background, it is equally beneficial to have basic information about religious background and/or orientation. If one does not know, ask.

Conclusion

Unless one is involved in some type of religious counseling, religion as a cultural variable is often overlooked. The truth of this statement is greater perhaps in the United States than it is in some other countries, which do not promote separation of church and government. Despite the separation of religion and governmental affairs, in the United States, for many people, religious doctrines provide considerable guidance and comfort. The influence of one's religious faith often is demonstrated at times of crisis and conflict. Despite the impact that religious faith can and does have on some persons' decisions and actions, especially in times of discomfort, helping professionals often overlook this important variable. Through the process of failing to recognize the influence and impact of this variable, the helping professional may be overlooking a component which can have significant influence on the outcome of the helping plan.

The purpose of this chapter was not to recommend a process by which the helping professional could incorporate religion in the helping plan, nor was it intended to recommend ways to minimize the impact religion may have in the helping process. The purpose of this chapter has been to make the helper aware of the possible importance of religious faith with regard to working with some clients. Additionally, the purpose was to increase the awareness of helping professionals with regard to the major religions in the world and their meanings and importance to those persons who live by their precepts.

There is no question in this author's mind that if we followed the major precepts of the five major religions we would have a peaceful and productive world where love and obedience would prevail. However, it is the wrongful interpretations and selfish intents that have caused religions to be used in ways not intended by the Holy ones and have caused many dreadful acts to be perpetrated in the name of religion.

Review Questions

1. What are the three (3) major religious divisions within the Christian faith?
2. What are the three (3) major beliefs of the Christian faith?
3. What are the three (3) major sects or versions of Judaism?
4. What is the name of the first five (5) books of the Hebrew Bible?

5. Within Judaism, what does Kosher mean?
6. What is the meaning of Yom Kippur?
7. Within the Islam faith, who is the Prophet Muhammad?
8. What are the Five Pillars of Islam?
9. What does the term "the middle way" mean in the faith of Buddhism?
10. What are the Four Nobel Truths in the faith of Buddhism?
11. Within the Hindu faith what does the term "Dharma" mean?
12. Within the Hindu faith what does the term "Karma" mean?

Suggested Activities

1. Discuss with someone of the Christian religion some of the basic beliefs of his/her religious faith.
2. Discuss with someone of the Jewish faith some of the basic beliefs of his/her religion.
3. Discuss with someone of the Islamic religion some of the basic beliefs of his/her faith.
4. Discuss with someone of the Buddhist faith some of the basic beliefs of his/her religion.
5. Discuss with someone of the Hindu religion some of the basic beliefs of his/her faith.

References

Allen R., & Toorawa, S. M. (2011). *Islam: A short guide to the faith.* Grand Rapid, MI: William B. Eerdmans Publishing Company.

Armstrong, K. (2001). *Buddha.* New York: Penguin Groups.

Asal, T. (1982): *The construction of religion as an anthropological category: in genealogies of religion: Discipline and reasons of power in Christianity and Islam* (2nd. ed.). Baltimore, MD: John Hopkins University Press.

Berry, D. L. (2007). *Pictures of Islam: A student's guide to Islam.* Macon, GA: Mercer University Press, p. 21.

Blainey, G. (2012): A short history of Christianity. *Policy, 28*(1) 57–60, http. Libraries ou.edu.

Bryan, W. V. (2007): *Multicultural aspects of disabilities.* Springfield, IL: Charles C. Thomas.

Denison, B. J., Kvisto, P., McClenon, J., & Swatos, W. H. (1998). *Encyclopedia of religion and society.* Walnut Creek, Calif. AltaMira Press.

Donin, H. (1972). *To be a Jew: A guide to Jewish observance in contemporary life.* New York: Basic Books.

Ganeri, A. (2001). Buddhism Srl, Florence, Italy: McRae Books.

Geertz, C. (1973). *Religion as a cultural system: In the interpretation of cultures:* (87) 12th. ed. London: Fontana Press.

Hardon, J. (2013). Retrieved from http://catholiceducation.org/karticles/religion/re0707.html

Johnstone, R. L. (2007). *Religion in society: A sociology of religion.* Upper Saddle River, NJ: Prentice Hall.

Makinde, J. A. (2013). *Religion.* Unpublished paper, University of Oklahoma.

Morrison, E. (2013). *Religion in today's society.* unpublished paper, University of Oklahoma

Nail, E., (2013). *A brief history of Christianity.* Unpublished paper. University of Oklahoma.

Novak, P., & Smith, H. (2003). *Buddhism: A concise introduction.* New York: Harper-Collins.

Rich, T. (2005). Judaism 101. Kashrut: Jewish dietary laws. Retrieved Jne 20, 2005. http://www.jewfag.org/kkashrut.htm

Robinson, R. (2004). *Sociology of religion in India.* New Delhi U.A.: Sage Publication.

Sabini, J. (1990). *Islam: A primer.* Washington, DC: Middle East Editorial Associates.

Trepp, L. (1980). *The complete book of Jewish observances: A practical manual for the modern Jew.* New York: Simon & Schuster.

Tylor, E. B. (1871). *Primitive culture: Research into the development of mythology, philosophy, religion, act, and custom* (1st. ed.). London: John Murray

Suggested Readings

Ali, S., Liu, W., & Humedian, M. (2004). Islam 101: Understanding the religion and therapy implications. *Professional Psychology: Research and Practice, 35,* 635–642

Ariel, Y. (2012). A different kind of dialogue: Messianic Judaism and Jewish-Christian Relations. *Cross Currents, 62*(3), 318–327.

Campbell, R. (2008). Leadership succession in early Islam: Exploring the nature and role of historical precedents. *The Leadership Quarterly, 19*(4), 426–438.

Holzman, G. (2006). Truth, tradition, and religion. The association between Judaism and Islam and the relation between religion and philosophy in medieval Jewish thought. *Al-Masaq, 18*(2), 191–200.

Johnson, S. D. (2006). Religion and Anti-Islamic Attitudes. *Review of Religious Research, 48*(1), 5–16.

Judaism–Religion Facts. (2012). Religion, World Religions, Comparative Religion–Just the facts on the world's religions.. Retrieved July 6, 2013.

Kimbal, C. (2002). *When religion becomes evil.* California: Harper Collins.

Larson, W. F. (2008). Jesus in Islam and Christianity: Discussing the Similarities and the Differences. *Missiology, 36*(3), 327–341.

Leaman, O. (2011). Judaism: An introduction. London and New York: I. B. Tauris, 2011.

McDowell, M., & Brown, N. (2009). *World religions at your fingertips.* NY: Penguin Group.

Muravchik, J., & Szrom, C. (2008). In search of moderate Muslims. *Commentary, 125*(2), 26–34.

Neusner, J. (2006). Judaism: The basics/Jacob Neusner. London; New York: Routledge.

Neusner, J. (2011). The Norms of Conviction of Rabbinic Judaism: Orthodoxy and Heresy. *Review Of Rabbinic Judaism, 14*(2), 235–247.

Ohlig, K. H., & Puin, G. R. (Eds.). (2010). *The hidden origins of Islam.* Amherst, NY: Prometheus Books.

Shapiro, E. S. (2013). The crisis of conservative Judaism. *First Things: A Monthly Journal Of Religion & Public Life* (233), 27–31.

Chapter 5

DISABILITY

Chapter Outline
• Introduction
• Development of Federal Rehabilitation Programs
• Definition of a disability
• Americans with Disabilities Act Amendments
• Who are persons with disabilities?
• Effects of labeling
• Disability among racial and ethnic groups and women
• Major health issues among American Indians

Chapter Objectives
• Present a definition of disability
• Provide an analysis of the disability definition
• Provide information with regard to the number of persons with a disability in America
• Identify prevalence of disabilities among racial and ethnic minorities
• Identify some of the impacts disabilities have on racial and ethnic minorities
• Identify key pieces of legislation that have contributed to the rehabilitation of persons with disabilities

Introduction

A holistic approach to treating and interacting with a client/patient in a helping relationship whether the helping relates to the field of rehabilitation, medicine, counseling, social work, or psychotherapy requires the helper to go beyond understanding the injury, the pathology of the disease, and/or the symptoms of the ailment and seek an understanding of the "whole" person. Most persons who consider themselves as professional helpers will quickly acknowledge that an understanding and awareness of many cultural factors influencing a person's life (educational, social, and family to mention only a few) provide the helper with a better basis for assisting the person being helped. In the quest for a complete understanding, one has to be equally vigilant of both positive and negative factors influencing the person's life. One of the most insidious negative impacts is discrimination.

Without evidence to the contrary, one is forced to assume that discrimination is not of recent origin. In fact, as discussed in the chapter on discrimination, there is overwhelming evidence to comfortably support the theory that discrimination is as old as humankind. Discrimination in some form has existed for many, many centuries. Not offered as a defense, but as a fact, humans have been at various times and often concurrently discriminated because of strength, or more precisely lack thereof, religious beliefs, gender, age, language, and physical stature to list only a few. Despite the fact that in America, as is true in most countries, there are a number of forms of discrimination; however, currently we too frequently hear about and concentrate on racial and gender discrimination. The changing demographic trends are prompting many aspects of American life to reevaluate and develop plans to reconstruct the ways in which we interact with persons heretofore ignored.

Persons with disabilities have been one of those groups that have been adversely affected by discrimination. Although modern-day discrimination of persons with disabilities does not have the malicious intent of elimination that early day "survival of the fittest," had. The fact remains that persons with disabilities have been discriminated in various ways that have had a negative impact upon their lives. Persons with disabilities who are from a minority group too frequently experience "dual discrimination," as a member of a racial/ethnic minority group and as a person with a disability. As helping professionals, we may overlook the duality of their life situation and concentrate upon the impact of the person's disability to the exclusion of the contributing factors of race and/or gender or the reverse may occur of focusing all attention on the person's race and/or gender overlooking the impact the disability has on the person's life. Clearly to maximize the potential of successfully rehabilitating clients, the rehabilitation/helping professional must take a holistic approach and examine various cultural aspects of the client's life situation.

What is a disability? How many people in America have a disability? At what point does a limitation become a disability? Who should be considered a person with a disability? And what is the appropriate terminology to use when referring to someone who is considered to have a disability? These are but a few of many questions the world of rehabilitation encounters frequently and society in general is attempting to answer.

As the medical and psychological professions have become better at diagnosing physical, mental, and emotional conditions, likewise, educational specialists have developed and learned more accurate ways of assessing learning styles and potential. Moreover, sociologists and social workers are contributing their knowledge toward the understanding of the impact social environmental factors have toward creating disabling conditions.

In the arena of education, increasing numbers of students are seeking assistance from counselors and teachers on the basis of having a learning disability. Stress-induced disabilities are being identified as a major problem by persons who work or have worked in jobs which are filled with high pressure activities such as the military, financial investors, and air traffic controllers to mention a few. To add to the list of stressed employees office workers, especially those who spend a considerable amount of time manipulating a computer terminal, are reporting various problems ranging from visual impairment to various forms of muscle strains. Given these problems, some new and others a variation of old physical, mental, or emotional issues, a relevant question is "What is the definition of a disability?" However, before we discuss a definition of disability we will take a historical view of the development of federal rehabilitation programs in the United States and following that I will define what a disability is.

Development of Federal Rehabilitation Programs

The American federal government can be credited with laying the foundation for the beginning of state and federal government's participation in the rehabilitation of persons with disabilities when in 1917 Congress passed the Smith-Hughes Act which established the Board of Vocational Education. This landmark act is considered an education act rather than a rehabilitation act; however, it indirectly provided services to persons with disabilities as a result of providing for vocational education. The initial venture into the area of the federal government authorizing and funding services to persons with disabilities was begun with the enactment of the Smith-Sears Veterans' Rehabilitation Act of 1918 and its main purpose was to provide "vocational" rehabilitation services and return to employment persons with disabilities who had been discharged from military service. It should be noted that to this point all of the federal rehabilitation efforts were established to provide service to veterans; therefore, persons with disabilities who had no connection to the military, if they could not afford services, had their rehabilitation services provided by charitable organizations and if they could afford was provided through private rehabilitation facilities.

Public rehabilitation programs came into existence in 1920 with the enactment of the Smith-Fess Act. As Bryan (1996) points out, the Act provided only for vocational guidance, training, occupational adjustment, prostheses, and placement services, thus establishing the guidelines that federal funding for rehabilitation services for persons with physical disabilities would be oriented toward preparing the person for employment. This meant that physical restoration, except providing prostheses which was provided to make the person more employable, and sociopsychological services were excluded. This philosophy continued for twenty-three years until the Barden-LaFollette Act of 1943 was enacted. This Act provided more funds and allowed additional program options such as providing physical restoration as well as funding research programs for in-depth study of more effective and efficient ways of rehabilitation and delivering rehabilitation services and finally it provided training funds for rehabilitation specialists such as physicians, nurses, rehabilitation counselors, physical therapists, occupational therapists, social workers, and psychologists.

The philosophy of directing vocational rehabilitation programs toward preparing persons for employment to the exclusion of other forms of rehabilitation was so deeply imbedded within the rehabilitation policy-makers and the United States Congress' mind that when the Mental Retardation Facilities and Community Health Centers Construction Act was passed in 1963, it was not placed within the vocational rehabilitation program partly because of its lack of emphasis on vocational goals. While maintaining its passion for strong emphasis on vocational goals as being a central theme of the vocational rehabilitation program, Congress continued to strengthen the program with the Vocational Rehabilitation Amendments Act of 1965. In this piece of legislation, Congress used three approaches to improve services: (1) Congress provided monies to states for innovative projects that developed new methods of providing services; (2) Congress created a broader base of services to people with disabilities, including individuals with socially handicapping conditions; and (3) Congress eliminated economic need as a requirement for rehabilitation services. It is noteworthy that prior to this amendment act, persons had to demonstrate that they could not pay for certain services; also social conditions were not considered a disability.

During the early and mid-1960s, persons with disabilities and various disability advocate groups began to give increased attention to the almost exclusive emphasis Congress was placing on vocational goals in most rehabilitation programs. The concerned community of persons with disabilities as well as many of their family members did not oppose "a" goal of employability, but believed that employment as "the" goal was rendering persons with severe disabilities who did not have much promise for sustained employment, to a life of dependency, institutionalization, and handouts. Additionally, these disability rights groups were equally concerned about other issues such as the lack of input persons with disabilities and their families had with the development of rehabilitation plans, deinstitutionalization, demedication and self-care to mention a few. An outgrowth of these concerns was the uniting of various groups of persons with disabilities for the purpose of demonstrating their concerns with a show of unity. Previously, one of the major weaknesses of efforts to promote the needs of persons with disabilities was the inability of the various groups to come together in a common cause. Two major obstacles existed—one was that advocacy was based along the lines of disability category associations such as polio, muscular dystrophy, multiple sclerosis, etc.; and two, most of these organizations were headed by persons who did not have a disability.

Gartner and Joe (1987) believe that one of the most notable features of the disability activism years was the central role played by persons with disabilities and the coalitions of people with different disabilities. They further inform us that perhaps for the first time persons with disabilities were the leaders of the movement. This was important because Congress and other rehabilitation policy makers were seeing persons with disabilities in new roles: as leaders and as their own advocates rather than in the passive subservient roles to which they had grown accustomed. The community of persons with disabilities had observed the success that African Americans and other racial minorities experienced through their marches and sit-ins which culminated in the passage of the Civil Rights Act of 1964.

As the community of persons with disabilities gained experience at coalition building and lobbying, their message began to be heard and heeded by rehabilitation policy makers. In 1975 the Education for All Handicapped Children Act (name later changed to Individuals with Disabilities Education Act—IDEA) was passed. The Act provided each child who had a disability a free, appropriate education in the least restrictive environment. Another important provision gave parents of children with disabilities the right to be involved in the process of determining the type and nature of their child's education.

During the early 1970s the community of persons with disabilities were not only concerned with education issues, they were also keenly aware that total rehabilitation meant independent living for those that were able to live independently. To this community, independent living was not restricted to those who were ambulatory or considered mentally competent, as was normally the restriction for independent housing. They strongly believed that persons with severe disabilities such as those with spinal cord injuries, mental and intellectual disabilities, as well as severe visual limitations should have the same opportunity as others, both with and without disabilities to be independent and exert control over their own lives. Stimulated by what they considered the failure of the traditional rehabilitation programs, they formed the American Coalition of Citizens with Disabilities (ACCD). One of the several acts that spurred the creation of the American Coalition of Citizens with Disabilities was the veto by President Nixon of the Vocational Rehabilitation Act of 1972 on the grounds the legislation "strayed too far from the essential vocational objective of the program." Of considerable importance to the community of persons with disabilities was that within the Act were provisions of federal financial support for independent living centers. Through the efforts of ACCD and others within the community of persons with disabilities as well as families, friends, and other advocates, independent living centers were funded through the Rehabilitation Comprehensive Services and Developmental Disabilities Act of 1978 (Rehabilitation Amendment of 1978).

Prior to the enactment of the Rehabilitation Amendment of 1978, there were nongovernment supported independent living centers which had been developed as a result of persons with severe disabilities moving into communities and contracting for services that they could not provide for themselves. Through this method of independence, persons with severe disabilities were able to exert considerable control over their lives. An obvious limitation to the nongovernment-supported programs was financial support. Therefore, to expand opportunities to a larger population, funding provided by state and the federal government was needed. This was achieved by the enactment of the Rehabilitation Amendment of 1978.

The independent living center concept has evolved into an important addition to the nation's rehabilitation program as well as a tremendous benefit to persons with disabilities. Currently there are over 300 centers representing every state in the country. This concept is also used throughout Europe. From a rehabilitation viewpoint, a relevant question is, "What are independent living centers?"

According to Bryan (1996), services vary in an effort to accommodate the needs of the population served; moreover, most centers reflect a common goal which Townsend and Ryan (1991) describe as advocating for "independence" in decisions about one's life which may not necessarily mean physically performing daily living tasks. With respect to the roles of independent living centers, they categorize them into four areas: (1) control and direct personal and community services including planning and organizing transportation, finances, paid work, cooking, laundry, housekeeping, and general assistance; (2) encourage regular participation in leisure and recreational activities including social skills, emotional stability, motivation, attitudes, and interaction support to participants at home or outside the home; (3) assist with the development and use of individual potential and talents, i.e., individual's vision of the possibilities for overcoming barriers which limit fulfillment of aspirations; and (4) contribute to the well-being and betterment of society, including the ability to give as well as take to combat a sense of dependency on others. Moreover, the major emphasis is on the consumer, in this case person with a disability, making choices about how he/she wants to live, choosing who or what will provide the services as well as how they will be provided.

The disability rights movement and the push for independent living centers developed simultaneously with the effort to pass the Rehabilitation Act of 1973 which would provide the greatest strength of the rehabilitation program that heretofore had existed. Title V, with its Sections 501-504 were the heart of the act:

Section 501: This section established the Interagency Committee on Handicapped Employees. This committee was charged with overseeing federal hiring, placement and job advancement of persons with disabilities within the federal government system.

Section 502: The Architectural and Transportation Barriers Compliance Board was established by this section to monitor the construction of new federal buildings and remodeling existing structures to ensure they were accessible to persons with disabilities.

Section 503: This section required every employer who entered into a contract for more than $2500 with the federal government to comply with affirmative action in hiring persons with disabilities.

Section 504: As a result of this section, every American institution receiving federal assistance had to take steps to ensure that persons with disabilities are not discriminated in employment.

There is little question that the Rehabilitation Act of 1973 was the strongest piece of legislation for protecting persons with disabilities from discrimination in the area of employment to that date; however, there was one major weakness–the act affected only those private and public employers who did business under contract with the federal government for $2500 or greater. Granted, this was sufficient to cover the Fortune 500 companies as well as most other large companies, but the majority of American businesses are small, many of whom do not necessarily contract with the federal government. Therefore, many neighborhood or local "mom and pop" businesses were not affected.

In 1990, this flaw was corrected with the enactment of the most comprehensive piece of legislation for persons with disabilities in the form of the Americans with Disabilities Act (ADA). This is a Civil Rights piece of legislation that prohibits discrimination against persons with disabilities and protects their civil rights by requiring all persons and all businesses to adhere to the provisions. A detailed explanation of the Americans with Disabilities Act and its amendments will be discussed later in this chapter; however next I want to explore definition of a disability.

Definition of a Disability

The definition of a disability appears to be dynamic; it has evolved over the past several decades as science and technology have revealed different methods of detecting and successfully treating many life situations which create limitations to one's abilities to successfully carry forward with life activities. In retrospect, we find that what was considered a disability depended upon the society in which the person(s) with the limitation lived. In some ancient societies such as Rome, just the fact that a person "significantly" deviated from the "norm" appeared to be grounds for declaring the person as disabled, thus warranting abandonment and exclusion from society. In other societies such as the period of time when America was primarily an agrarian society, the classification of persons as being disabled, to a large degree, was predicated upon their abilities to be physically productive. If they were able to work the land and extract a living from the soil, they were accepted, perhaps viewed as being "different" but not disabled. Therefore, early definitions of disability emphasized a person who had a physical or mental condition which limited his/her ability to be gainfully employed. Later, emotional conditions were added as part of the evolving definition of disability.

In referring to Beatrice Wright's early works on defining the difference between a disability and handicap, Charlene P. DeLoach and Associates (1983) provide the following as further evidence of how our thinking has evolved with regard to what constitutes a disability:

First, a disability has an "objective aspect," in contrast to a handicap, which is relative in nature. The second important point is that a disability is a "condition" resulting from illness, injury or congenital causes. Often people equate disability with illness. Disability should be understood as an ongoing condition that is a result of an injury, illness or congenital cause. And finally, a disability limits or impairs physical or mental functioning. A person with a disability will have functional limitations and these limitations are used as a means of describing the effects of the disability upon the person.

Though lengthy, this explanation of a disability remains fairly accurate but has one major limitation that being the foundation for a disability is a medical condition or more precisely, one that can be defined through medical interrogation. This was also the limitations of a definition given by Henderson and Bryan (1984). They defined a disability as a condition of impairment, physical or mental, having an objective aspect that can usually be described by a physician. This limitation of describing a disability solely on the basis of medical observations is a vivid indication of the evolution of the description of a disability as we view the currently acceptable definition which was issued as part of the 1990 Americans with Disabilities Act (ADA).

The Americans with Disabilities Act provides what is considered a "three-pronged" definition. The following is an identification of each prong and a brief analysis.

First Prong

DEFINITION–A person with a physical or mental impairment that substantially limits one or more major life activities such as walking, seeing, hearing, speaking, breathing, learning, working, or caring for one's self.

ANALYSIS–the key words are "substantially limits." As an example, a broken leg is usually temporary, therefore, not considered a disability because it does not substantially impair walking on a permanent basis. However, if the break is severe enough to require permanent or long-term use of a mobility aid, it may be considered a disability.

As one reviews the major life activities, it will be noticed that the inability to perform is often determined by medical review; however, one life activity–learning–is often determined by educational specialists. It is true that the causes of some forms of learning problems such as intellectual limitations and brain damage are medically and/or psychologically determined, but several others such as Attention Deficit Disorder are often determined by non-medical personnel. The point made is that the inclusion of learning as a disability, or more precisely, the lack thereof is an evolution in the thinking of what constitutes a disability.

Second Prong

DEFINITION–a person is considered to have a disability if he/she has a record of such a physical or mental impairment.

ANALYSIS–this definition deals in part with the stigma attached to having a disability. It speaks to "one who has a record of such a physical or mental impairment." This means that even though the person's condition may be controlled by medication or through rehabilitation, he/she can still be considered as having a disability because society's perception and reaction probably will continue to be one of viewing the person as having a disability. An illustration of this is a person who controls his epileptic seizures with medication is considered to have a disability because there is a record of seizures even though they are medically controlled; employers and others may think of him as having a disability. This will probably be the case despite his education and the fact that training has prepared him for employment in areas which, if he were to have a seizure, would be at minimum risk to himself and others. Another example is this book's author had polio many years ago which resulted in a weak right leg and a limp. Although he has a doctorate, has been a college professor and administrator and the effects of polio have not impaired his ability to carry out any major life activities, he is considered as having a disability because, in this case, there is both a record of having a disability and there is visual evidence of same. Therefore, society does perceive him to be a person with a disability.

Third Prong

DEFINITION–a person is considered as having a disability if he/she is regarded as having such an impairment.

ANALYSIS–Similar to the second prong, this also deals with perception and to some extent, stigma; however, it differs in that it is referring to persons who may not have a disability but have conditions that are perceived as being disabling. For example, a person who has a large visible birthmark on his face which does not limit any of his major life activities may be perceived or stigmatized by employers and others as a person with a disability; therefore, he can be classified as having a disability.

As an overall analysis of the latest definition (ADA), we find that it differs from the older definitions in that they were based upon the limitations being clinically proven and the older definition did not take into consideration the impact of stigma and perception; whereas the ADA definition is more inclusive allowing more conditions to be considered.

Americans with Disabilities Act Amendments

The Americans with Disabilities Act was amended by the United States Congress in 2008 and became effective January 01, 2009. The Equal Employment Opportunity Commission (EEOC) was instructed to issue final regulation which it did in 2011. The following is a brief overview of the final regulations for implementation of the Americans with Disabilities Act Amendments (ADAAA).

The following points relate to some of the regulations issued by the Equal Employment Opportunity Commission. For a more detailed discussion the reader is encouraged to go to the U.S. Equal Employment Opportunity Commission web site.

Point One: In enacting the Americans with Disabilities Act Amendments (ADAAA), Congress made it easier for an individual seeking protection under the ADA to establish that he or she has a disability within the meaning of the statute.

Point Two: The Equal Employment Opportunity Commission (EEOC) regulations implement of the ADAAA; in particular Congress mandates that the definition of disability be construed broadly.

Point Three: The term "substantially limits" requires a lower degree of functional limitation than the standard previously applied by the courts. Stated differently, the term "substantially" limits is to be construed broadly.

Point Four: With one exception (ordinary eyeglasses or contact lenses), the determination of whether an impairment substantially limits a major life activity shall be made without regard to the ameliorative effects of mitigating measures, such as medication or hearing aids.

Point Five: An impairment that is episodic or in remission is a disability if it would substantially limit a major life activity when active.

Point Six: In keeping with Congress's direction that the primary focus of the Americans with Disabilities Act should be to determine whether discrimination has occurred, the determination of whether a disability exists should not require extensive analysis.

As previously mentioned there are other determination put forth by the Equal Employment Opportunity Commission, thus the reader is encourage to review the complete set of regulations.

Is "Handicap" an Offensive Word?

Some persons within the disability rights movement believe that applying the word "handicap" to a person with a disability should never be done. The major reason behind the rejection of the label is the negative images projected by the word handicap. The word "handicap" is derived from an old English term which means cap-in-hand or stated more succinctly–beggar. Many years ago in England, one of the few groups which were allowed to beg in the streets were persons with disabilities; therefore, to a large extent the terms "handicap" and "beggar" have become synonymous.

Bryan (1996) convincingly argues that both terms "handicap" and "disability" for the uninformed illuminate negative images of persons with disabilities. He concludes his comments with the following:

> Many people believe the words "handicap" and "disability" mean the same: two words used to describe the same human condition. Too often the words "handicap" and "disability" create images of a person who cannot work and cannot take care of daily life functions. This image may be altered somewhat when they encounter a person with a disability; however, the image of a person unable to function at the same level as someone who does not have a disability is often the replacement. These ideas about handicap and disability are what most nondisabled persons use to judge persons with disabilities.

Perhaps Wright (1960) has the correct approach to handicap when she referred to the term meaning the obstacle that one faces in pursuing one's life goals. This view does not place handicap either as an extremely negative term or in the exclusive domain of persons with disabilities. In reality, every human faces many handicaps in his or her lifetime.

Undoubtedly scholars, rehabilitation professionals and others will continue the debate with regard to the usefulness or lack thereof of the terms handicap and disability. Until a definitive answer emerges, the most appropriate and least offensive approach is to place the person first and the limitation as secondary, thus "a person with a disability or a person with a handicap" is preferred.

When Is a Person Rehabilitated?

If a person is considered to have a disability if he/she has a physical or mental impairment that substantially limits one or more major life activity, then is he rehabilitated when there is no longer a limitation to a major life activity? Is the person rehabilitated when he is gainfully employed, thus able to provide for his basic needs? Is a person to be considered rehabilitated when, through the use of assistive devices or personal assistance, he is able to carry through with his major life activities?

These are only a few of the valid questions rehabilitation and other helping professionals encounter as they develop rehabilitation plans. In any academic course such as planning or evaluation and measurement, students are told that to determine success or failure one must establish his or her objectives in measurable terms; therefore, we return to the question, "How does one determine when a client is rehabilitated?" Some rehabilitation professionals define rehabilitation as the restoration of the person to the fullest physical, mental, social, vocational, and economic usefulness of which he or she is capable. This appears to be a comprehensive and reasonable definition in that it does not limit rehabilitation to any one life function. In the past, many vocational rehabilitation agencies considered a client to be rehabilitated when the client had been employed on a job for a specific period of time. The employment generally occurred after the client had been trained in an area commensurate with her abilities and/or had been provided physical restoration services that allowed her to become employable. The limitations of this approach to defining rehabilitation is obvious in that for those because of the severity of their disability employment is not realistic, it is virtually impossible for them to be considered rehabilitated.

Who Are Persons with Disabilities?

Membership in the world of disability is open and has no boundaries. Anyone, regardless of race, gender, ethnicity, social or economic status, faith and age is subject to become a member at any time in his/her life. It is true, as will be discussed later, that some groups have a greater chance of becoming a member than others and from a parity standpoint, is overrepresented; equity of inclusion notwithstanding, people with disabilities are the largest open-class minority group in the world.

Class of People

In passing the 1990 Americans with Disabilities Act, the United States Congress recognized persons with disabilities as a class who has been discriminated, similar to the way ethnic minorities have experienced discrimination. To support this pronouncement, Congress acknowledged the following realities:

1. Society has isolated and segregated individuals with disabilities;
2. Persons with disabilities have been victims of serious discrimination;
3. Discrimination against persons with disabilities continues to be a pervasive social problem;
4. The result of discrimination against persons with disabilities continues to be problematic in the critical areas of employment, housing, public accommodation, education, transportation, communication, institutionalization, health services, voting, and access to public services;
5. There has been no legal recourse for persons with disabilities who have been victims of discrimination;
6. Some of the acts of discrimination encountered by persons with disabilities are blatant and intentionally exclusionary;
7. Persons with disabilities occupy an inferior status in the American society;
8. Persons with disabilities are a minority group which has been relegated to a position lacking political power in the American society.

In passing the Rehabilitation Act Amendment of 1992, the American Congress reemphasized its belief that persons with disabilities are treated as an underclass of people by stating:

1. Individuals with disabilities constitute one of the most disadvantaged groups in society; and

2. Individuals with disabilities continually encounter various forms of discrimination.

With the statements from the Americans with Disabilities Act and the Rehabilitation Act Amendments of 1992, Congress appears to be describing persons with disabilities as a class of people who have been continually and consistently denied their civil rights.

Number of Persons with Disabilities

It is difficult at best to provide an accurate count of the number of persons with disabilities in America. The methods of identifying persons with disabilities are the major obstacle to receiving a complete and accurate count. As one reviews the methods used to collect statistics with regard to persons with disabilities a myriad of data-collecting techniques come into view. Some statistics are based on "self-identification," others may be work related, while others exclude persons who are institutionalized. Still others are based upon a certain age range, generally age 14–64, while some researchers consider a person as being disabled if he/she was injured or sick and unable to work for a given period of time. Finally, none of these methods are able to include the person who has an "invisible" disability, such as heart condition, diabetes, various forms of seizures, and some mental and emotional problems unless the person is willing to disclose the disability.

An excellent example of discrepancies in the estimate of the population of persons with disabilities occurs when one views the 1990 statistics. The Americans with Disabilities Act estimated the number of persons with disabilities to be 43 million, while in the same year, the National Health Interview Survey (NHIS) estimated the population to be 33.8 million. The problem of accurately counting or projection the number of persons with a disability continues today. One can see the number of persons with disabilities ranging from 43 million to 54 million. The fact is no one knows the accurate number of persons with a disability because of the reasons previously mentioned. The number depends on how the count is conducted and for what purpose the count is conducted.

Despite the various methods and their shortcomings, with regard to determining the number of persons with disabilities in America, the most widely accepted estimate is that approximately one-fifth of the American population has a disability. An obvious observation of the percentage of persons with disabilities is that the community of persons with disabilities represents a significant portion of the American population. This causes one to consider the impact a population of this size can have toward improving their life conditions when they unite to pursue common causes. The sphere of influence increases dramatically as one considers the number of persons with disabilities plus for every person with a disability there is at least one significant other who has concerns with regard to that person's well-being and one can also conservatively estimate that there are a significant number of people in America that make all or a part of their income from working with persons with disabilities. As one contemplates these facts it is abundantly clear that the community of persons with disabilities and those that care for and have an interest in their well-being comprise a considerable portion of the American population. Therefore, all of these forces working together can cause significant change to occur in American society.

Effects of Labeling

As a society of categorizers, attaching labels to help describe events, ideas, theories, individuals, and groups are important to establishing and maintaining an orderly society. This, in theory, is correct and would remain so if all of our labels are "neutral" bestowing neither good nor bad significance to the individual or object being labeled. Of course, we recognize that this is not the case and in reality is not practical in many instances. Significance of good or bad, right or wrong, as well as degrees in-between in some cases is very useful. For instance, labeling or identifying an action such as smoking as being bad for one's health is useful; also labeling certain behaviors in public as inappropriate is useful in socializing children toward that society's acceptable behaviors. Therefore, labeling, in most instances, is a useful process.

The use of labeling similar to the use of medicine, while developed to be helpful, if used incorrectly it can have the opposite effect and do more harm than good. Perhaps the most obvious negative impact of attaching a label to describe humans can be seen in the various meanings society has associated with the terms used to describe and identify persons with disabilities. First, the contemporary terms used are disabled and handicapped. These terms, along with many others which thankfully are not used as often as in past years such as crippled, impaired, lunatic, deformed, stupid, and crazy all leave the impression of an inferior person. Robert Funk (1987) described the influence of persistent negative labeling such as persons with disabilities as being deviants, incompetent, unhealthy objects of fear who are dependent upon the welfare and charity of others as sufficient societal justification for exclusionary action, such as segregation of persons with disabilities and denial of equal opportunities.

Most of the negative labeling terms used to describe persons with disabilities are not original creations of the current generations of our population;

these terms have been associated with persons with disabilities for decades. If one reviews old hospital records of mental institutions the use of terms such as lunatic, deranged and imbecile were considered to be acceptable medical terms of the time. Similarly, the word "crippled" was liberally used in most hospitals; in fact, in the not too distant past many pediatric orthopedic hospitals were named "crippled children's" hospital. As previously stated, all of these terms imply inferiority. Myron Eisenberg and associates (1982) believe we construct an ideology to explain the perceived inferiority of persons with disabilities by using stigmatic terms such as cripple, moron, and gimp in our daily language. The noted author Beatrice A. Wright (1988) believes this type of labeling develops a negative bias and this bias steers perception, thoughts, and feelings along negative lines to such a degree that positive qualities remain hidden. She continues by stating that the negative bias becomes a powerful source of prejudice that ill serves those who are already disadvantaged.

Perhaps the ultimate tragedy of negative labeling is what Eisenberg and associates (1982) describe as "buying into the stigmatization process" and they describe the process as the stigmatized individual holding the same beliefs and self-identity as does the rest of society. As we review the following comments of Joseph Stubbins (1988), one gains the impression he agrees with Eisenberg's point:

> The toughest item on the agenda of disabling is that modern America has no need for most disabled persons. In the rehabilitation community this conclusion is unthinkable, although such a conclusion is both plausible and real. Even those disabled citizens who lead conventional lives tend to repress their status and patronizing attitudes of the able-bodied and internalize the value of the straight world.

It is the internalization of the values of the nondisabled that is of concern to rehabilitation professionals and rehabilitation advocates. By accepting nondisabled persons descriptions, views, and attitudes toward them, persons with disabilities are in effect allowing the nondisabled population to exert unwarranted control over their lives. The following comments by Joseph Stubbins (1988) succinctly place in perspective the hazards of persons with disabilities buying into the nondisabled labeling:

> Disability can be viewed as a particular kind of relationship between a person with an impairment and the social and physical environment. What kind of relationship is this? (1) It is a superordinate subordinate one; able-bodied persons have power over those with impairments. (2) This power relationship is manifested by the able-bodied population's defining critical words from their

perspective, e.g., in saying that disability is in the person rather than the relationship, and having control of the environment. (3) The relationship is characterized by the able-bodied person's asserting the right to determine what kind of rehabilitation services disabled people need.

These three points appear to have been key elements in the rise of the disability rights movement. While the attitudes expressed within these points do not represent a mean-spirited approach of the nondisabled, in interacting with persons who have disabilities, it nevertheless represents oppression; and this and other forms of oppression was considered by the disability rights movement leadership as stumbling blocks which had to be removed before rehabilitation services could be considered effective and meeting the needs of the population it was intended to serve.

The chapter will now shift attention to special groups who have experienced disabilities. The discussion will provide information of the impact upon persons within these groups by virtue of them having a disability.

Disability Among Racial and Ethnic Groups and Women

The results of most surveys of the percentage of disabilities in America reveal a picture of a higher rate of disabilities among racial minorities and women than Caucasian males.

When viewed from the standpoint of ranking the prevalence of disabilities among racial minority groups, Native Americans have the highest rate followed by African Americans with Caucasians being third; persons of Hispanic origin ranked fourth and Asian or Pacific Americans fifth. This same rank order occurs as one compares women and their racial background. When women are viewed as an aggregate without respect for racial background survey results confirms that women have a higher rate of disabilities than men.

As one views the living and working conditions of some minorities and women, plausible reasons for the high rate of disabilities are revealed: with respect to American Indians, alcohol and alcohol-related accidents and violence account for a significant number of disabilities, also the fact that many American Indians appear to be susceptible to diabetes contributes to the increased rate. A significant number of disabilities among African Americans and Hispanic/Latino Americans can be contributed to the fact that many persons of these groups work in jobs where the accident rates are abnormally high. Also, many Hispanic/Latino are agricultural workers and agricultural accidents are among the highest among all occupations. Working conditions and the stress of being mother, spouse, and employee contribute heavily to the high disability rate for women.

African Americans and Disabilities

According to a U.S. Census Bureau report, among the ethnic and racial groups of Asian or Pacific Americans, Caucasians, and Hispanic/Latino, African Americans have the greatest prevalence of disabilities. The same is true when severe disabilities are considered.

A review of data indicates that too many African Americans continue to experience the same or similar problems that have plagued them for decades. These problems answer the question of why there is a high rate of disabilities among African Americans. The following provides clues that also answer the question of why:

1. Since over 50 percent of the working African American population work as unskilled laborers, they are more susceptible to disabling injuries. Except for farm labor, African Americans work under some of the most dangerous conditions, most with a high probability of producing employee injuries.
2. Approximately 50 percent of the African American population's income places them in what is considered the low-socioeconomic class. This generally means their living environment is consistent with their income level, relegating them to live in areas where there may be physical exposure to lead and other chemical hazards as well as being at greater risk of physical violence. These hazards, added to poor lighting, heating, and ventilation provide an environment conducive to acquiring a disability.
3. Lack of access to and/or utilization of adequate health care have historically been a major problem for African Americans. Additionally inability to afford health insurance causes those in need of health care to delay attending to health needs until the problems are critical. Hopefully with the Affordable Health Care Act the previously mentioned problem will become less of a problem.
4. Poor dietary habits such as excessive consumption of fatty foods, salt, and/or high sodium content is a major contributor to development of health conditions leading to disabilities.
5. Unhealthy lifestyles such as smoking and excessive use of alcohol.

Asian and Pacific Americans and Disabilities

Although the Asian and Pacific American population trails African Americans and Hispanic/Latino, they are one of the fastest growing ethnic minority groups in America. To illustrate, the 2000 U.S. Census Bureau count indicated that Asians were 3.6 percent of the U.S. population, four years later in

2004 the population had increased to 4.2 percent and in 2010 the Asian population was 4.8 percent. The population growth of Asian and Pacific Americans as projected is continuing to increase.

With regard to disabilities, Asian and Pacific Americans have the lowest rate of disabilities among the racial/ethnic minorities of African Americans, Hispanic/Latino, and American Indians. Also they have the lowest rate of severe disabilities.

Hispanic/Latino Americans and Disabilities

It is estimated by the U.S. Bureau of the Census that persons of Hispanic/ Latino origin have a lower (15.3%) rate of disabilities than Native American Indians and African Americans. For several reasons, the author has questions with regard to the accuracy of the Hispanic/Latino rates. First, the type of employment in which many Mexican Americans are engaged, i.e., farm labor, has the highest rate of accidents of any U.S. occupation. Second, many injuries that lead to disabilities goes unreported by some undocumented Hispanic/Latino workers because of their fear of being removed from the United States. Third, there have been cases of employers not reporting accidents and not allowing the employees to report or seek medical care.

Health Issues Among Hispanic/Latinos

There are a number of health issues of major concern within the Hispanic/ Latino communities, such as cancer, cardiovascular disease, diabetes, HIV/ AIDS, and substance abuse. Each will be addressed briefly. However, Aida Giachello (1994) summarizes the single greatest problem Hispanic/Latino persons face in regard to health care is the lack of access to the health care system, while dated this assessment remain true today. She points out that "Latinos lack access to a broad array of health services, especially primary care." She continues by stating, "This lack results from financial, cultural and institutional barriers. Poor and uninsured Latinos confront high fees for both preventive and acute care, a lack of bilingual/bicultural services, long-time gaps between calling for an appointment and actually seeing a physician and long waits once they get to the clinic." She concluded her comments by saying these facts contribute to Hispanic/Latinos disproportionate use of more costly services such as hospital emergency rooms when symptoms of illness persist or when the illness has reached an advanced stage.

In Valdez and associates' (1993) research while also dated, the results remain true and serve as foundation for Giachello's comments with regard to lack of insurance being a major barrier to adequate access to health care for Hispanic/Latinos. Valdez found that 39 percent of Hispanic/Latinos under the age of 65 were uninsured. Giachello (1994) convincingly argues the problem of lack of insurance is related to employment status. To be more precise, uninsured Hispanic/Latinos are more likely to work in industries which lack insurance coverage or at best offer inadequate coverage and because of the low income associated with many of the jobs, their abilities to secure adequate health insurance is greatly diminished.

Aiuda Giachello (1994) adds to our understanding of uninsured Hispanic/Latinos by providing the following facts and statistics on uninsured by national origin, sex, and age.

> Insurance coverage varies among Latinos by national origin, with Central and South Americans and Mexicans being worst off. As reported by the National Council of La Raza (NCLR), 40% of persons from Central and South Americans were uninsured in 1990, as were 36% of those of Mexican origin. The percentage of uninsured Puerto Ricans was the lowest (14%); perhaps owing to their higher levels of poverty and greater dependence on public assistance and Medicaid coverage. Hopefully the Affordable Health Care Act will provide hope for these groups.

The lack of access to appropriate health care for Hispanic/Latinos causes health problems, such as the ones to be discussed, to become a major concern because they are often not attended until they reach advanced stages. This along with inadequate primary and secondary prevention efforts and education often places many Hispanic/Latinos at risk for treatable conditions becoming lethal. Hopefully the Affordable Health Care Act will significantly eliminate some if not all of the previously mentioned problems related to health care and lack of health insurance. At this point it is too early to make a definitive declaration.

Smoking

The message that cigarette smoking is harmful has been clearly made by Surgeon General Reports as well as other responsible health officials. Still, an alarming number of both youth and adults, particularly ethnic minorities, continue to engage in the harmful habit. There have been numerous claims (all denied by the tobacco industry) that the tobacco industry, in its advertising, has targeted ethnic and racial minorities, particularly the young and women. In other words, their advertising campaigns are designed to encourage them to begin and/or continue using tobacco products. Whether the industry is guilty of these charges is debatable, also it can be debated that health educators have not done as effective job discouraging people from smoking as the tobacco groups have done encouraging people to smoke.

Some researchers like Gerardo Marin and his colleagues (1995) convincingly argue that "Although cigarette smoking is the single most important preventable cause of death and disability in the United States, little has been done to develop culturally appropriate intervention for ethnic minority groups, particularly for Hispanics." What this means is that there continues to be a high percentage of Hispanic/Latinos who smoke despite the health warnings and possible negative consequences. Also, it appears that the rate may increase in the future rather than decrease. Again, because of the risk to one's health with regard to possible death and disabilities, this fact becomes more and more alarming, especially since the negative aspects can be prevented by abstaining from cigarette smoking. Some of the many disabling conditions resulting from smoking are cancer and cardiovascular disease—two of the top ten causes of death regardless of racial or ethnic background.

Cancer

At the present time, the Hispanic/Latino population appears to contract cancer at the same rate as Euro-Americans. The most prevalent cancers among Hispanic/Latino males are cancers of the prostate, lung, and colon; most common among women are cancers of the breast, colon, and cervix.

Cardiovascular Disease

Although studies of the rate of cardiovascular diseases among Hispanic/Latinos are somewhat meager and limited, according to Doctor Eliseo Perez-Stable (1994), the data that does exist shows the incidence and prevalence of cardiovascular disease among Hispanic/Latino men in the United States is somewhat lower than for Euro-American males and African American males. No similar data appears to be available for Hispanic/Latino females.

Even though this health condition does not appear at this time to be more prevalent among Hispanic/Latinos than in the general population, there is cause for concern for two reasons: one, as previously stated, cardiovascular disease is one of the top ten causes of death of humankind; and two, lifestyles of some Hispanic/Latinos, particularly cigarette smoking and dietary habits which lead to obesity, if not decreased could very well trigger a dramatic increase in cardiovascular diseases among Hispanic/Latinos.

Diabetes

Diabetes ranks as one of the top ten causes of death of humans. Diabetes is a major health issue among Hispanic/Latinos. Henrietta Bernall and Eliseo Perez-Stable (1994) provide us with information which indicates that

Hispanic/Latinos living in the United States have shown higher than expected prevalence of diabetes. Extracting information from a 1983-1984 Hispanic Health and Nutrition Examination survey (HHANES) report, the authors discovered that Mexicans between the ages of 20 to 74 years had two to three times the prevalence of diabetes than Euro-Americans and African Americans. In the same report, Puerto Ricans had a diagnosed rate of diabetes similar to Mexicans and they found the prevalence of diabetes to be higher for Puerto Ricans and Mexicans than for Cubans.

Human Immunodeficiency Virus (HIV) and Acquired Immunodeficiency Syndrome (AIDS)

Emilio Carrillo and Steven Uranga-McKane (1994) classify the rate of HIV infections and cases of AIDS among Hispanic/Latinos as an epidemic. Unfortunately, this statement remains true. Social, economic, and cultural factors contribute to the magnitude of the problem; therefore, helping professionals and rehabilitation specialists must identify what these contributing factors are and devise ways of assisting those in need of help. Until appropriate attention is given to this epidemic it will continue to be a major health issue among Hispanic/Latino people.

American Indians and Disabilities

While the total population of American Indians is set at approximately one percent of the entire U.S. population, the rate of disabilities is disproportionately high, being estimated by some sources as high as 22 percent. Comparatively, the U.S. disability percentage considering all ethnic and racial groups is in the 19 percent range. The 20 percent rate of disability among the American Indian population makes their percentage not only higher than the national percentage; it is also higher than any other ethnic and racial groups.

American Indians, as a population of people, are younger than Euro-Americans as well as younger than the other major racial and ethnic groups. The median age for American Indians, in 2000 was approximately 28 years, whereas the median age for U.S. all races is approximately 36 years The American Indian population is a young population with the majority being in the child-bearing age; therefore, one may expect to see an increase in the future population statistics.

Given the fact that American Indians have a disproportionate rate of disabilities, the most logical question is, "Why?" At the risk of oversimplifying a complex question, perhaps the answer can be summarized by stating "lifestyle." In this situation, lifestyle is not intended to be negative or imply immoral behaviors but is intended to assert that the living conditions and the manner of life that society has forced upon many Native Americans places them "at risk" for various types of disabilities. To be more specific, many American Indians live on reservations and many of the reservations are in isolated locations with few chances for employment. Consequently, the boredom and lack of off-reservation socialization cause some to abuse alcohol which may lead to diseases such as cirrhosis of the liver and other liver diseases, automobile and other accidents, attempted suicide, and homicides. By no means do all disabilities occur on and to persons living on reservations. For American Indians on and off reservations, racism and discrimination cause stress and despair which can have similar results as the isolation and loneliness of the reservation. Additionally, the economic realities for many American Indians mean they have to live on minimal incomes; consequently, many of the foods they consume have a high fat and caloric content. As will be discussed in health issues, American Indians have a high rate of obesity, which along with inappropriate dietary habits, is a major contributor to the development of diabetes. Relatedly, diabetes is a major contributor to blindness as well as amputations. Also, diet and obesity are major causes of heart conditions as well as hypertension and this can lead to cerebrovascular diseases.

The obvious bad news is that American Indians rank high on many of the indices of poor health conditions; however, the good news is that these conditions are caused by lifestyle conditions that can be corrected by altering these lifestyle conditions. The author would like to point out that this is not an "Indian problem" but a national problem that will require cooperation and collaboration of Indians and the appropriate local, state, and federal governmental agencies and organizations. After all, American Indians did not create the problem of lifestyle in isolation; therefore, they should not be expected to solve all of the problems without appropriate assistance.

Major Health Issues Among American Indians

"On almost every indicator of morbidity, mortality, and quality of life, American Indians are substantially worse off than the dominant culture and as bad or worse off than other minorities." This observation was made by McCubbin and his associates (1993) as they attempted to provide a summary of the health conditions of Native Americans and the observation remains true today. They continued their observations with the following comments:

Although the death rate for Native American infants is approximately equal to that for all races, post neonatal deaths and death from Sudden Infant Death

Syndrome (SIDS) are nearly twice as common among Native Americans as in the general population. The prevalence of diabetes among Native Americans exceeds 20 percent in many tribes. The Native American death rate for alcoholism is four times higher than the national average. Alcoholism is also related to incidences of Fetal Alcohol Syndrome (FAS) six times greater than in the general population, to over 60 percent of cases of child abuse and neglect, to 75 percent of accidents and a homicide rate 60 percent higher than that of the general population. The suicide rates among various Native American tribes (also related to alcoholism) are three times the rate for general population.

In addition to the previously mentioned health issues, American Indians experience greater problems than the national average with: heart disease, accidents, cancer and diabetes. Moreover, they have higher incidence rates, according to the Indian Health Service (1994), of tuberculosis (five times higher than the national average), alcoholism (43.5 times higher), homicide (71 times higher), suicide (54 times higher) and pneumonia/influenza (44 percent higher). At this point I will provide a brief discussion of several of the major health issues: alcoholism, fetal alcohol syndrome, diabetes, obesity, and drug use.

Alcoholism

According to Carpenter et al. (1985), alcohol abuse constitutes the single most significant health problem among American Indians. Excessive consumption of alcohol appears to be the norm among some American Indians and, unfortunately, this pattern of rapid and excessive drinking becomes part of adolescent American Indians who begin to drink in peer groups where drinking may be sanctioned. Recent evidence indicates that problem drinking is quite prevalent among adolescents and younger Indian children.

The fact that there is a high rate of alcoholism among American Indians should in no way be considered as low moral standards and a lack of self-control. There are some major contributing factors that have caused some American Indians to become dependent upon alcohol. (1) Poverty–In a message to the United States Congress in 1970, President Richard M. Nixon described Native Americans as "the most deprived and most isolated minority group in our nation." Indian reservations have been described as "America's third world" and American Indians have described themselves as "beggars in our land." Some public health officials contend that the depth of poverty among American Indians is reflected in that American Indian's homes were five times more likely to be lacking plumbing and nearly fourteen times more likely to be without sewage disposal than other homes in America. (2) Reservation life–With regard to reservation life slightly less than half of the

American Indian population lives on reservations and, according to Beauvis and LaBoueff (1988), poverty and its attendant ills of poor nutrition, poor health, and inadequate housing and transportation are still a way of life on most reservations. It is postulated that these conditions, coupled with the isolation of many reservations, lead to chronic stress which put many American Indians in a vulnerable position when confronted with opportunities to use alcohol and/or drugs. Allen Cheadle and associates (1994) support Fred Beauvis and his associate's position with these comments, "Reasons for the high levels of alcohol abuse among Indians on reservations have been attributed to the poverty and hopelessness associated with reservation life and with problems of adapting traditional Indian values to a culture that is predominantly white with contrasting values." (3) Peer pressure–the combination of pressure from one's peers "to be social," and the lack of anyone discouraging the use of alcohol leads many adults and, more particular, adolescents down the path toward excessive drinking.

As destructive as excessive alcohol consumption is, it can be a double disaster for females, particularly those within the child-bearing ages. The consumption of alcohol affects both the female and her unborn child. This condition is called Fetal Alcohol Syndrome (FAS).

Fetal Alcohol Syndrome

The consumption of alcohol while pregnant has been known to be a danger to babies for many centuries. In Judges 13:7, the Bible states, "Behold, thou shalt conceive and bear a son: and now drink no wine or strong drink." Alcohol consumed during pregnancy reaches the fetus in a very short time; thus, as Streissguth et al. (1988) correctly contend, "Prenatal exposure to alcohol can damage the baby and have profound and lasting effects on its development."

The National Organization on Mental Retardation (1992) explains that Fetal Alcohol Syndrome refers to a group of physical and mental birth defects resulting from a woman drinking alcohol during pregnancy. Fetal Alcohol Syndrome, according to Masis and May (1991), is the leading known cause of mental retardation. Other symptoms can include organ dysfunction, growth deficiencies before and after birth, central nervous dysfunction resulting in learning disabilities and lower intelligence, and physical malformation in the face and cranial areas (Streissguth, LaDue, Randels, 1988). In addition, children may experience behavioral and mental problems which may progress into adulthood.

An Association representing persons with mental and intellectual disabilities provides valuable information with regard to how alcohol affects the development of the fetus. It is believed that alcohol may affect the way cells grow and arrange themselves as they multiply, altering tissue growth in the part of the fetus that is developing at the time of exposure. The brain is particularly sensitive to alcohol which diminishes the development of cells.

Frequently, children born with fetal alcohol syndrome have low birth weight. As the infant grows, it is not uncommon for various symptoms to develop, such as muscle problems, bone and joint problems, genital defects, and heart defects.

Other less obvious symptoms such as intellectual and other developmental delays may also occur. Frequently, social adaptions are difficult for persons with Fetal Alcohol Syndrome. Studies have shown that persons with fetal alcohol syndrome have long-term disabilities enduring into adolescence and adulthood. Perhaps the most handicapping long-term disability is poor adaptive behavior. In addition to endangering their children, American Indian women who drink alcohol to an excess are at risk for advanced liver disease, decreased life expectancy, and because of depression, are at risk to be involved in domestic violence.

As a result of the various problems associated with excessive drinking and the high rate of alcoholism among American Indians, tribal leaders and public health official have declared alcoholism the number one health problem. The magnitude of the problem has promoted some Indians to say that alcoholism is a form of genocide.

Diabetes

Health complications from diabetes make it the sixth leading cause of death among American Indians (Healthy People 2000). Relatedly, the prevalence rate for diabetes in American Indians is higher than any of the other ethnic minority groups—African Americans, Hispanic/Latino Americans, and Asian and Pacific Americans.

A deficiency in the body's ability to produce insulin is a simplified definition of diabetes. Bogardus and Lillioja (1992) explain that diabetes is classified into two categories: insulin-dependent diabetes mellitus (IDDM) and noninsulin-dependent diabetes mellitus (NIDDM). They further point out that there are approximately ten million people in the United States who are considered diabetic. Noninsulin-dependent diabetes appears to be the most prevalent form of diabetes, comprising approximately 90 percent of the cases.

The noninsulin-dependent diabetes is the most prevalent form among American Indians (Orchard et al., 1992). As there is significant cultural and ethnic diversity among American Indian tribes, there are wide variations in the prevalence of diabetes among American Indians. As an example, the

Pima Indians have the highest reported prevalence rate of noninsulin-dependent diabetes in the world, as high as 50 percent of those 35 years of age and older (Sugarman et al., 1993); whereas, according to Newman (1992), Alaska Natives have the lowest rates in America, only half that of the United States population all races and ethnic groups. A major reason for the difference appears to be difference in lifestyles, particularly dietary habits.

Both forms of diabetes, insulin-dependent (Type I) and noninsulin-dependent (Type II) can and do cause disabilities such as amputees (neuropathy), blindness (retinopathy), cardiovascular disease (CVD), and End Stage Renal Disease (nephropathy).

Amputations–Persons with diabetes are at significant risk for lower extremity amputations; such procedures are 15 times more common among persons with diabetes; relatedly persons with diabetes account for approximately 50,000 (50%) of all non-traumatic amputations performed in the United States.

Blindness–Diabetes mellitus is a major cause of blindness in the United States and is the leading cause of new blindness in working-aged Americans. Diabetic retinopathy accounts for approximately 12 percent of new cases of blindness each year in the United States. Persons who have diabetes are 25 times more at risk for blindness than the general population. It is projected that, if untreated, 70 percent of American Indians persons with diabetes will develop retinopathy which may lead to more serious visual problems.

Cardiovascular Disease–Diabetes may lead to cardiovascular disease which is the leading cause of morbidity and mortality among persons with diabetes. The annual risk for death or disability from cardiovascular disease is two to three times greater for persons with diabetes than for persons without diabetes. Additionally, persons with diabetes are at risk for cerebrovascular disease and for coronary artery disease at a rate that is two to three times greater than the general population.

One of the suspected contributing causal factors for development of diabetes is obesity. In many cases, obesity is a result of lifestyle, thus is preventable.

Obesity

Welty (1991) reminds us that American Indian have experienced an epidemic of diabetes, increasing rates of cardiovascular disease and hypertension, and poor survival rates for breast cancer–all partially attributed to the increasing prevalence of obesity over the past generation. Further comments by Welty indicate that obesity may be a contributing factor to gallstones, arthritis, and to adverse outcomes of pregnancy. Additionally, research points to obesity as one of the most common risk factors predisposing persons to certain cancers, as well as osteoarthritis.

In summary, according to Barbara Erickson (1993), obesity is more prevalent in American Indians than in the U.S. population in practically all age groups. Adult American Indian men and women are significantly more overweight than the comparable U.S. population. Obesity rates in Native American adolescents and preschool children are higher than the respective rate for U.S., all races combined. The rates of obesity differ among the various tribal regions. A possible explanation is that their cultures have undergone significant changes over the past half century and as a consequence, their lifestyles and diets have changed. Studies indicate that factors shown to influence the development and maintenance of obesity include lack of physical activity, diet, ethnicity, income, education, and genetic susceptibility.

Drug Use

There appears to be a higher rate of drug use among reservation youth than the American Indian youth living off reservations (Beauvis 1992). One possible reason is again the isolation and poor living conditions found on some reservations.

While the statistics regarding drug use are cause for concern, one should not lose sight that more American Indian youth do not use drugs on a daily basis than those who do use them; therefore, an appropriate intervention would be to mobilize those who abstain and have them work with the users in an effort to convince them to become drug free. As Beauvis and LaBoueff postulate, "Among younger children, at least, there is practically no use if friends do not encourage drug use and if friends would actively try to prevent one from using drugs."

Providers of Health Care Services

MEDICINE MEN. Long before we had primary care physicians and managed care, medicine men provided the health care for American Indians. Through the use of herbs, spiritual and religious ceremonies, as well as many other methods, the medicine man provided for the health needs of his people. During the period of assimilation where the U.S. government and others were attempting to strip Native American people of their culture, one of the things that was almost lost was the tradition of the medicine man. Fortunately, some of the traditions were retained; consequently, some American Indians rely to some degree upon the efforts and knowledge of the medicine man. There are those who question the effectiveness of these practices; however, as with any healing process, it is aided by faith.

INDIAN HEALTH SERVICES. The following statements by Hershman and Campion (1985) are dated however these comments remain true today. They said that Native Americans are faced with many chronic health problems. Because of the migration and changing ways of life, many of the traditional ways of diagnosing and treating illnesses have been lost. They continue by stating that despite the changes, Indian people are more receptive to modern medicine; however, some will resort to the medicine man or other traditional medicine if a cure is not forthcoming. Relatedly, the Indian Health Service is the agency designated to provide health care to American Indians.

A student in one of the author's classes made the following astute analysis regarding the way many American Indians handle their personal health:

> Typically, the Native American live in circumstances where habitual lifestyles develop. Proportionately, health is a concern. Untreated illness is commonplace. From self-diagnosing and self-medicating to self-care these become patterns of response. One buys time with these methods. Eventually, conditions develop leading to a severely compromised health status. A true state of emergency occurs and the individual becomes a patient. (Theresa Prairie Chief, 1993)

HISTORICAL BACKGROUND. In 1954, Public Health Service took over the Bureau of Indian Affair's role of providing Indian health care. To help determine some of the health needs and concerns and to become prepared to deliver health care to American Indians, in 1957, a comprehensive health survey was conducted. The results were stunning in that there were significant statistical differences existing relative to other populations in the United States. Virtually all comparisons were undesirable.

Not until 1976 were issues created by the study addressed. The Indian Health Care Improvement Act was formulated to provide corrections to the disparities. Because of inadequate funding, some of the problems remained to be corrected. In 1988, reauthorization of the act gave the Indian Health Service agency status within the Public Health Service.

Conclusion

Cultural diversity in America is inevitable; cultural diversity in America is good and desirable, and because of cultural diversity many aspects of American society will experience change. Another fact about cultural diversity is that persons with disabilities, including persons with disabilities from ethnic/racial minority backgrounds, are part of this diversity; thus a relevant question is, "What are some of the changes that will have to occur to accommodate persons with disabilities and what will be some of the effects of more and more persons with disabilities becoming part of the American mainstream?" Books are written on changes that will take place in the twenty-first century as a result of America becoming more diverse; therefore, this conclusion cannot adequately address the many changes. However major changes must occur for persons with disabilities to feel as part of the mainstream of American society.

The major problem that most persons with disabilities encounter is the negative attitudes of others with regard to what the person with a disability can do. As a society, too often we think of disability as "can't" such as blind people can't see, deaf people can't hear, paraplegic people can't walk, mute people can't talk and the list could continue. While it is true there are things that a person with a disability cannot do, is this not true for all humans? We do not observe persons without disabilities and think of the things they cannot do, when in fact, if careful analysis were made, there are probably as many things they cannot do as there are things the person with a disability cannot do. It is true that one of the reasons we think of what the person with a disability cannot do is that his limitations are often visible, while so-called nondisabled person's limitations are hidden. Regardless, thinking of a person's inabilities is acquired through a socialization process and can be unlearned and not perpetuated by passing on to the next generation. Instead, our society must learn to acknowledge the limitation(s) of a person with a disability and concentrate upon the things he can do, encouraging and assisting him to strengthen his assets just as we would a person without a disability.

Closely associated with removal of negative attitudes toward persons with disabilities is removing the stigma associated with having a disability. Persons with disabilities learn to dislike themselves because society too often views them as inferior humans. Some of the words we use to describe disabilities and those that possess them give some clue to the intensity of the stigma attached—words such as "cripple," "crazy," "dumb," and "gimp" can be devastating. The exclusion of many life activities and events; the denial of opportunities, and benign neglect that many persons with disabilities experience have the effect of deepening the feeling of inferiority.

To eliminate stigma attached to disabilities, our society must teach our children that there is nothing shameful about having a disability. We must impress upon these future adults that there is nothing wrong with having friends who are different and there is nothing bad about socializing, dating, and marrying persons with disabilities. Most of all, we must emphasize that persons with disabilities are as good and useful as persons without a disability. Once children learn to accept persons with disabilities and their limitations, they will experience few, if any, difficulties working, socializing, loving and living with persons who have disabilities.

Because of technical advances, the world of work is changing and opportunities for persons with disabilities are increasing and will continue to do so.

For persons with disabilities to take advantage of these employment opportunities equal opportunity to quality education must be made available. New methods of assessing intelligence and abilities are being acquired and concurrent with this is the need for new attitudes and perceptions of persons with disabilities' intellectual capabilities so that they can have fair and reasonable opportunities to be educated and trained for present and future jobs. Finally, as persons with disabilities are able to successfully compete for career-type jobs, they will have the resources to enjoy the many fine resources of America.

Review Questions

1. How does the Americans with Disabilities Act define disability?
2. How does the Americans with Disabilities Act's definition of disability differ from previous definitions?
3. What are some of the difficulties encountered in attempting to obtain an accurate count with regard to the number of persons with disabilities in America?
4. The first federal legislation with regard to rehabilitation of persons with disabilities was established for which group?
5. What are the five (5) titles that constitute the 1990 Americans with Disabilities Act?

Suggested Activities

1. Conduct an informal survey by interviewing at least five (5) persons, asking them to give you their definition of a disability; also ask them to identify five (5) disabilities.
2. In the previously mentioned survey, ask the participants at what point would they consider a person to be rehabilitated?
3. Research information on the Americans with Disabilities Act and identify relevant facts with regard to each title, then list how each title impacts persons with disabilities.
4. Visit a rehabilitation center and learn about the latest techniques used to rehabilitate persons with disabilities.
5. Interview a rehabilitation counselor with regard to the types of services provided to persons with disabilities by his/her agency.

References

Beauvis, F., & LaBoueff, S. (1985). Drug and alcohol abuse interventions in American Indian communities. *International Journal of Addictions, 20*(1), 139–171, January.

Bernall, H., & Perez-Stable, E. J. (1994). Diabetes mellitus. In M. Molina & C. Molina (Eds.), *Latino health in the U.S.: A growing challenge.* Washington DC: American Public Health Association.

Bogardus, C., & Lillioja, S. (1992). Pima Indians as a model to study the genetics of NIDOM. *Journal of Cellular Biochemistry, 48*(40), 337–343.

Bryan, W. V. (1996). *In search of freedom.* Springfield, IL: Charles C Thomas.

Carpenter, R. Lyons, C., & Miller, W. (1985). Peer-managed self-control program for prevention of alcohol abuse in American Indian high school students: A pilot evaluation study. *International Journal of the Addictions, 20*(2), 299–310, February.

Carrillo, E., & Uranga-McKanne, S. (1994). HIV/AIDS. In M. Molina & S. Molina (Eds.), *Latino health in the U.S.: A growing challenge.* Washington DC: American Public Health Association.

Cheadle, A., Pearson, D., Wagner, E., & Psaty, B. (1994). Relationship between socioeconomic status, health status, and lifestyle practices of American Indians: Evidence from a plains reservation population. *Public Health Reports, 109*(3), 405–413.

DeLoach, C., Wilkins, R. D., & Walker, G. W. (1983). *Independent living, philosophy, process and services.* Baltimore: University Park Press.

Eisenberg, M., Giggins, C., & Duval, R. (Eds.). (1982). *Disabled people as second-class citizens.* New York: Springer

Erickson, B. (1993). *Obesity in Native Americans.* Unpublished paper, University of Oklahoma Health Sciences Center, Oklahoma City, OK.

Funk, R. (1987). From caste to class in the context of civil rights. In A. Gartner & T. Joe (Eds.), *Images of the disabled.* New York: Praeger.

Gartner, A., & Joe, T., (Eds.). (1987). *Images of the disabled.* New York: Praeger.

Giachello, A. L. M. (1994). Issues of access and use. In M. Molina & C. Molina (Eds.), *Latino health in the U.S.: A growing challenge.* Washington DC: American Public Health Association.

Henderson, G., & Bryan, W. V. (1984). *Psychosocial aspects of disability.* Springfield, IL: Charles C Thomas.

Kent, D. (1988). In search of a heroine: Images of women with disabilities in fiction and drama. In M. Fine & A. Asch (Eds.), *Women with disablities.* Philadelphia: Temple University Press.

Marin, G., Marin, B. V., Pérez-Stable, E. J., Sabogal, F., & Sabogal-Otero, R. (1995). Cultural differences in attitudes and expectancies between Hispanic and Non-Hispanic white smokers. In A. M. Padilla (Ed.), *Hispanic psychology: Critical issues in theory and research.* Thousand Oaks, CA: Sage.

Masis, K. B., & May, P. A. (1991). A comprehensive local program for the prevention of fetal alcohol syndrome. *Public Health Reports, 106*(5), 484–489.

McCubbin, H. I., Thompson, E. A., Thompson, A. I., McCubbin, M. A., & Kaston, A. J. (1993). Culture, ethnicity and the family: Critical factors in childhood chronic illnesses and disabilities. *Pediatrics, 91,* 1063–1070, May.

National Organization on Mental Retardation. (1992). *Facts about alcohol use during pregnancy.* The Arc.

Orchard, T. J. LaPorte, R. E., & Dorman, J. S. (1992). Diabetes. In J. M. & R. D. Wallace (Eds.), *Public health and preventive medicine.* Norwalk, CT: Appleton and Lange, pp. 873–883.

Pérez-Stable, E. J. (1994). Cardiovascular disease. In M. Molina & C. Molina (Eds.), *Latino health in the U.S.: A growing challenge.* Washington DC: American Public Health Association.

Prairie Chief, T. (1993). U.S. health care of Native Americans: The impossibility is the reality. Unpublished paper, University of Oklahoma Health Sciences Center, Oklahoma City, OK.

Streissguth, A. P., LaDue, R. A., & Randels, S. P. (1988). A manual on adolescents and adults with fetal alcohol syndrome with special reference to American Indians. *Indian Health Service,* Contract #240-83-0035.

Stubbins, J. (1988). The politics of disability. In H. E. Yuker (Ed.), *Attitudes toward persons with disabilities.* New York: Springer.

Townsend, E., & Ryan, B. (1991). Assessing independence in community living. *Canadian Journal of Public Health, 82,* 52–57.

Valdez, R. B., Morgenstern, H., Brown, E. R., Wyn, R., Wang C., & Cumberland, W. (1994). Insuring Latinos against the cost of illness. In M. Molina & C. Molina (Eds.), *Latino health in the U.S.: A growing challenge.* Washington DC: American Public Health Association.

Welty, T. (1991). Health implications of obesity in American Indians and Alaska Natives. *American Journal of Clinical Nutrition, 53*(6 Suppl).

Wright, B. (1960). *Physical disability: A psychological approach.* New York: Harper and Row.

Wright, B. A. (1988). Attitudes and the fundamental negative bias: Conditions and corrections. In H. E. Yuker (Ed.), *Attitudes toward persons with disabilities.* New York: Springer.

Suggested Readings

Bryan, W. V. (1996). *In search of freedom.* Springfield, IL: Charles C Thomas.

Eisenberg, M. G., Giggins, C., & Duval, R. J. (Eds.). (1982). *Disabled people as second-class citizens.* New York: Springer.

Fine, M., & Asch, A. (1988). Disabilities beyond stigma: Social interaction, discrimination and activism. *Journal of Social Issues, 44,* 3–21.

Funk, R (1987). From caste to class in the context of civil rights. In A. Gartner & T. Joe (Eds.), *Images of the disabled.*

Henderson, G., & Bryan, W. V. (1997). *Psychosocial aspects of disability* (2nd ed.). Springfield, IL: Charles C Thomas.

Stubbins, J. (1988). The politics of disability. In H. E. Yuker (Ed.), *Attitudes toward persons with disabilities.* New York: Springer.

Chapter 6

AFRICAN AMERICANS

Chapter Outline
- Introduction
- Historical Perspective
- Social Issues Impacting African Americans
- Educational Issues
- Employment and Economic Issues
- Major Health Issues
- Family Dynamics
- Intervention Strategies
- Assessment
- Conclusion

Chapter Objectives
- Identify significant historical events which have impacted the lives of African Americans
- Identify the prevalence of disabilities among the African American population in the United States
- Identify, social, educational, and economical issues which impact the lives of African Americans
- Identify how social, educational and economic issues affect the lives of African Americans

Introduction

Although Africans were ship crew members of expeditions from what is now Europe, and to this author's knowledge, they were not enslaved to the land that was being explored or intended to be explored. This fact means that the first Africans or persons of African descent were not brought to what is now the United States of America as slaves. However, later ships did bring Africans and others to America to be slaves and/or indentured servants. This fact means that African, black people, have been part of the fabric of the United States for over 390 years. The point being made is that African Americans have been a significant part of the building of the United States culture. Despite the noble attempts of past generations of African slaves and descendants of slaves to keep alive memories, history, and traditions of the African motherland, much of this information has been lost simply by virtue of time, the inability to commit this information in written form as well as influences from new experiences which have added and embedded new cultural thoughts, views and beliefs into the minds of decedents of persons shackled by the cruel institution of slavery. This means that African Americans have, as is the case for other nationalities that have come to the United States developed, by virtue of the experiences to which they have been exposed, some new cultural views which are more in line with the overall culture of the host country. This does not mean that the new citizens have totally abandoned or in many cases willfully abandoned their homeland cultural views; however given enough time in a new cultural environment, in most cases, it is natural that they will lose many, if not much, of the old country culture and take on and contribute to the culture of their new homeland.

In this chapter I will discuss some of the significant events which have helped shape the cultural views of current African Americans. The following is not intended to be a complete discussion of events and actions which have contributed to the cultural views of current African Americans. Space will not allow a complete or comprehensive discussion of African American history. This author has selected certain events to illustrate some of the things that have had significant impacts on the cultural development of African Americans in the United States of America.

Historical Perspective

The author of this book has chosen to segment the existence of African Americans in America into five periods; some periods are overlapping: (1) Slavery 1619–1865, (2) Reconstruction 1865–1877, (3) Segregation 1877–1964, (4) Black Nationalism 1930–1964, and (5) Integration 1964 to present. Certainly these are arbitrary segments of periods of time and events; others may choose to use different classifications. Offered as an example, the integration period of 1964 to present includes the significant period of Affirmative Action; some may wish to add a unique time period for this era.

Slavery (1619–1865)

The cruelty of indentured servitude and slavery has been part of the human experience for thousands of years. There is ample evidence that the first appearance of Africans and persons of African descent in America was not as slaves but as explorers and ship navigators sailing to North America among other areas in the territory to become known as the United States of America. This noble entrance of black people in America notwithstanding, the beginning of the permanent existence of persons of African descent began in August 1619 when the colonial government at Jamestown, Virginia, purchased twenty blacks from a Dutch frigate. Some historians indicate that the first Africans were indentured servants. This event opened the period of slavery which linked America to the long list of nations, empires, countries, and territories which had engaged in the inhumane practice of human bondage.

The purpose of slavery in America is clear, that being able to provide an inexpensive and steady, controlled labor force to work the fields, shops, and homes of the owners. Meager as the efforts were, questions can be raised as to the cheapness of feeding, clothing, housing, and the occasional medical care of the slaves; however, certainly slavery to their owners had one major advantage that made the institution more desirable than employing persons for wages–the ability to control the work force. Slavery did not allow for demands of higher wages and work stoppage if the demands were not met. Slavery was never intended to be an on-the-job training program; therefore, the impact was as emotionally and psychologically devastating as the practice was cruel. The emotional and psychological costs to the slaves were so severe that the impact has been felt by generations of their offspring. Additionally, the impact has affected the entire nation of American citizens in various ways. Some of the major impacts upon the slaves and their generations to follow are: (1) labeled as inferior, (2) branded as immoral, (3) stereotyped as unable to be educated, and (4) deprived of normal family relationships.

To make the institution of slavery work effectively, the slave owners had to cause their human subjects to feel inferior thus allowing themselves to be dominated by "superior beings" who would determine what was best for their lives and provide accordingly. One may incorrectly think that physical intimidation was the only means the slave owners used to force their wills upon slaves; however, physical intimidation was only one of several methods. The process of destroying the slaves' self-worth began on the slave ship where persons from the same tribe and/or spoke the same language were separated so that communication would be difficult. This form of separation was continued once they were placed under the control of the purchaser. The unfamiliar surroundings, inability to communicate effectively, and punishment for behaving in ways which were natural to them was more than enough to confuse and intimidate the slaves. Add to what has been stated, years of humiliating living conditions as well as consistently being referred to as sub-human and stupid, one can easily sketch a picture where feelings of inferiority served as the primary background of life for the slaves.

Other actions taken during the slavery period which had profound effects upon future generations of African Americans were: (1) the practice of separating families, particularly not allowing most males to establish normal family ties, thus bonding with their children; (2) forcing many of the males and females to serve as producers of future laborers by forcing the males to mate with numerous females and then the slave owner selling the offspring. The act of using some males as breeders is a classic example of the concept of "blaming the victim" in that despite being forced to live in this manner they were branded as immoral for their actions; (3) degrading the institution of marriage by not allowing couples to participate in the religious ceremony associated with marriage, instead having them jump over a broom handle or some other meaningless act; (4) not allowing slaves to be educated; and (5) treating the slaves as livestock to be bought and sold with their last name changing to the name of their current owner.

These, as well as other actions had the effect of causing the person who was forced to be a slave to feel inferior to the person who proclaimed to own him. Additionally, it sowed the seeds for a matriarchal dominated family and the process of African Americans being deficient in the educational arena was begun. As one might expect, as years have passed, many of these negatives have been continued and in some instances such as poor educational attainment have been magnified while other groups have made steady progress.

Undoubtedly, slavery has had many negative effects on the persons who were enslaved as well as their progeny; however, there is a growing voice within America which is expressing the belief that over 100 years of "freedom" should have erased many of the deficits. This is perhaps a reasonable assumption to make, but inaccurate none-the-less. One could argue that it is unreasonable to think that 100 plus years could erase over 200 years of deprivation. A more effective argument is that because of the discrimination to which African Americans have been subjected they have not experienced 100 years of freedom.

Slavery was certainly a cruel and inhumane form of discrimination, and the period of reconstruction was no less discriminatory for the African American.

Reconstruction (1865–1877)

With the end of slavery in 1865, persons who had been enslaved were legally free. While freedom had long been the dream of African Americans who were not free, it was unfortunate that most were not prepared to live as free individuals. They knew how to farm but most were not knowledgeable of the ways of managing a farm, additionally if they had possessed the management tools they would have had difficulty implementing them, because as a result of the Civil War, much of the infrastructure of the Southern states had been destroyed. In short, if they were able to raise crops, how would they market them? These were some of the conditions that the period of reconstruction began for persons who had been considered slaves. It is true that promises of land and livestock had been made, but very few saw those promises become reality. Instead of being a period of time when the Southern states were rebuilt and persons who had previously been enslaved were being prepared to live lives free from discrimination and intimidation, selfish intentions and greedy-minded persons chose to use the situation for their benefits.

History correctly records that some progress was made with regard to African Americans, such as being elected to Congress and to important local positions in several southern state legislatures. Ironically it was this trend toward moving from being powerless to having some voice in the building of their lives that cut short this phase of reconstruction. Former slave owners and their descendants had hopes of the "South" returning to its former position of southern grandeur and the slight elevation of their former human property was a definite threat to those dreams. To place an end to what they considered "foolish efforts," they began to devise ways to place fear within the hearts and minds of the ex-slaves, the results of which were the establishment of the Ku Klux Klan (KKK) and other white supremacy groups. The Klan had as its major goal putting "blacks" in their place, which was being subservient to white people and they attempted to do this through beating, burning of blacks' homes and churches, as well as lynching. Unfortunately, these activities were condoned by many of the southern local and state authorities. Their activities to a large extent brought to an end the experiment of reconstruction of the South, particularly any positive involvement by African Americans. Instead, began the new era of segregation or separation of the races, particularly the black and white races. No doubt, one of the legacies of the reconstruction period with regard to African Americans was the deepening realization that either as slave or ex-slave they had very little control of their lives and that they were at best second-class citizens who had very little recourse to seek grievance for wrongful acts committed against their person. In other terms, the seeds of distrust of the dominant society had begun to grow.

Segregation (1877–1964)

As the southern politics and other day-to-day activities returned to the control of the former land owners, two things high on their agenda were to insure that the ex-slaves were powerless and that there was complete separation of the black and white races as much as possible. The impact of these decisions was to last for many years and to a considerable extent continues to play a role in the daily lives of many African Americans today. Some of the measures taken were: (1) denial of the right of African Americans to vote in the former Confederate states; (2) segregated public school systems with the black schools inadequately funded; (3) segregated public and private facilities such as denying African Americans the right to dine in facilities where whites dined and separate restroom facilities to mention a couple; (4) the denial of African Americans the right to purchase homes wherever they could afford; (5) the denial of the right to worship wherever one desired; (6) the basic denial of free speech; and (7) relegation to menial tasks and receiving lower salaries than their white counterparts.

In fairness to the southern states, it must be noted that African Americans were to some degree denied these same rights in virtually every state of the Union. It was the southern states that most vigorously and aggressively promoted and practiced these discriminations. They were the ones who held on to these practices long after other parts of the country had begun to experiment with different ways of interaction between the two races. It is interesting to note that these same states which held the hardest line with regard to race relations today appear to be making better adjustment in this area than some of the states which did not practice segregation with the same fervor as the former Confederate states.

The impact of the denial of these rights have had and continue to have an impact upon the lives of African Americans in the areas of education, economics, employment, and the social realm. These impacts will be explored later in this chapter. At this point, we are establishing a historical basis for why the lives of many African Americans have been affected in the ways they are.

Black Nationalism (1930–1964)

Considering the many restrictions and denial of rights, the ex-slaves and their descendants must have been asking the question, "What is freedom for black people?" As generations of African Americans continued to experience the effects of segregation, several trains of thought began to develop with regard to the question of what is freedom for black people—one was Black Nationalism. Black Nationalism had different meanings to the various groups seriously debating the plight of the African American. Representing the two extremes, one group led by a fiery black man from the West Indies, Marcus Garvey, it meant returning to Africa, other groups proposed that several southern states be given to African Americans to be turned into "all-black" states. Neither the "back to Africa" movement nor the "all-black states" efforts succeeded. Mr. Garvey was deported from the United States and perhaps the all-black state idea was doomed from conception. Since neither effort met with much success is not the point; the idea worth keeping in one's mind is that African Americans' dream of exerting control over their lives was kept alive. Later movements such as the Nation of Islam (Black Muslim) promoted similar ideals.

The period of Black Nationalism overlaps the segregation period and, as previously stated, the exclusion of African Americans from the mainstream of American society gave rise to the Black Nationalism movement. A significant impact of the Black Nationalism movement was the questioning by African Americans of whether American society would ever accept them and allow them to truly be free. Further, the thought of many African Americans was that if they were not going to be accepted into American society as first-class citizens, they should separate themselves from mainstream America. In short, the roots of distrust of the dominant society were beginning to deepen.

Integration (1964 to Present)

Perhaps not as loudly heard during the peak period of the black national movement, but certainly a persistent voice for moderation, living within and changing from within the system were voices such as the National Association for the Advancement of Colored People (NAACP) and the Urban League to mention only two groups promoting working within the system. These voices became louder and would later be joined by other forceful organizations such as the Southern Christian Leadership Conference of which Dr. Martin Luther King, Jr. emerged as a leader.

The NAACP legal defense fund led by Thurgood Marshall was successful in winning the *Brown vs. Topeka Board of Education* decision which was the beginning of the end of segregated school system. Through marches, sit-ins, demonstrations, work stoppages, and refusing to shop at the segregated facilities and ride city busses, segregated facilities were integrated. The brevity of this account tends to make the efforts and results appear easy, which is not the case, as many lives were lost and/or destroyed in the struggle. Most certainly, America went through a social transformation it had not experienced since the Civil War.

Social Issues Impacting African Americans

During the twentieth century and continuing into the twenty-first century a major social issue faced by Americans of African heritage has been and continues to be "inclusion" acceptance into a society which at best has viewed and to some degrees continue to view them as second-class citizens. As discussed previously, many years after legalized slavery was abolished, the posture of the nation was segregating black people into what was farcically called "separate but equal" facilities. This separation has created a societal imbalance which, in most cases, favors Euro-Americans. Certainly much has been accomplished toward reducing the inequality that exists between African Americans and Euro-Americans. Laws and attitudinal changes have accounted for much of the progress. However, despite this progress, as the twenty-first century has become a reality, inclusion and equality remains a major "social issue of the day."

Equality struggles have been a hallmark of African American existence in America. While the efforts have met with some degree of success, such as access to educational opportunities, advancements in employment and personal security, the difficulties of the struggles, coupled with the slow pace of progression, has been attributed for some of the social issues that will be continued for quite some time. The failure of integration to produce a color-blind society as well as the regression in civil rights during the decades of the 1980s and 1990s as well as into the twenty-first century has produced considerable frustration on the part of many African Americans. For some, this frustration has led to their abandonment of the age-old principle of delayed gratification practiced by many African Americans. Particularly, some younger African Americans appear to have taken the attitude that if their paths to the American dream are going to be blocked, they will create their own roads to success. Too frequently and unfortunately, those roads have led to negative encounters with law enforcement and too often have resulted in disastrous results.

While the overwhelming majority of young and older African Americans are law abiding, concern has been voiced by African Americans with regard to the number of African Americans who are being lost to violence, crime, substance abuse, and overreactive law enforcement. Statistics indicate that violence involving America's youth is increasing. Although dated the following comments by Gordon, Gordon, and Nembhard (1994) remain true that

African American males have a disproportionate involvement in violence and violent behavior.

Because a large number of African American males, particularly between 18–34 years of age have been killed, many African Americans consider this a form of genocide. One may ask, "If this is a form of genocide, isn't it self-imposed and why are African American males disproportionately involved in violence and violent behavior?" In an attempt to address these and other relevant questions, Earl Washington (1996) conducted a survey of the literature and gleaned the following sociologic theories and concepts: (1) poverty-social disorganization theory, (2) racial oppression-displaced aggression theory, (3) subculture of violence theory, and (4) compulsive masculinity theory. It should be noted that these concepts and theories are by no means the extent of speculation of why African American males are disproportionately involved in violence and violent behaviors. These will provide the reader with some of the current thought with regard to this subject.

Theories

Poverty-Social Disorganization Theory

According to Voss and Hepburn (1968), this theory indicates that there is a correlation between the high rate of criminal involvement among African American men and the high rate of poverty within African American communities. Those that place credence in this theory postulate that poverty contributes to social conditions that are conducive to criminal violence, such as chronic unemployment, teen pregnancy, female-headed families, academic failure, welfare dependency, inadequate socialization, and substance abuse.

Racial Oppression Displaced Aggression Theory

This theory posits that anger and frustration built up within African American men and youth as legitimate means to success, such as academic achievement, upward mobility, financial success and gainful employment, are blocked by society. As a result, the inability to attain goals creates anger; however, fear of retaliation by Euro-Americans forces African Americans to internalize the anger; consequently the frustration is displaced in the form of violence against other African Americans and African American communities.

Subculture of Violence Theory

This theory maintains that the majority of African Americans is law abiding and maintain values that promote conforming to the prevailing laws;

however, there are subculture values and norms which condone violence as an acceptable means of resolving interpersonal conflicts. The theory also emphasizes that during late adolescence to middle-age, African Americans develop attitudes that view trouble, toughness, sexual conquests, manipulation, autonomy, and excitement as ways of confirming one's manhood.

Compulsive Masculinity Theory

First proposed by Parson in 1947 and intended to explain male behavior in general, not specifically any ethnic groups, this theory put forth the proposition that all males at some point in their lives attempt to repudiate identification with their mothers and identify with what is considered masculine; thus his behavior becomes the antithesis of what he perceives as feminine. If one subscribes to this theory, an important factor will be to identify the male influences in the young man's life, in that his perception of masculinity will be greatly influenced by those contacts.

Broken Promise Theory

This author proposes his own theory which postulates that the over involvement of young African American males in violence and violent behavior is not based upon low morals or lack of self-control but upon anger and frustration relating to society's broken promises. As African Americans emerged from the cruel bonds of slavery and began the struggle to build lives within whatever framework the American society allowed, a guiding principle that sustained black people in America has been the societal promise that if one obeys the laws, becomes employable and works hard, there would be no limitations to obtaining the key to the door marked "success." Many African American youth heard stories of their grandparents' struggles and they observed their parents' struggles, only to realize that each generation basically begins the struggle in the same position or at a less-advantageous position than the previous generation. As they contemplate their futures, they see a similar situation awaiting them. Unwilling to accept the same fate, they take charge (in their belief) of their lives. For too many, taking charge translates into violent and illegal behavior. Unfortunately, this behavior will continue until society "makes good on its promises."

Teenage Pregnancy

Regardless of race, teenage pregnancy occupies the nation's concerns. According to the American March of Dimes Birth Defect Foundation, almost one million teenagers become pregnant annually and more than half give birth. Teenagers of African American descent have a high rate of pregnancy. The March of Dimes provides the following information with regard to health risks to teenage mothers, health risks to the baby, and consequences of a teenage pregnancy. All issues deal with why there is considerable concern within the African American community.

Health risks to a teenage mother and her baby:

- Teenage mothers are more at risk of pregnancy complications such as premature labor, anemia, high blood pressure, as well as placental problems.
- Because of immaturity, teens are at risk for sexually transmitted diseases such as chlamydia, syphilis, and AIDS.
- Of all maternal age groups, pregnant teens are least likely to get early and regular prenatal care.
- Because of poor dietary habits, pregnant teens increase the risk of their babies being born with health problems.
- Of all maternal age groups, pregnant teens are less likely to gain an adequate amount of weight which increases the risk of delivering a baby with low birth weight.

CONSEQUENCES OF TEENAGE PREGNANCY. The results of teenage pregnancy frequently impact counselors and other helping professionals in that teen mothers are more likely to drop out of high school. The absence of a high school diploma generally leads to other problems such as inability to secure employment that will adequately support a family, causing the family to rely in part on some type of public assistance. Also, interrupted high school education can result in securing what is considered unskilled jobs which too often have elements of danger possibly leading to disabilities. Due to immaturity, teens often have not had the time or experience to develop good parenting skills. Sadly, a by-product of the inability to deal with the stress of rearing a child is child abuse.

Family

Changing Influence of the Family

Another social issue which certainly is not unique to African Americans or any other ethnic minority group is the changing influence of the family. As America has become more mobile and information about distant shores more accessible, the closeness that families enjoyed particularly during our agrarian period has diminished considerably. This same scenario has impacted African Americans, but perhaps the greatest threat to family stability among African Americans are the things that have previously been discussed, the youth being influenced by gangs and teen pregnancies robbing young girls of their formative years.

Educational Issues

Few, if any, would disagree that education is one of the keys to the survival of any society. Whether the education is a primitive group passing along knowledge of hunting and shelter preparation or an industrialized nation brainstorming with regard to ways of improving access and participation to its kindergarten through college educational programs, education occurs. Therefore, there is no question that education occurs; rather the questions are to what extent, how accessible, quality thereof, and level of participation. The answers determine how far a society advances.

The United States of America, one of the most technologically advanced countries in the world, has reached this enviable status by having an advanced national education system. Many would argue that the United States is not as advanced as it should be given its resources. As evidence critics point to America's educational ranking among other industrialized nations. Questions have been raised with respect to the quality of education as well as whether the educational system is demanding enough regarding demonstrations of educational competency. These are valid and legitimate questions and concerns. Another concern is the rate of participation of the minority/ethnic groups, particularly, African Americans, Asian and Pacific Americans, Hispanic/Latino Americans, and American Indians.

With regard to African Americans, as previously stated, during legalized slavery, it was illegal for slaves to be formally educated. After its abolishment, African Americans were educated in separate facilities from Euro-Americans and without question; their education was not equal to their Euro-American counterparts. Legal education segregation continued until the landmark *Brown vs. Topeka Board of Education* ruling in 1954.

While morally wrong, prior to the 1960s, America could afford to have an unequally educated population in that jobs requiring unskilled laborers were plentiful. Unfortunately, America accepted ethnic minority groups as being less educated, thus filling the roles of unskilled workers. With current technological advances, countries wishing to compete in the global market cannot afford to undereducated any segment of their population.

African Americans in Higher Education

Distinguished Scholar Reginald Wilson identifies two major events which have had a significant impact upon African Americans attending college.

The first was the passage of the G.I. Bill for educational benefits in 1945. This bill was not specifically designed to increase minority attendance in colleges; it was established to avoid millions of veterans from saturating the job market after the Korean War. Regardless of the intent, it has had the effect of making higher education affordable for many African Americans as well as other ethnic minorities. The second event was the 1964 Civil Rights Act which placed emphasis on equality for all American citizens. Following the passage of this landmark Civil Rights Act, acknowledgment was given that ethnic minorities in general, and specifically African Americans, had not been afforded equal opportunities to attain formal education. With this acknowledgment also came the realization that special services would be helpful to many African American college students eliminate the effects of past discrimination; therefore, programs such as Upward Bound, Talent Search, and Affirmative Action came into existence.

Today, considerable discourse is conducted with regard to the need for and fairness of having such programs for specific groups of people. Despite these discussions, these programs, as well as other efforts, appear to have produced positive results. The positive results were proclaimed in a 1997 issue of *Black Issues in Higher Education* as the article announced that African American baccalaureates surged by 30 percent from 1991 to 1995.

Reginald Wilson informs us that African American females are the primary cause of this phenomenal growth in African American baccalaureate recipients. The following comments by Professor Wilson provide additional analysis of the growth and what it means:

> For African American men there has been an incremental increase of 2,000 new baccalaureates a year, but African American women have gained by 4,000 a year.
>
> During the same period of time, the number of whites receiving baccalaureate degrees declined slightly, meaning that African Americans represented a larger percentage of the college-going population.

The impressive growth of African American baccalaureate recipients has to a large extent been made possible through the efforts of Historically Black Colleges and Universities (HBCU). Although increased enrollment of African Americans in community and junior colleges as well as increased enrollment at predominantly white institutions (PWI) has decreased the historically black colleges and universities share of African American student enrollment, they continue to produce the majority of African American baccalaureates as well as awarding a significant number of graduate degrees.

HISTORICALLY BLACK COLLEGES AND UNIVERSITIES. A Quaker group in Philadelphia established the first public black college in 1837, Cheyney State

College (Payne 1994). Later in that century, in 1862, the Morrill Land Grant Act was passed which established grants of land to each state (30,000 acres for each member of congress). The proceeds were to be used to establish what is known as Agricultural and Mechanical Colleges (A&M). In the 1862 act, only one black college (Alcorn State) was established. The other colleges established were white institutions of higher education. In 1890, another Morrill Land Grant Act was passed which created 16 black colleges (Wilson 1994).

During the period of legal segregation, historically black colleges and universities were the primary means of obtaining higher education for African Americans. Additionally, these institutions served as the principle employers of black intellectuals. With regard to educating African Americans, Reginald Wilson reminds us that during their over 100-year history, historically black colleges and universities not only were the primary access to higher education for African Americans, but with its open door policy, they accepted both the best prepared students and many that were not as well prepared which would not have been admissible to other colleges and universities. With the end of legal segregation access to traditionally white institutions became somewhat easier resulting in a decline in the position of African Americans who attended historically black institutions. Despite the decline, most historically black colleges and universities remain viable institutions.

Education is of considerable importance to most every American and of particular value to African Americans in that for many years, education has been promoted as their ticket out of poverty and a weapon to be used in the war against oppression and discrimination. In most instances, increased education is associated with increased opportunities, specifically employment opportunities.

Employment and Economic Issues

In an economic-based society such as exists in the United States, gainful employment is essential. Work, to a large degree, defines who we are, how we feel about ourselves, and how others perceive us, as well as our ability to purchase goods and services. In identifying how work helps satisfy the basic needs, Ann Roe (1956) outlined Abraham Maslow's hierarchy of needs:

> In our society there is no single situation which is potentially so capable of giving some satisfaction at all levels of basic needs as is the occupation. With respect to the physiological needs, it is clear that in our culture the usual means for allaying hunger and thirst, and to some extent, sexual needs and other is through the job, which provides the money that can be exchanged for food and drink. The same is true for safety needs. The need to be a member of a group

and to give and receive love is also one which can be satisfied in part by the occupation. To work with a congenial group, to be an extrinsic part of the function to the group, to be needed and welcomed by the group are important aspects of the satisfactory job.

Perhaps satisfaction of the need for esteem from self and others is most easily seen as a big part of the occupation. In the first place, entering upon an occupation is generally seen in our culture as a symbol of adulthood and an indication that a young man or woman has reached a stage of some independence and freedom. Having a job in itself carries a measure of esteem. What importance it has is seen most clearly in the devastating effects upon the individual of being out of work. Occupation as a source of need satisfaction is of extreme importance in our culture. It may be that occupations have become so important in our culture just because so many needs are so well satisfied by them.

Given the important role employment plays in our lives, African Americans tend to be at risk for experiencing difficulties in fulfilling some of life's basic needs in that they experience high rates of unemployment and underemployment. The following will identify some of the effects of unemployment.

Unemployment

The high rate of unemployment of African Americans, particularly African American males, has such a long standing history that the figures tend to have lost their shock value. Because of the changing nature of employment, the quoting of current employment or unemployment statistics becomes of little value; however, what are of vital importance are the trends. At any point in time, one comparing Euro-American and African American employment/unemployment rates will see that the unemployment rate for African Americans is twice that of Euro-Americans. To paint an even more distressing picture, the unemployment rate for African American teenagers is consistently in the 20-plus percent range.

Gang activity and violent behavior, as well as other illegal actions committed by African American youth have been a byproduct of unemployment. While no excuse justifies disregarding just laws, as a society, we must look at the impact of a segment of our population being denied equal opportunities. Teenage unemployment generally is considerably higher than adult unemployment, but for African American youth the rate is triple that of their Euro-American counterparts.

Family Dynamics

Historical Perspective of African American Families

The African American family, its effectiveness, its roles, and values have been greatly maligned in the American society. Considerable amount of misperceptions and injurious information concerning African American families began with slavery where, in most cases, marriage among slaves was treated lightly. To formalize a union between two slaves, jumping over a broomstick was considered sufficient and this action in no way guaranteed that the union and their offspring would not be separated through selling one partner and/ or some or all the children. According to Blassingame (1972), although some slave owners did not view slave marriages in the same light as their own, they had a tendency to keep slave families together in that from the slave owner's viewpoint, a married slave who was concerned about his or her family was less likely to revolt. Because slave families had little, if any, control over their destinies, it has been theorized by some behavioral scientists that slave families were unstable and set into motion destructive psychological and sociological tendencies which impact some African Americans today—factors such as absentee fathers, single parent families, and female-dominated families. John Blassingame (1972) argues that despite these theories of the destruction of the family system under slavery, the African American slave family was a most important survival mechanism for slaves. Abzug (1971), in his earlier work, laid the foundation for Blassingame's point of view with the following comments:

> It was in the family that the slave received affection, companionship, love and empathy with his suffering under this peculiar institution. Through the family he learned how to avoid punishment, cooperate with his fellow slaves, and retain some semblance of his self-esteem. The socialization of the slave child was another important function for the slave parents. They could cushion the shock of bondage for him, inculcate in him values different than those the master attempted to teach him, and represent another frame of reference for his self-esteem besides the master.

The primary nurturing role in the slave family was the responsibility of the mother and that role has not appreciably changed in today's society. However, some feel that the role of today's African American mothers has expanded considerably beyond being the emotional glue that bonds the family together.

ROLE OF MOTHER. A major flaw in analyzing African American families, particularly segmenting individual roles, is that the family and its members' roles are compared to Euro-American, middle-class families and family members' roles. Because of unequal access to education, employment, and housing as well as income, in this author's opinion, this makes a comparison harmful; harmful because conclusions are reached which often place African American families and the members' roles in negative positions. Perhaps a good example is to view the African American mother as domineering. This concept has been fostered in that a large percentage of African American married women are employed and in some cases are more gainfully employed (in terms of income) than their husbands. In comparison, it has been within the last several decades that a significant number of Euro-American females worked. Because African American females have been in the paid labor force since the abolishment of slavery, their status has been elevated by social scientists. The African American male's status has been devalued, thus the unfair labeling of African American females as being bossy and dominant within the family.

While it is an untrue characterization of African American females as being aggressive, domineering, and demanding, it is true that in many instances it is easier for an African American female to secure employment than African American males. Therefore, African American females may be visible to those who are not familiar with some of the oppressive struggles African American females face as being the primary economic provider for the family again perpetuating the myth that the female within an African American family is the dominant force. Robert Staples (1988) effectively debunks the myth of the dominating black female with the following:

> From the time of slavery onward, she has resisted the destructive forces that she has encountered in American society. During the period of slavery, she fought and survived the attack on her dignity by the slave system, relinquished the passive role ascribed to members of her gender to insure the survival of her people, and tolerated the culturally endured irresponsibility of her man in recognition of this country's relentless attempts to castrate him. Too often, the only result of her sacrifices and suffering has been the invidious and inaccurate labeling of her as a matriarch, a figure deserving respect but not love. The objective reality of the black women in America is that she occupies the lowest rung of the socioeconomic ladder of all sex-race groups and has the least prestige. The double burden of gender and race has put her in the category of a super-oppressed entity.

Also adding to the myth of the dominating female is that approximately one-third of the African American households are headed by a female (no male present). At this junction, several points should be made with regard to female-headed households:

- When we think of female-headed households, we logically think of absence of a male, and visions of "deadbeat dads" quickly enter the picture. There is no question that a high percentage of the households are void of a male (husband and father) because of no marriage, divorce, and/or abandonment; however, there is a considerable number who are widowed. The African American female is expected to live almost nine years longer than the African American male; therefore, there is a good chance that a considerable number of female-headed households are results of death of the male.

- Niara Sudarkasa (1993) contends the increase in female-headed households is of recent origin and is a result of the welfare policy and public housing policies. The point is that in past generations (pre 1960s), unwed teenagers would live with other adults, parents, grandparents, or other relatives; however, today public assistance programs along with housing authority policy encourages unwed mothers to live apart from relatives, thus being counted as heads of households.

- Female-headed households can and most often are stable households. Generations of advice and experience are passed down from parent to daughter with regard to surviving within the American society. Moreover, considerable resources such as kinfolk, church members, and friends are available to assist with household-related matters.

- Female-headed household does not mean absence of male influence. Brothers, uncles, and grandfathers as well as male friends and other male relatives are available to assist with the guidance of children.

- As Sudarkasa points out, female-headed households are not totally the result of teen pregnancy, but in part females reacting to the demographic, economic, political and social plight of black life in America.

Considering the several myths surrounding the role of African American women, it is not surprising that there is misunderstanding of their roles within the family setting. Succinctly stated, African American women are co-providers sharing equal roles and status with their male partners in the handling of family matters.

ROLE OF FATHER. Similar to the African American female's role, the African American male's role is shrouded in misperceptions, some of which have their roots in the treatment of African American males during slavery. In slavery, to maintain control over the black male, he was generally degraded. He was helpless in defending himself from being whipped like a child, he was unable to protect his family from any action the slave master decided to perform, and he was labeled as lazy, ignorant, and not worthy of trust. Some of these labels are applied to the current generation of African American males. The following comments by Robert Staples (1988) clearly identify some of the perceptions held with regard to African American males.

> Along with the economic conditions that impinge on their role performance, black men are saddled with a number of stereotypes that label them as irresponsible, criminalistics, hypersexual, and lacking in masculine traits. Some of these stereotypes become self-fulfilling prophecies because the dominant society is structured in a way that prevents many black men from achieving the goals of manhood. At the same time, the notion of the castrated black male is largely a myth. Although mainstream culture has deprived many black men of the economic wherewithal for normal, masculine functions, most function in a way that gains the respect of their mates, children and community.

The lack of economic prowess to which Professor Staples refers is a major obstacle faced by African American men's' quest to provide a better standard of living for their families. Factors such as high unemployment and low salaries for those who are employed create situations that decrease the African American males' chances of fulfilling the role of primary economic provider for his family.

Staples (1988), while using the works of Lewis (1975), Scanzoni (1971), Cazanave (1979) and Daneal (1975), makes two important points. First, recent literature has refuted the long-held view that African American males are ineffective and indifferent to their children. Instead, current literature produced by Lewis and Scanzoni indicates that black fathers are warm, nurturing, and play a vital role in the rearing of their offspring. Second, the works of Cazanave and Daneal found better parenting patterns among middle class, African American fathers. Thus, indicating that when African American fathers have the economic resources to provide for the family, they are able to be more effective parents.

African American Family Characteristics and Child-Rearing Practices

It is well documented that the family serves as a major force in the psychological, social, and emotional development of children; therefore, the manner in which the parents react to events, the belief system they promote, the attitudes they project, the behaviors they display, and the values they embrace influence the maturation of the children. Robert Hill (1972) identifies strong kinship bonds, strong achievement orientation, adaptability of family roles, strong religious orientation, and strong work orientation as strengths of African American families. Janice Hale-Benson (1988) contends that the following are common characteristics of many African Americans: People-oriented, authoritarian in their child-rearing practices, positive attitudes toward child bearing (meaning little, if any, stigma is attached to bearing a child outside of wedlock), strong attention to nonverbal communication and style orientation (importance is not only placed on what one does but how one does it).

KINSHIP BONDS. Parental type influence upon African American children generally extends beyond the immediate family members. A long-standing practice of many African American parents has been to seek and accept advice and emotional and sometimes financial support from their parents, grandparents, uncles, aunts, highly respected cousins as well as non-relatives such as close friends and select church members. It is not uncommon for close friends, especially church member acquaintances, to be referred to as uncle, aunt, or in some cases as the person's "play mother." This informal adoption of non-relatives into the family circle is a means of showing respect and acknowledgment of the level of the family's regard of their friendship. Children grow up hearing of these persons being referred to as relatives and treat them with the same respect and regard they have for blood relatives.

ACHIEVEMENT ORIENTED. Education has always played a prominent role in the lives of African Americans. As stated before, most African Americans view education as the key to unlock the doors of success. Most African American parents stress to their children they want them to have a better life than their lives and emphasize that being educated will help ensure that they are able to secure jobs that will afford them the better things in life.

WORK ORIENTED. Despite the stereotype of African Americans, particularly African American males, as lazy persons, African Americans have a very strong work ethic. The high unemployment rate of African Americans is most often a result of discrimination, lack of education, and lack of skills necessary to successfully compete for certain jobs than it is of lack of ambition and drive. Most families emphasize work as much as education, in that work is viewed as the reward for being educated.

ADAPTABILITY OF FAMILY ROLES. Versatility has been one of the keys to the survival of the African American family. This is evident as African American females have stepped forward to provide economic support in times when the male is either unemployed or underemployed. Similarly the male may assume many of the housekeeping duties as the female is keep busy with work outside of the home. African American children learn early to be adaptable in that the older children are quite often called upon to take care of the younger children, serving as substitute parents–providing services ranging from basic babysitting to determining appropriate discipline.

PEOPLE ORIENTED. Janice Hale-Benson (1988) contends that black children are taught to be aware of people's moods, emotions, and body language as much, if not more, than actual words. Therefore, African American children learn to be excellent readers of nonverbal communication. Sometimes African Americans who are quiet are viewed by the uninformed as being inattentive and nonaggressive, when they do not ask many questions, in actuality they do not feel the need to ask questions when they have obtained the answers through observance of nonverbal communication.

AUTHORITARIANISM. Many African American parents are very direct in their child-rearing practices. In disciplinary situations, "talking back" is often not tolerated. Stated in other terms, when the parent is disciplining a child, he/she does not allow nor does the child expect to give a lengthy discussion on how unfair he/she believes the punishment to be. The parent will tolerate some discussion, but when the decision on punishment has been made, the parent expects (and generally receives) compliance without much input from the child. Physical discipline is not uncommon in African American families. In most cases, the physical part of the punishment does not reach the stage of being a beating; however, in an age where corporal punishment may be considered child abuse, more than one black parent has been shocked to learn that what they consider firm direct punishment is considered by others to be abusive.

ATTITUDES TOWARD CHILDBEARING. Although childbearing outside of wedlock is not encouraged by African Americans, when it does occur, the child is not considered illegitimate. The child is generally accepted and loved as any child would be. Most often unwed females are not encouraged to have an abortion or place the child for adoption. This is not to imply that there are only a few abortions or adoptions, but to emphasize that the abortions and adoptions are often not driven by shame but more because the person or family determines that they do not have the resources to adequately care for the child.

STYLE. From a very early age, black children learn that what one does is important and the style with which one does things is equally important. Style is a way the black child puts his personal signature to whatever he/she is doing. This emphasis is carried over into adult life. A very good example is the personal touch black basketball players put into dunking a ball or the way in which a professional football player reacts when he has made a spectacular play.

Intervention Strategies

Persons in the helping professions, such as rehabilitation counselors, social workers, psychologists, teachers and educational counselors to mention a few, would love to have a "menu" type book that would identify a group, list the characteristics of that group, and based upon those characteristics the helper would be provided with a how-to-do list of techniques that will be applicable in the situation at hand. Because we are dealing with humans and currently no two are exactly alike, therefore this approach is not practical. Despite this common-sense knowledge, too frequently books, journals, and articles list common characteristics of African Americans, Asian and Pacific Americans, etc. as though all persons in those groups have had the same experiences, have the same backgrounds, and came from the same social and economic background. Most helping professionals probably have read that Asians are polite, quiet, and reserved and African Americans are loud and concrete thinkers. The truth is that some Asians are quiet and some African Americans are loud; likewise, some Asian Pacific Americans are loud while some African Americans are very good at abstract thinking. The point is that there is no one set of characteristics which adequately describe all members of any group. There are a variety of factors to consider when attempting assessing a client to determine the appropriate helping approach.

Assessment

In assessing a client one must get to know the person, his background, and his experiences so that he does not rely on identifying the client through stereotypical ideas of the person and the group to which he is associated. The concept of giving consideration to one's cultural background when engaged in the helping process is of tremendous value; it frees the professional helper from the tunnel vision of observing everything from one perspective, primarily the dominant culture's viewpoint. As liberating as this concept is, it can also be equally destructive if the helper takes a monolithic view of minority group attitudes and behaviors as stated by Donald Atkinson and his associates (1989). By this they mean disregarding within group differences and viewing all members of a particular minority group as having the same experiences, beliefs, attitudes, and value systems. One can easily see that this point of view is as unproductive as judging everyone by the dominant culture's standards.

To avoid making either of the previously mentioned mistakes, the professional helper would be wise to assess the client from a variety of diagnostic viewpoints: pride and identification with one's culture and heritage, level of acculturation, communication styles, expectations of the helping process, value orientation, and situational control (influence of family, religious influence, and social influence).

Pride In and Identification with One's Culture and Heritage

Because of the reasons why African Americans became permanent residents of America, pride in who they are and from where they originated was degraded by the majority of Euro-Americans. In essence, African Americans were taught to hate themselves and loathe their black identity. In too many cases, this effort was very successful, resulting in African Americans attempting to emulate Euro-Americans. As discussed in the historical background section, considerable effort has been made to restore pride in being black people. Consequently, African Americans are at various stages of pride, identification, and acceptance or rejection of their culture and heritage.

Several distinguished scholars, including Thomas (1971) and Cross (1971), have contributed to the literature with regard to African Americans moving from a Euro-American orientation to a black identity orientation and this concept has been referred to as the Black Identity Model. Social scientists such as Janet Helms (1985) believe that the racial identity model has potential diagnostic value. Additionally, Derald Sue and David Sue (1990) indicate that research now suggests that a minority individual's reaction to counseling, the counseling process, and the counselor is influenced by his/her cultural/racial identity and not simply linked to minority-group membership. They further point out the high failure-to-return rate of many culturally different clients seems intimately linked to the mental health professional's inability to accurately assess the cultural identity of the client.

Perhaps William Cross (1971), in his original work and in his revisions (1991) which he calls Nigrescense, has done as much as anyone to promote this model as a technique by which professional helpers may trace the developmental stages blacks encounter in moving from a form of self-hating to a self-healing and culturally affirming self-concept. One can certainly question the model and Cross acknowledges that not all African Americans engage in a self-hatred process. Some persons will correctly point out that many African Americans do not indulge in self-hatred and that their self-concept is firmly rooted in pride in being a black person.

The author is suggesting that helping professionals can use this model as a tool in evaluating the stage of black racial identity of their African American clients. It should also be recognized that the author believes a value of this model is not that each African American goes through all of the stages, but that each African American client when being seen by the helper is at some stage of black identity and development and this model serves as a valuable tool in understanding the stage.

Conclusion

Many African Americans' world views have been influenced by the manner in which they have been treated by the dominant culture. For example, older African Americans who experienced the period of segregation have his/her views influenced by strict separation of the African American and Euro-American races. In many instances, these experiences affect the level of trust the African American client will have in a Euro-American helping professional.

Many African American communities are attempting to address critical issues such as gangs, gang-related activities, and teen pregnancy. Gang violence and young girls cutting their formative years short through having babies are problems of monumental proportion that require the expertise of helping professionals. Helping professionals' expertise is needed when these situations go beyond being problems and become debilitating.

Review Questions

1. What, if any, are the benefits of a helping professional understanding the historical background of African Americans?
2. What impact is violence having on African American youth and what is the relevance of violence among African American youth to the helping process?
3. To what do the following theories and concept relate: Poverty-Social Disorganization theory, Compulsive Masculinity theory, and Broken Promise concept?
4. What are some of the negative stereotypes of African Americans and how can they impact the helping process?
5. How can the helping professional insure that the client's expectations of the helping process and his expectations are congruent

Suggested Activities

1. Determine the number and/or percentage of African Americans living in your state.
2. Make a list of at least five agencies and/or organizations in your state that specialize in assisting African Americans. Also, identify the type of services these organizations provide. This can be the beginning of a community service file that you can use as a helping professional.

References

Blassingame, J. (1972). *The slave community*. New York: Oxford University Press.

Carter, D. J., & Wilson, R. (1990). *Minorities in higher education–Ninth annual statistics report*. Washington, DC: American Council on Education.

Cazanave, N. (1979). Middle-income black fathers: An analysis of the provider role, the family coordinator, 28 (November) In C. H. Mindel et al. (Eds.), *Ethnic families in America* (3rd ed.). Englewood Cliffs, NJ: Prentice-Hall.

Cross, Jr., W. E. (1971). The Negro-to-black conversion experience. *Black World, 20,* 13–27.

Daneal, J. E. (1975). A definition of fatherhood as expressed by black fathers. Ph.D. Dissertation, University of Pittsburg. In C. H. Mindel et al. (Eds.), *Ethnic families.*

Hale-Benson, J. E. (1988). *Black children: Their roots, culture and learning styles* (rev. ed.). Baltimore: Johns Hopkins University Press.

Helms, J. E. (1990). Black and white racial identity. Westport, CT: Greenwood Press.

Mindel, C. H. et al. (1990). *Ethnic families in America* (3rd ed.). Engelwood Cliffs, NJ: Prentice-Hall.

Parsons, T. (1947). Certain primary sources of aggression in the social structure of the western world. *Psychiatry, 10,* 167–181.

Payne, N. J. (1994). Maintaining the competitive tradition. In M. J. Justiz et al. (Eds.), *Minorities in higher education.* Phoenix, AZ: Oryx Press.

Roe, A. (1956). The psychology of occupations. New York: John Wiley and Sons.

Scanzoni, J. (1971). The black family in modern society. In C. H. Mindel et al. (Eds.), *Ethnic families in America* (3rd ed.). Englewood Cliffs, NJ: Prentice-Hall.

Staples, R. (1988). The black American family. In C. H. Mindel et al. (Eds.), *Ethnic families in America* (3rd ed.). Englewood Cliffs, NJ: Prentice-Hall.

Sudarkasa, N. (1993). Female-headed African American households. In H. P. McAdoo (Ed.), *Family ethnicity.* Newbury Park, CA: Sage.

Sue, D. W., & Sue, D. (1990). *Counseling the culturally different* (2nd ed.). New York: John Wiley and Sons.

Thomas, C. W. (1971). *Boys no more.* Beverly Hills, CA: Glencoe.

Voss, H., & Hepburn, J. R. (1968). Patterns of criminal homicide in Chicago. *Journal of Criminal Law, Criminology, and Police Science, 59,* 499–508.

Washington, E. M. (1996). A survey of the literature on theories and prevention of black male youth involvement in violence. *The Journal of Negro Education, 65*(4), Fall.

Wilson, R. (1994). The participation of African Americans in American higher education. In J. M. Justiz et al. (Eds.), *Minorities in higher education.* Phoenix, AZ: Oryx Press.

Suggested Readings

Cross, Jr., W. E. (1991). *Shades of black.* Philadelphia: Temple University Press.

Gutman, H. (1976). *The black family in slavery and freedom 1750–1925.* New York: Pantheon.

Helms, J. E. (1990). *Black and white racial identity.* Westport, CT: Greenwood Press.

Phinney, J. Stages of ethnic identity development in minority group adolescence. *Journal of Early Adolescence, 9,* 34–49.

Massey, D. S., & Eggers, M. L. (1990). The ecology of inequality: Minorities and the concentration of poverty, 1970–1980. A*merican Journal of Sociology, 95*(5), 1153–1188, March.

Ponterotto, J. G., & Pedersen, P. B. (1993). *Preventing prejudice: A guide for counselors and educators.* Newbury Park, CA: Sage.

Staples, R. The black American family. In C. H. Mindel et al. (Eds.), *Ethnic families in America: Patterns and variations* (3rd ed., pp. 303–324). Englewood Cliffs, NJ: Prentice-Hall.

Sudarkasa, N. Female-headed African American households: Some neglected dimensions. In H. P. McAdoo (Ed.), *Family ethnicity: Strength in diversity* (pp. 81–89). Newbury Park, CA: Sage.

Chapter 7

AMERICAN INDIANS

Chapter Outline
- Introduction
- Historical Perspective
- Social Issues Impacting American Indians
- Employment Issues
- Economic Issues
- Family Dynamics
- Intervention Strategies
- Conclusion

Chapter Objectives
- Identify significant historical events which have impacted the lives of American Indians
- Identify the diversity of American Indians
- Identify, social, educational, and economical issues which impact the lives of American Indians
- Identify critical cultural information of which helping professionals must be aware

Introduction

Most historians and anthropologists consider American Indians as the first people of what is now the United States of America; thus they are the Natives of America. At the time of Columbus' voyage to the Western Hemisphere, it is estimated that there were approximately 10 million Native Americans (Harjo, 1993). Robert John (1988) informs us that at the time of the Native Americans' first contact with Europeans, there were approximately 300 languages spoken, and Susan Harjo points out that Native Americans still maintain 300 separate languages and dialects even though the author notes they are not all the same 300 languages that existed at the time of Columbus.

Quite often, when we think of American Indians, we think of them as a single culture; however, to the contrary, there are over 500 tribes in America with approximately 300 of them being federally recognized (Porter, 1983). Instead of viewing American Indians as a homogeneous group, one must realize many American Indians tribes are nations. In other words, they are nations within a nation. Susan Harjo reminds us that Indian nations are inherently sovereign and have negotiated approximately 600 treaties with the U.S. government. Therefore, trying to assign a single culture to American Indians would be similar to assigning a single culture to North America. Just as one would be lumping Mexicans, American Indians, African Americans, and Canadians into one category, we make a similar mistake by trying to determine a common culture for all American Indian tribes.

Historical Background

In retrospect, at the time of first European contact, there were well over 300 tribes in America, each having its own form of government, living as what we might consider independent nations. As a result of this contact, the independence was to come to an end for most American Indian tribes. Richardson (1981) correctly points out that the American Indian population has been dramatically decreased as a result of two things—disease and war. By the end of the eighteenth century, the American Indian population had been decreased by at least 10 percent of the numbers that existed at the time of first contact with Europeans. Relatedly, the American Indian population is increasing in that the 2010 census report placed the population of American Indians and Alaskan Natives at almost three million; this means they are approximately one percent of the United States population. It is further estimated that by 2050 the population of American Indians and Alaskan Natives will be two percent of the United States population.

A large percentage of the decrease in population, previously mentioned can be attributed to the European introduction of diseases such as diphtheria, smallpox, measles, chickenpox, influenza, scarlet fever, malaria, typhus, and typhoid fever. When I say introduced, this does not mean that this was a deliberate act. American Indians had no immunity to these diseases. The death toll from these diseases and others was so great that Susan Harjo has labeled it as one of the greatest natural catastrophes of all times.

The other major event that added to the decimation of the American Indian population was wars which generally were fought as a result of the Europeans attempting to seize American Indians land. The process of taking Indian land not only impacted the number of American Indians, but also had an impact on their entire way of life. Despite numerous treaties and promises that assured Indians that their lands were safe from the encroachment of Euro-Americans, their land base has been significantly reduced. Their land was taken and generally they were forced to relocate to land which the United States government considered as unsuitable for Euro-American inhabitation.

Susan Harjo (1988) provides an excellent overview of what has happened to the American Indian's land base:

> The Indian land base has gone from 138 million acres in 1887 to approximately 50 million acres today. There are many reasons for land loss, including flooding for Corps of Engineer projects, creation of national monuments, taking of land for tax defaults and welfare payment, invalidation of wills, and Bureau of Indian Affairs (BIA) forced sales on the open market. The 1917 Allotment Act or Dawes Act alone resulted in the loss of more than half the Indian land. Of the 48 million acres left after the Allotment Act took its toll, 20 million acres were desert or semiarid and not suitable for cultivation. The federal government promised to irrigate these lands and "to make the deserts bloom." For most of these arid reservations, this promise remains unfulfilled.

The Allotment Act allocated land on reservations that had been guaranteed by treaties. Every family head was to receive 160 acres and a single person 80 acres. The idea was that Indians should become farmers and thereby become more civilized. This notion of farming was not well received by many tribes and was particularly onerous to many Indians in the Great Plains. The land was to be held in trust for 25 years. Indians deemed "competent" by the federal government could end the trust status, own the land in fee simple, and become U.S. Citizens. Any land outside the allotted acreage was declared to be "excess" and sold to non-Indian settlers.

The relocation of the American Indian is without a doubt one of the most shameful acts forced upon any group of people. Thousands of people were removed from places and ways of living that were familiar to them and forced to adjust to environments and surroundings that were unfamiliar. Additionally, many were required to adopt a new lifestyle that was foreign to them. Perhaps the most familiar acts of relocation to Americans are the "Trail of Tears" where the Cherokee people and other Indian tribes were moved from the Southeast area of the United States to Oklahoma. During this move, thousands of Indians died and many more suffered debilitating illness. While this forced march is the most often discussed relocation, there were many more. In fact, all of the "Five Civilized Tribes" (Cherokee, Creek, Chickasaw, Choctaw, and Seminole) as well as several others were relocated to what was titled Indian Territory, later to be named Oklahoma (meaning home of the red man).

The promise of an "Indian Land," where they would be free from further white encroachment, ended in 1889 when parts of what is now Oklahoma were opened for non-Indian settlement. The frontier dash for free land further depleted the Indian's land base. In 1936, the Indian Reorganization Act was passed by the U.S. Congress and the result was the ending of the allotment policy and as Susan Harjo points out, the Indian land base has remained relatively constant since that time.

As strange as it may seem today, America's first people were not considered citizens as the U.S. government was formed. During the previously mentioned allotment period, if the American Indian's land was held in "fee status," they were given citizenship. American Indian World War I veterans were granted citizenship by a law passed in 1919. Finally, in 1924, the Indian Citizenship Act was passed.

Assimilation

Susan Harjo (1988) identifies what she considers three major ways in which the goals of assimilation were to be programmed with American Indians: (1) Allowing Christian groups to establish their denominations on Indian land to convert Indians to Christianity, thus getting them to forsake their religious beliefs and practices and various religious ceremonies which to many of the Euro Americans were paganistic. (2) Imposing an educational system upon the children that had as its primary objective to instill non-Indian values. This was done through a boarding school system which required the children to be separated from their parents for up to twelve years. The children were forbidden to speak their tribal language or practice any of the tribal traditions. Parents and relatives were not allowed to visit the children during the school year. The boarding school staff impressed upon the children that their tribal traditions were savage. Blanchard (1983) says these deplorable efforts were attempts to "civilize" the children. Scholars such as Lowrey (1983), Josephy (1982), Blanchard (1983), and Kleinfeld and Bloom (1977) feel that this experience, along with others, had a definite impact upon weakening the various American Indian cultures. Federal efforts were made to break up tribal land holdings and turn Indians into individual land owners, imposing taxes on their lands.

Again, I rely on the knowledge base of Susan Harjo to provide an explanation of the termination period.

During the period from World War II to 1961, a series of disruptive assimilation efforts occurred to force Indians into the melting pot. This era is referred to as the "termination period." During the 1950s federal Indian policy involved the termination of the tribal-federal relationship with certain Indian governments, the liquidation of their estates; the transfer of federal responsibility and jurisdiction to states and the physical relocation of Indian people from reservations to urban areas. Termination legislation affected more than 100 tribes, bands and rancheros; some 12,000 individual Indians were disenfranchised, and 2.5 million acres of Indian land were removed from trust status.

It is abundantly clear that all of these efforts were to destroy the various cultures and instill a belief that the new ways were superior and better. The current conditions of some American Indian people are vivid and compelling evidence that many of these efforts were successful.

Recent laws such as Public Law 93-638, Indian Self-Determination and Educational Assistance Act, Indian Child Welfare Act, and the American Indian Religious Freedom Act are attempts by the U.S. government to allow American Indians to have the freedom to determine their own destinies.

Indian Self-Determination and Educational Assistance Act give tribes the right to contract with the appropriate agencies to conduct and administer programs which are needed.

Indian Child Welfare Act forbid the removal of Indian children from their homes and placed with non-Indian families.

American Indian Religious Freedom Act protects Indians' rights to believe, express, and exercise the traditional religions of the American Indian, Eskimo, Aleut, and Native Hawaiians.

Social Issues

A major social issue for most American Indian tribes has been the regaining and/or maintenance of their cultures. If there is one common thread that weaves its way through all American Indian tribes, it is a belief in harmony with mind, body, spirit, and Mother Earth. Most American Indians view the earth as a living entity which has a spirit, thus, land is an important part of their cultural ways of life as is their spiritual and religious ceremonies. Several tribes have filed law suit in an attempt to regain land that was taken from them and opened for non-Indian settlement. Additionally, other tribes are engaged in discussion with the U.S. government over the ownership of Indian land on which the government has placed national monuments. Moreover, considerable concern exists among many tribes over the disturbance of sacred grounds, particularly the removal of Indian artifacts, including the bones of Indian ancestors.

Giving consideration to the facts presented in the historical background section, with regard to loss of land base, the efforts to destroy their religious beliefs and the attempt to degrade and remove other aspects of their culture by removing children from the home and placing them with non-Indian fam-

ilies and/or sending them to boarding schools, one can imagine the inner tur-
moil and confusion that many American Indians feel. Confusion is often
heightened as American Indians engage in an emotional tug-of-war over the
desires to maintain traditional values and the need to adjust to the dominant
society values. The results of this emotional struggle tend to appear in some
of the behaviors of American Indians, particularly in the form of substance
abuse. Susan Harjo (1993) views substance abuse as the number one social
issue among Indian people and alcohol-related diseases and accidents as the
biggest killers of Indians. It is estimated that approximately nine percent of
the American adult population experience significant drinking problems, in
contrast on some reservations the drinking problem is as high as 50 percent
(Carpenter et al., 1985). Beauvis and LaBoueff (1985) feel that 80 to 90 percent of the problems Indian people have are related to abuse of alcohol and
drugs.

Louise Sinclair (1987) provides a to-the-point summary of American Indian
cultures and substance abuse:

> To be an adolescent and an Indian is to be in a state of crisis, of social and cul-
> tural confusion. The Indians belong to a cultural group that is undergoing its
> own identity crisis; Native people as a whole experience conflict and confu-
> sion, as they find themselves gradually immersed in white society. The pres-
> sure to conform to the way of life of the majority is great, yet the importance
> of the Native culture is equally great. The results of this conflict are saddening:
> drug and alcohol abuse affects as much as 70 percent of the Native population,
> and fatalities related to drug and alcohol occurs more than three times as fre-
> quently to Natives as to the rest of the population.

Substance abuse appears to be the genesis of many problems Indian people encounter, including the high rate of accidents and homicides. Reasons
for the high rate of substance abuse, particularly alcohol and drugs, will be
explored. Also other issues which could be considered as social issues such
as high unemployment rate, school dropout rate, and teen pregnancy will be
discussed in other sections.

Employment Issues

Traditionally, American Indians have had a much higher rate of unemployment than most other races and ethnic groups. One of the reasons for
the high unemployment rate is that there are not many job opportunities on
reservations and since some reservations are in remote areas, traveling to a
job site outside of the reservation boundaries becomes challenging, especial-

ly if one has limited transportation options. Similar to African American youth, American Indian youth unemployment is double the Euro-American youth unemployment rate.

In discussing problems of American Indians frequently the issue of Indian reservations, their remoteness and lack of opportunities become points for discussion. Too frequently, this discussion is slanted because it is felt that those living on reservations are disadvantaged. While this may be true in some and perhaps many aspects, one has also to realize approximately 50 percent of American Indians do not live on reservations. Consequently, their employment possibilities are enhanced. The point is that part of the reason for high unemployment rates for American Indians is prejudice against Indians. Until the nation effectively addresses the problem of employment discrimination based upon ethnicity, American Indians and African Americans will continue to have unemployment rates that are double and triple that of their Euro-American counterparts.

Economic Issues

Some tribes and their members are improving economically, especially since they have become involved in gaming (bingo, lotto, pull tabs, casinos, etc.). Additionally and more prevalent than gaming, many tribes have developed various industries such as ownership of hotels, motels, plant nurseries, and convenience stores, to mention a few. Obviously, this is a giant step forward in that it produces revenue and provides employment for Indian people.

A final point is that there are some misperceptions concerning American Indians and money. First, it is not true that by virtue of being an Indian one automatically receives a check from the government. Some American Indians receive checks for oil, mineral and/or grazing leases on land that the U.S. government holds in trust for them or their tribe. Second, American Indians do not pay taxes similar to other American citizens. The misperceptions perhaps come from the fact that Indians do not pay federal income taxes on income from trust lands held for them by the United States, nor do they pay state income taxes on income earned on an Indian reservation. Third, being an Indian does not constitute a tuition-free college education.

American Indians receive very few special economic concessions. The ones they do receive are more than justified given the extent of the resources they had to give to the government, which some would say was taken and/or stolen from them.

Family Dynamics

Historical Perspective of American Indian Families

Because of the diversity among American Indian tribes, over 500 different tribes, each having its own cultural background, it is with extreme difficulty one encounters in attempting to describe American Indian families. In reality, it is impossible to condense American Indian family characteristics into a neat concise overview. Deloria (1969) attempts to dispel the myth of American Indians as a homogeneous group with these terse comments, "People can tell just by looking at us what we want, what should be done to help us, how we feel and what a real Indian is like."

The stereotyping of Indian people perhaps began with and continues through the media. The image of American Indian family life is that of the tribal leaders sitting around a fire making decisions for all the tribal people, thus the idea is that Indian family life was dictated to and controlled by the tribal leaders and elders. When the image is magnified beyond the tribal fire and counsel activities to the family unit, it was projected as the male-dominated family where the father was the hunter and provider and the female's roles were subordinate to the male. No doubt in some tribes, this is a fairly accurate view of family life; however, in other tribes, this is quite distorted in that women were not totally subservient to the males. The point is that it is difficult at best to portray American Indian family life in a homogeneous fashion.

As already discussed, as American Indian people encountered European immigrants, the Europeans attempted to destroy the American Indian's cultures and "civilize" them. One of the ways was to remove the children from their homes and send them to boarding schools where they were educated in the "white man's ways."

Susan Shown Harjo (1993) effectively describes the intent of the boarding schools: The establishment of boarding schools for children was a deliberate attempt to disrupt traditional child-rearing practices. Children were forcibly removed from their homes for up to 12 years, and parents and other relatives were not allowed to visit the children during the school year. Children were taught that their traditions were savage and immoral. There are many accounts of parents camping outside the gates of boarding schools to get a glimpse of their children.

Harjo continues by pointing out other impacts the boarding school systems have had on the American Indian family dynamics in that most grandparents and many current Indian parents are the product of boarding and other governmental schools. She contends that for those who spent a considerable portion of their formative years in the schools away from their families, they have very little in the way of family rearing role models. Harjo concludes her comments by explaining that in past years there have been attempts to recover from past experiences and reestablish traditional Indian family values. These values, according to Harjo, include extended family concept. She believes the extended family identification is central to citizens of Indian nations.

Mother Role

As is true in most segments of American societies, the mother's role in Native American families is one of nurturing the young; however, there is evidence that in the past several years, this role has expanded toward becoming co-responsible with the male (again levels of acculturation come into play in this matter). American Indian women tend to be employed at approximately the same percentage as males and there is increasing numbers of female-headed households.

Father Role

The idea of the male as the primary provider within any family, regardless of race or ethnicity, is no longer a realistic view of family life in America. American Indian males, similar to African American males, experience considerable difficulties in securing and maintaining gainful employment. (This is evident by the high rate of unemployment among American Indian males.) Therefore, the roles of American Indian males are beginning to be restructured. As the American Indian females are sharing provider responsibilities, the males are beginning to share in the nurturing and household responsibilities.

Intervention

As was discussed in the historical background of this chapter, American Indians have experience numerous attempts at degrading and destroying their heritages and cultures. Sandra Choney and her associates (1995) convincingly argue that it is more appropriate to consider American Indians' levels of acculturation rather than attempt to develop a theory or model of Indian identity. Their primary reason for taking this position is that because of the diversity among American Indians with regard to their tribal affiliations, American Indians derive their cultural base more from tribal association than from any concept of "Indianness." They further point out that the fact there is no homogeneous world view complicates the determination of a single description of Indianness or racial identity and makes its use as a defining concept problematic. Consequently, Choney et al. believe that attempts to explain American Indians through racial identity does more harm than good, in that it has the potential of perpetuating the stereotypical thinking of American Indians as a homogeneous group of people. Conclusively, they urge helpers to assess American Indian clients on the basis of levels of acculturation.

Levels of Acculturation

In assessing level of acculturation of American Indians, determining tribal affiliation, and whether the person originates and/or lives in a rural, urban, or reservation area are necessary. Once tribal affiliation is determined, the helper should determine the following:

1. Does the person participate in tribal activities?
2. What type of tribal activities does the person participate?
3. What are some of the customs and beliefs of the tribe?
4. How does the person feel with regard to the customs and beliefs?
5. What is the tribal language?
6. Does the person speak the language?
7. When does the person speak the language?
8. Does anyone in the family (including extended family) speak the language?
9. Which language is spoken the most in the home and at tribal events, English or tribal language?
10. What does being an Indian mean to him/her?

It is also helpful to determine the type of schooling, whether the person attended a missionary school, tribal school, and/or traditional American school. Additional information that help determine level of acculturation is asking questions with regard to how and with whom the person socializes, as well as the types of entertainment in which the person engages.

Initially, the professional helper will be able to determine some aspects of level of acculturation by the way the person is dressed, speech patterns, and mannerisms. A word of caution is appropriate at this point in that the helper should not expect all traditional American Indians to enter his office wearing moccasins, buckskin pants and shirt, beads, and speak in the movie stereotype manner. However, if the person appears in a three-piece suit, it is an indication his level of acculturation is high. Even so, it is not uncommon for American Indians to live in two worlds: during week days, they function as a nontraditional American Indian; however, on the weekends, they become more involved in traditional tribal customs. The best and really the only way for the helper to know is to ask the person how does he/she view him or herself?

The point for determining rural, urban or reservation background provides information with regard to lifestyle and opportunities. This information can be used to help determine level of acculturation but also can be used by the helper to determine resources available to be used in the helping process.

William Martin, Jr., and his colleagues (1988), reporting from a survey of vocational rehabilitation counselors who work with American Indians, identified the following barriers in delivering rehabilitation services to American Indians living on reservations (this author would like to point out that this information is good for all levels and kinds of professional helpers):

1. Lack of understanding cultural differences
2. Transportation problems
3. Lack of employment opportunities
4. Lack of commitment to Vocational Rehabilitation goals
5. Language barriers, and
6. Substance abuse problems.

Communication Style

In reading books that discuss culture of minority groups, quite frequently these documents state that American Indians value silence, thus they tend to be more nonverbal than verbal. Often to the amazement of a professional helper, he encounters a very articulate American Indian. The point being made is that this is a generalization that the helping professional cannot afford to become trapped into believing. The truth is American Indians' communication styles and abilities have the same range as Euro-Americans.

The stereotype of American Indians as nonverbal is an interesting myth because the reality is that the history of most American Indian tribes is based in oral communication. To be more specific, most American Indian history has been transferred from generation to generation orally; therefore, many American Indians are great storytellers. One suspects this myth of the nonverbal American Indian began because their communication styles were different than Euro-Americans; thus rather than acknowledging the differences, American Indians were tagged as nonverbal.

Similar to other ethnic minorities, in a helping relationship, American Indians may be very "guarded" with their information and release small bits at any given time. The reason for this is that they are very suspicious of giving information to "officials," in that in the past this receipt of such information by government officials and missionaries was used against them. In fact, in some cases they lost their land and children from officials knowing too much of their business.

Another fact that the helper should be aware is that some American Indians, similar to African Americans, are often very good at reading body language. This is not a generalization because the reason for this is simple; for a group of people who were restricted in their communication and interaction with Euro-Americans, they learned to read body language to determine fact from fiction when dealing with Euro-Americans. This means that the helping professional must be very aware of his/her body language and insure that what is communicated verbally is congruent with what his/her body is communicating.

The final point with regard to communication style is that the helping professionals should assess the communication style of the American Indian client and develop the helping efforts within that style rather than attempting to change the style, unless communication is an aspect of the helping plan.

Expectations

Realizing that the clients' level of understanding with regard to the helping process will vary depending upon prior experiences with the mental health process as well as prior experiences with illness and disability, the helping professional must determine what the American Indian client expects from the helping process. The helping professional will be aided in his process of helping if he becomes familiar with the Indian Health Service which is a unique setting that is not available to other ethnic minorities (see Chapter 5, "Disabilities"). The helping professional and particularly the rehabilitation professional should also be aware that there are varying opinions held by American Indians with regard to the usefulness of the Indian Health Service. Additionally, the clients' expectations may in fact have been influenced (good or bad) by previous experiences with this health service agency. Moreover, the helper should be aware of the faith or lack thereof the American Indian client places in the medicine man. The helpers' efforts may be disregarded by the client if he believes the medicine man can help and further believes the helping professional's work is contrary to what has been prescribed by the medicine man. The helping professional would be wise in this type of situation to include the medicine man in the helping process.

The final point with regard to expectations is made via the following recommendation offered by Sandra Choney and her colleagues (1995):

1. Some Native Americans, particularly those with more traditional beliefs about health, may respond better to treatment if traditional healers are involved.

2. The use of the extended family can have a positive therapeutic outcome. The counselor, however, should be aware that using the Indian family will be somewhat different than when working with non-Indians. Sessions may occur outside the clinic or office setting. The Indian family may be less motivated to engage in "talk therapy" and more willing to be active agents of change.

3. Differences in communication styles, perceptions of trustworthiness, gender role definitions, medicine and social support networks including family relationships all provide major considerations when undertaking problem identification and treatment planning for Native American clients.

4. Caution must be taken when using standardized tests to assess Native Americans. Life experiences, cognitive structure, use of nonstandard English, differences in epistemologies and economic hardship characterize the lives of many Indian people.

Value Orientation

Similar to the other minority groups discussed in this book, knowledge of history, traditions, and customs, along with asking appropriate questions, will aid the professional helper in identifying some of the client's values. The professional helper should be accepting of these values and whenever possible use them in the helping plan rather than attempting to force the client to change his values to conform to those that are most comfortable for the professional helper. Additionally, the helper can improve his chances of success with an American Indian client if he will recognize that quite often the client is attempting to live in two cultures—one the dominant society culture, and two, his tribal culture. The professional helper should be sensitive to this and assist the client with this balancing act. In some instances, the most difficult part of this balancing act, especially for a younger American Indian, is remaining connected to his family, particularly the parents who may be more traditionally oriented than he. Some behavioral science specialists in American Indian affairs suggest that the helper can provide support to the client by encouraging him to maintain those things in his culture that have endured over the ages but also learn to adapt to the new techniques and technology of the dominant culture.

Situational Controls

Family, religious beliefs and activities, as well as social environment may be more influential in the lives of some American Indians than in the lives of many Euro-Americans as well as other helpers of different ethnic group than the American Indian. Depending upon the tribe, religious beliefs dictate tribal members' response to illness, disease, and disabilities. Religious activities, medicine men, and church elders may exert considerable influence, especially for American Indians who are traditional in their beliefs. Family and family elders also will provide advice and counsel to some American Indian clients. The professional helper in these instances may need to include these significant influences in the helping process.

Conclusion

With over 500 tribes, many of which are sovereign nations and many having their own language, American Indians are among the most diverse group of people in the United States. Many attempts have been made by both governmental and non-governmental entities to strip the various tribes and their people of their cultures. Boarding schools, forced relocations to unfamiliar environments, as well as attempts to force tribes to not speak their native language are but a few of the things that were done to force American Indians to abandon their ways of life and adapt the Euro-American standards. Even today, some American Indian tribes engage in dialogue with the United States government, attempting to regain land and other property taken from them. Some mental health professionals indicate that the stress of dealing with day-to-day discrimination as well as the isolation and lack of resources on reservations has contributed to the epidemic of alcoholism prevalent among some American Indians. It should be noted that alcoholism occurs at high rates among American Indians who do not live on reservations; therefore, alcoholism is not a reservation problem. Reservation life appears to be a contributing factor.

Alcoholism too frequently is the major contributing factor to accidents and violence. These situations, as well as the emotional problems caused by excessive drinking, are issues helping professionals will encounter when working with some American Indians. Pregnant American Indian women who drink to an excess also risk having babies who suffer from fetal alcohol syndrome.

Noninsulin diabetes also is a major problem among many American Indians. Helping professionals need to be aware of the effects of diabetes, which include amputations and blindness, and other impact upon their American Indian clients.

Unemployment and underemployment creates problems for some American Indians with regard to their abilities to provide safe living environments for their families. Also because of the types of jobs in which many are employed, they are at risk of injuries which may lead to disabilities.

All of these previously mentioned factors have resulted in American Indians having the highest rate of disabilities of any ethnic and/or racial group in America.

Review Questions

1. What were some of the methods used by Euro-Americans to acculturate American Indians?
2. Why should American Indians be considered a diverse group of people?
3. What are some of the major health problems among American Indians?
4. What are some of the obstacles a helping professional may encounter with regard to working with an American Indian client who lives on a reservation?
5. What impact(s) may occur if you were working with an American Indian who utilizes the services of a Medicine Man?
6. In a helping relationship what are some of the reasons an American Indian may limit his/her verbal communication?
7. What do you believe are important and relevant cultural factors of American Indians in the helping process?

Suggested Activities

1. Determine the number and/or percentage of American Indians living in your state.
2. Determine how many tribes are represented in your state.
3. Determine whether your state has reservations. If yes, visit at least two and observe and make notes with regard to the following: living conditions, employment opportunities, educational opportunities and language commonly spoken on the reservation.
4. Make a list of five agencies and/or organizations in your state that specialize in assisting American Indians.

References

Beauvis, F., & LaBoueff, S. (1985). Drug and alcohol abuse interventions in American Indian communities. *International Journal of Addictions, 20*(1), 139–171, January.

Beauvis, F. (1992). Comparison of drug use rates for reservation Indians, non-reservation Indians and Anglo youth. *American Indian and Alaska native mental health research, 5*(1), 13–31.

Blanchard, E. L. (1983) (1990). In D. W. Sue & D. Su (Eds.), *Counseling the culturally different* (2nd ed.). New York: John Wiley and Sons.

Carpenter, R., Lyons, C., & Miller, W. (1985). Peer-managed self-control program for prevention of alcohol abuse in American Indian high school students: A pilot evaluation study. *International Journal of the Addictions, 20*(2), 299–310, February.

Choney, S. K., Berryhill-Paapke, E., & Robbins, R. R. (1995). The acculturation of American Indians: Developing frameworks for research and practice. In J. G. Ponterotto et al. (Eds.), *Handbook of multicultural counseling.* Thousand Oaks, CA: Sage.

Deloria, V. (1969). *Custer died for your sins: An Indian manifesto.* New York: Macmillan.

Harjo, S. S. (1993). The American Indian experience. In H. P. McAdoo (Ed.), *Family ethnicity.* Newbury Park, CA: Sage.

John, R. (1988). The Native American family. In C. H. Mindel et al. (Eds.), *Ethnic families in America* (3rd ed.). Englewood Cliffs, NJ: Prentice-Hall.

Josephy, A. M. (1982). *Now that the buffalo's gone: A study of today's American Indians.* New York: Knopf.

Kleinfield, J., & Bloom, J. (1977). Boarding schools: Effects on the mental health of Eskimo adolescents. *American Journal of Psychiatry, 134,* 411–417.

Lowrey, L. (1983). Bridging a culture in counseling. *Journal of Applied Rehabilitation Counseling, 14,* 69–73.

Martin, W. E., Jr., Frank, L. W., Minkler, S., & Johnson, M. (1988). A survey of vocational rehabilitation counselors who work with American Indians. *Journal of Applied Rehabilitation Counseling, 19*(4), 29–34.

Porter, F. W. (1988). In C. H. Mindel et al. (Eds.), *Ethnic families in America* (3rd ed.). Englewood Cliffs, NJ: Prentice-Hall.

Richardson, E. H. (1981). In D. W. Sue & D. Sue (Eds.), *Counseling the culturally different* (2nd ed.). New York: John Wiley and Sons.

Sinclair, L. (1987). Native adolescents in crisis. *Canadian Nurse, 83*(8), 28–29, September.

Suggested Readings

Choney, S. K., Berryhill-Paapke, E., & Robbins, R. R. (1995). The acculturation of American Indians: Developing frameworks for research and practice. In J. G. Ponterotto et al. (Eds.), *Handbook of multicultural counseling.* Thousand Oaks, CA: Sage.

Dauphinais, P., Dauphinais, L., & Rowe, W. (1981). Effects of race and communication style on Indian perceptions of counselor effectiveness. *Counselor Education and Supervision, 21,* 72–80.

Dauphinais, P. (1993). Boarding schools: Fond memories of anguish and heartache. *Focus, 1,* 11–12.

DuFrene, P., & Coleman, V. (1992). Counseling Native Americans: Guidelines for group process. *Journal for Specialists in Group Work, 17,* 229–234.

Harjo, S. S. (1993). The American Indian experience. In H. N. McAdoo (Ed.), *Family ethnicity: Strength in diversity* (pp. 199–207). Newbury Park, CA: Sage.

John, R. (1988). The Native American family. In C. H. Mindel et al. (Eds.), *Ethnic families in America: Patterns and variations* (3rd ed., pp. 325–363). Englewood Cliffs, NJ: Prentice-Hall.

Redhorse, J. G. (1978). Family behavior of urban American Indians. *Social Work, 59*(2), 67–72.

Wagner, J. K. (1976). The role of intermarriage in the acculturation of selected urban American women. *Anthropologica, 18*(2), 215–229.

Chapter 8

ASIAN AND PACIFIC AMERICANS

Chapter Outline
• Introduction
• Historical Perspective
• Social Issues Impacting Asian and Pacific Americans
• Economic and Employment Issues
• Educational Issues
• Family Dynamics
• Intervention
• Communication Style
• Expectation
• Value Orientation
• Conclusion

Chapter Objectives
• Identify significant historical events which have impacted the lives of Chinese, Japanese, Korean and Filipino Americans
• Identify the diversity of Asian and Pacific Americans
• Identify, social, educational and economical issues which impact the lives of Asian Pacific Ameircans

Introduction

While Asian and Pacific Americans constitute approximately three percent of the United States population, there has been a phenomenal growth of approximately 800 percent increase in the population over the past 35 years. Similar to the Hispanic/Latino ethnic group, Asian or Pacific Americans are not a homogeneous group. In fact, Asian or Pacific Americans are a much more diverse group than most Americans realize. The group consists of those whom we normally consider as Asian or Pacific Island countries such as China, Japan, Korea, and the Philippines. In addition, there are a number of other countries included as Asian Pacific and they include India, Brunei, Burma, Indonesia, Malaysia, Bangladesh, Pakistan, Sri Lanka, Vietnam, Cambodia, Laos, Thailand, and there are others that could be named; however, the author's intent is to make the point of Asian and Pacific Americans as being a very diverse group of people. Once again, the author wishes to caution the reader not to overgeneralize by assuming that there is a single Asian and Pacific American culture. Unfortunately, space does not permit a discussion of each of the various subgroups that comprise the Asian and Pacific American ethnic groups. As a result of the aforementioned limitation, most of the discussion will relate to the subgroups of Chinese Americans, Filipino Americans, Japanese Americans, and Korean Americans. Books and journal articles will be listed in the suggested reading section of this chapter which will provide the reader with information regarding some of those subgroups not extensively covered.

Historical Background

Similar to the debate as to exactly when and under what conditions Africans first tread water and walked on American soil, it is unclear as to the date and circumstances surrounding Asian Pacific Islanders' entry into America. Cordova (1983) contends that in the 1760s a few natives of the Philippines removed themselves from a Spanish merchant ship in Louisiana and found their way to what is now New Orleans. Similarly, Jensen (1988) contends that during this same period a few, Asian Indians were delivered as indentured servants to the East Coast of America. While these accounts are probably based upon documented facts, the official beginning of Asian and Pacific immigration to the United States began in the 1840s and Rowena Fong (1992) lets us know that there were a variety of reasons for the immigration: political freedom, economic advancement, personal aspirations, and/or family pressure.

Chinese Americans

Of the Asian groups, the Chinese were the first of the Asian Pacific subgroups to immigrate to the United States in significant numbers. The discovery of gold in the Sacramento Valley attracted the attention of many groups, both domestic and international. In addition to seeking their fortunes in the gold fields of California, many Chinese helped build the transcontinental railroad.

There has been some debate with regard to the intent of many of the Chinese immigrants; some say most of the early immigrants came as sojourners, meaning they intended to return to China, and those proponents of their immigration point out that the majority of these immigrants were males who, if they were married, had left their families behind. On the other hand, some researchers indicate that the immigrants' intentions were to send for their families after they had secured enough money to establish a home in America. Whatever the intent, it is clear that they came to take advantage of the employment opportunities that were available in America. In the early days of immigration, while they were not exactly welcomed by the frontiersmen, they were accepted because they were a source of cheap labor, particularly to mine and railroad owners. In the late 1860s, circumstances began to change and Sue and Sue (1990) inform us that a series of business recessions, coupled with the completion of the Union Central Pacific Railroad, began to create competition for jobs. Morrison Wong (1995) adds to our understanding of the attitudes being displayed at that time by Euro-Americans regarding Chinese immigrants by pointing out that xenophobic and racist attitudes begin to be common among the general population which caused considerable anti-Asian feelings. Rowena Fong (1992) succinctly places the Euro-Americans' self-serving views in perspective as she states, "The main complaint was that Chinese immigrants worked too hard for wages that were too low and thereby undercut the wages of Euro-American workers."

A result of this anti-Chinese sentiment there was physical violence against Chinese people such as the riot in Los Angeles's, Chinatown that Sandermeyer (1973) described, or the physical attack upon Chinese immigrants in Rock Spring, Wyoming that was outlined by Kitano (1969). Additionally, laws that were detrimental to Chinese people were being passed throughout the United States such as the 1853 California Foreign Miner's Tax which imposed a tax on noncitizen miners. In 1870, San Francisco implemented a Cubic Air Ordinance which was designed to eliminate large numbers of Chinese sleeping in a single room together. In 1852, California levied a $50 per head tax on each Chinese arriving ship passenger. In 1882, the United States Congress passed the Chinese Exclusion Act which Morrison Wong (1995) describes as "the first and only immigration act to specifically designate an ethnic, racial or nationality group for exclusion." Wong provides further information with regard to the act in these comments, "The act prohibited all Chinese laborers, whether skilled or unskilled, from entering the United States for ten years. All other Chinese entering the United States had to have identification certificates issued by the Chinese government. The Chinese Exclusion Act was extended by the U.S. Congress for another ten years with the 1892 Geary Act, and in 1902, Congress passed legislation that made permanent the exclusion of immigration of Chinese persons. Not until the 1943 Magnuson Act was passed by the United States Congress was the Chinese Exclusion Act of 1882 effectively repealed."

Because of the early discrimination Chinese immigrants faced, coupled with the lack of protection from harm received from local, state, and/or federal authorities, Chinese individuals and families banned together for self-protection and survival. This resulted in the development of what we now call Chinatowns. In addition, other Chinese organizations such as Chinese Consolidated Benevolent Association were formed to maintain Chinese culture and serve as a voice for the Chinese people to the Euro-American authority structure (Fong, 1992). There have been several other legislative acts since the 1943 repeal of the Chinese Exclusion Act that have impacted Chinese immigration to the United States. Perhaps the greatest impact has occurred as a result of the 1965 Immigration Act which lifted many of the immigration quotas and according to Morrison Wong (1995), "By abolishing the national origins system, this act became the first immigration policy that practiced the principles of racial equality." The Immigration Act of 1965 was amended in 1981 which also had the effect of increasing Chinese immigration. In 2011 the Chinese population in America exceeded four million. It must be noted that not all are as a result of immigration. A significant portion of this number is a result of family growth.

Japanese Americans

Following the immigration efforts of the Chinese were the Japanese; however, as Rowena Fong (1992) reminds us, the Japanese government attempted to avoid some of the pitfalls that the Chinese immigrants encountered by screening the Japanese men who were to immigrate to the United States. Once in the states the Japanese government would consult with the U.S. government on behalf of Japanese immigrants. The first large immigration of Japanese occurred in the 1880s as Malays were recruited and contracted to work in the Hawaiian sugar cane fields. As a result, the Japanese eventually became the largest ethnic minority on the Hawaiian Islands. In the 1890s, Japanese began to arrive on the U.S. mainland, primarily in California, to work the farm fields and the gold mines.

Similar to what had happened to the Chinese; the Japanese began to experience prejudice and discrimination, especially from Euro-American workers. Some Euro-American workers began to advocate violent actions to exclude Japanese from working. In part to avoid confrontation, beginning in 1900 President Theodore Roosevelt and the Japanese government developed what was called a "Gentleman's Agreement" which in simple terms restricted the immigration of Japanese for the purpose of being a laborer. This agreement was renewed in 1905 and in 1908.

Setsuko Nishi (1995) reminds us that in 1924, the Oriental Exclusion Act was passed by the United States which had the effect of virtually stopping

Japanese immigration for the next thirty years. In 1952, immigration of Japanese began again with the passage of the McCarren-Walter Immigration Act. The next major immigration of Japanese came as a result of the passage of the 1965 Immigration Act.

Without a doubt, the most devastating insult to Japanese Americans was the collecting and virtually imprisoning of over one hundred thousand persons after the government of Japan attacked Pearl Harbor in 1941. These Japanese American citizens were taken from their homes, supposedly out of fear they would aid the Japanese government, although they were American citizens and had no loyalty to the Japanese government. This act has had a tremendous psychological impact upon Japanese Americans which is felt even today. This is a fact to which helping professionals should be aware. More discussion will occur later in the chapter. Currently, the Japanese American population exceeds one million.

Filipino Americans

The second largest population of Asian or Pacific American subgroup is Filipino Americans. Currently their population count exceeds three million. As mentioned at the beginning of the chapter, persons from the Philippine Islands may have been the first Asian Pacific persons to come to the United States. Pauline Agbayani-Siewert and Linda Revilla, (1995) using Cordova (1983) and Espina (1982) work as documentation, propose that "the first Filipino settlements in the United States began in the late eighteenth century," when Filipinos escaped from Spanish ships and found their way to Louisiana.

There is a significant Spanish influence in most Filipino heritage as a result of Spain's colonization of the Philippines for over 300 years. Thus, the majority of Filipinos are of the Catholic faith. Spain's rule of the Philippine Islands ended as they were defeated by America in the Spanish-American war. At the end of this war, the Philippine government declared itself as an independent nation, which lead to the Philippine-American War, or as the American government preferred to label it, the Philippine Insurrection.

The Philippine Islands became an American colony after losing the insurrection/war, thus making Filipino persons U.S. nationals with the right to open entry into the United States. The period of America's colonization of the Philippines continued until 1946 when the country was granted its independence.

Agbayani-Siewert and Revilla (1995) separate the Filipino immigration to the United States into two waves–the first came as a result of the U.S. Congress passing the 1903 Pensionado Act which, according to those authors, "Provided support to send young Filipinos to the United States for education on American life." They further pointed out that many of this group returned to the Philippines after they had completed their education. The second wave consisted primarily of Filipinos immigrating to the U.S. to work. They were often recruited as cheap labor in Hawaii, Alaska, and in the western United States.

Rowena Fong (1992) provides an idea of where Filipino individuals worked in the United States with the following comments:

> As Japanese and Korean labor immigration ended about 1905, Hawaiian plantation owners began to look elsewhere for cheap workers. Like the Chinese and Japanese laborers, the Filipinos were persuaded by sugar plantation owners to go to Hawaii and work under contract. In 1907, 150 Filipinos were sent to Hawaii. Others soon arrived on the mainland and the Filipinos became successors to Chinese and Japanese on western farms and canneries. They numbered about 100,000 from the 1930s through the 1950s, with about equal numbers on the mainland and in Hawaii. Besides working on farms and in canneries, Filipinos also worked as cooks and did domestic labor.

Although Filipinos were United States nationals, they also experienced discrimination. Sue and Sue (1990) reports Filipino immigrants experienced discrimination from labor unions led by the American Federation of Labor who espoused the idea that Filipinos were cheap labor lowering the standard of living for Euro-American workers. In addition, Fong (1992) points out that there was physical violence such as a mob attack on a California Filipino club, including beatings and one murder.

Despite the hardships imposed by violence and discriminatory behavior, Filipinos continued to immigrate to the United States. Besides economic opportunities, there are primarily two reasons Filipinos immigrated to the United States and continue to do so—one, because of the Unites States' early colonial involvement, most Filipinos have a good understanding and feel comfortable with many U.S. customs and values; and two, because of the U.S. military presence in the area, Filipinos marry service personnel and become United States citizens.

Korean Americans

The noted Asian Pacific American scholar Pyong Gap Min (1995) divides Korean immigration to the United States into three distinct periods: Old immigration (pioneer period), intermediate period, and new immigration. The dissection of Korean's migration to the U.S. into these three periods provides an excellent overview of the reasons behind their immigration to the United States:

Old Immigration (1903–1905): Similar to many Chinese and Japanese immigrants, the first Koreans appear to have immigrated to Hawaii to work on the sugar plantations. During the early 1900s to 1905, Professor Min (1995) informs us that a modest number of Koreans were recruited by the sugar plantation owners to replace Japanese workers who had moved to California or were engaged in strikes or work stoppages. This period of immigration ended partly because the Korean government halted immigration from Korea upon suspicion that Koreans in America were being mistreated and partly because of pressure applied by the Japanese government. Upon winning the Russo-Japanese War, Korea became a colony of Japan in a sense, which afforded the Japanese government considerable control over Korea's affairs.

Intermediate Period (1950–1965): There appears to have been two major groups of immigrants during this period. First group were brides of U.S. servicemen who were stationed in South Korea during the Korean War and the second group were orphans of the Korean War. Soldiers adopted children who had lost both parents as a result of the war. According to Min (1995) later non-military U.S. citizens began to adopt Korean orphans.

New Immigration (1965–Present): As was the case in increases in Chinese and Japanese immigration, the 1965 Immigration and Naturalization Act has had the greatest impact upon increasing Korean immigration.

Currently there are about one and one half million Korean Americans. As is the case with the other Asian American groups discussed the numbers are increasing primarily because of family growth and of course some immigration.

Social Issues Impacting Asian and Pacific Americans

Collectively, Asian and Pacific Americans have been characterized by the mass media as the "model minority." With this title those that subscribe to this belief are saying that Asian and Pacific Americans have either reached or succeeded the national median of indicators which are often used as measures of success in America such as income and education to mention only two. The overall concept is that Asian and Pacific Americans have been discriminated similar to other ethnic and racial minorities in America and have overcome this hideous stumbling block and achieved the "American dream."

The distinguished authors Derald Sue and David Sue (1990) take exception to this characterization of Asian and Pacific Americans but point out that at first glance this concept of the successful minority appears to have validity. They allude to the fact that the Chinese, Japanese and Filipinos have either equaled or exceeded the national median income and with regard to education, collectively the Asian and Pacific American subgroups complete a higher median number of grades than all other groups in America. Additionally, Asian or Pacific Americans appear to be better accepted by Euro-Americans than the other ethnic, racial minority groups in that interracial marriage between Asian or Pacific Americans and Euro-Americans appears to be more acceptable than any other ethnic racial group. Stated more succinctly, the "social distance" (prejudice and discrimination) seem to be less than for the other groups. Finally, Sue and Sue tell us that a variety of studies show that Asian and Pacific Americans demonstrate very few problems in areas such as juvenile delinquency and psychiatric disorders which serve as indicators of good mental health. All of these things taken together seem to indicate a minority group which has made a successful adjustment to life in America despite having to deal with prejudice and discrimination.

As previously stated, Derald and David Sue do not subscribe to the concept of model minority. Other authors and scholars Min (1995), Tsukada (1988), Wong (1982), Cabezas et al. (1987), and Toji and Johnson (1992) also take exception to the media-made concept of model minority. As one analyzes some of the areas previously mention as proof of the successful or model minority concept, one obtains a better perspective as to Asian and Pacific American life in America.

As previously stated, those who subscribe to the idea that Asian and Pacific Americans are a model minority point to the fact that their median family income exceeds that of Euro-Americans; however, upon close observation, the primary reason for this is in many cases there are more wage earners in the Asian or Pacific American family than in the Euro-American family. Additionally, authors such as Wong (1982), Cabezas et al. (1987), and Tsukada (1988) convincingly argue that despite the educational attainment and/or training, Asian and Pacific Americans' labor positions and salary received are less than Euro-Americans with comparable education and training. In other words, Asian and Pacific Americans experience similar, glass ceilings and prejudicial career path blocks as other ethnic, racial minorities and women.

Sue and Sue (1990) continue to debunk the model minority myth by alluding to the fact that from an educational standpoint, many Asian and Pacific Americans continue to experience difficulty with English. They refer to a finding of Watanabe (1976) which indicates that some Asians who have lived in the United States for several generations continue to have difficulty mastering the English language.

While some may point to the ethnic gatherings that have produced Chinatowns, Japantowns, etc. as economic success, they too frequently forget that these areas came into existence as effort to avoid prejudice, discrimination, and violence. Additionally, as Sue and Sue (1998) remind us, some of these areas represent ghetto areas with prevalent unemployment, poverty, health problems, and juvenile delinquency.

In addition to misrepresenting the life situation of many Asian and Pacific Americans, other potentially damaging effects are: (1) Possible resentment by other ethnic and racial minority groups toward Asian and Pacific Americans. By stating that Asian Pacific Americans have overcome all obstacles placed in their paths, this is implying that other minority groups could do the same if they had the motivation and determination to do so. (2) Denial of services to Asian Pacific Americans. Because of the positive stereotype, public officials and other policy makers may tend to exclude Asian and Pacific Americans from things such as health and human service assistance programs and federal student financial aid for needy and/or underrepresented students to mention only two. (3) Hurh and Kim (1982) argue that as Asian and Pacific Americans begin to believe the concept of being a model minority, they began to develop "false consciousness," thinking they have attained middle-class status, failing to recognize that they are underemployed and over-worked.

Economic and Employment Issues

As previously stated, the Asian and Pacific American median income is greater than the national average which gives the appearance of a highly economically successful group. A growing number of researchers and knowledgeable authorities with regard to Asian Pacific affairs indicate the economic success is an illusion in that the income figures are quite often generated by more family members than what generates the family income of Euro-Americans. Because economists and others have viewed the family income of Asian Pacific Americans as being above average, very little research exists to identify the standard of living these families experience.

Beth Hess and her associates (1995) discuss the economic position of Asian and Pacific Americans from the standpoint of their preparation for an entry into business, particularly businesses which they own. The authors point out that among Chinese Americans, the clustering together to form the Chinatowns has had a mixed blessing. On one hand, it has provided employment and a basis for bank and mortgage loans for new businesses and homes; however, on the other hand, they argue, for many of those who do not remove themselves from the Chinatown environment, especially new immigrants, they tend to live in poverty and are exploited at work. They continue by emphasizing that local merchants quite often become targets for groups of young Asians involved in the protection racket as well as drugs, gambling, and prostitution. With regard to the Japanese Americans, it appears they have become more diversified as they have become more socially mobile, moving into mid-level management jobs, particularly in the electronics and engineering areas.

With respect to the other Asian Pacific subgroups, Hess and her colleagues (1995) have this to say:

> In contrast, Asians from the Indian subcontinent entered the United States with educational credentials and technical skills and have found their economic foothold in the pharmaceutical industry and health-care facilities. Although they, too, have experienced discrimination, their economic success allows greater choice of where to live. Recent arrivals, from the Philippine Islands are also relatively well educated, with professional degrees in medicine, law and engineering, even though most have had to settle for less prestigious jobs. Immigrants from Korea lack the educational background of the Asian Indians and Filipinos, but compensate with a powerful commitment to self-employment for the entire family. Koreans have been successful in operating small grocery stores in urban neighborhoods, although this often brings them into conflict with other minority groups resentful of the Korean's presence.

This summary supports the idea that many Asian and Pacific Americans either come to the United States well prepared or prepare themselves for prestigious jobs but often discover that because of bias and discrimination, they are both underemployed and underpaid. Therefore, despite the myth of the model minority, Asian and Pacific Americans continue to experience discrimination in the workplace which has an impact upon their ability to earn so that their standard of living will be equal to their personal efforts.

Education Issues

The concept of model minority appears to permeate all aspects of Asian Pacific Americans' lives and education certainly is no exception. Bob Suzuki (1994) discusses the impact with the following comments:

> Due to the model minority stereotype, to even suggest that serious problems exist for Asians in higher education may seem to border on the absurd to many people, especially educators. Asian Pacific Americans, both students and faculty, are viewed as "overrepresented" in higher education in comparison with their proportion in the general population.

To be objective, let's look at both sides of the issue, why Asian and Pacific Americans appear to be successful and what are their strengths and what are their problems within the education area.

Strengths

- Asian and Pacific Americans' parents place considerable emphasis on education; therefore, many Asian and Pacific students are well prepared academically.
- A large percentage of Asian and Pacific Americans take college preparatory courses in the public schools.
- Because of the type of courses many Asian Pacific students take in elementary, middle, and high school, they are well prepared in analytical thinking which is the basis for many standardized tests.
- A larger proportion of Asian Pacific students take the Scholastic Aptitude Test (SAT) than students in general (HSIA 1988).

Weaknesses

- As Suzuki (1994) points out, the statistics on Asian and Pacific Americans with regard to enrollment into college would suggest that Asian Pacific students have no problem with gaining entry into U.S. colleges and universities, he indicates that this is true for some of the subgroups such as Chinese and Japanese, but for others as the southeast Asians and Filipinos, they in fact may be underrepresented.
- The return (salary) on the educational investment does not equal their Euro-American counterparts.

Family Dynamics

Because of their diversity, it would be a significant mistake to attempt a summarization of all Asian Pacific families by generalizing specific principles and values that this or any other author feels the various subgroups have in common. Therefore, I shall discuss each of the Asian Pacific American subgroups of Chinese American, Japanese American, Korean American, and Filipino American separately.

Chinese Americans

Since most of the current Chinese Americans are descendants of those first Chinese people to immigrate to America in the mid-1800s, a glimpse of the traditional Chinese family provides a foundation for understanding current behaviors. In particular, according to Morrison Wong (1988), we should look at customs that continue to influence Chinese Americans' lives as well as the degree to which the current generation has deviated from them by accepting Western values. Some of the traditional Chinese family dynamics are as follows:

- Extended kinship groups;
- Patriarchal–father and eldest son had the dominant roles in the family;
- Patrilocal, the married couple lived with the husband's parents;
- Filal Piety (respect) considered of paramount importance–The family came first; therefore, family obligations were more important than individual accomplishments;
- Arranged marriages.

As previously stated these were the roots which anchored the traditional Chinese family. Next, let's look at the modern Chinese American family dynamics. Wong (1988) separates the modern Chinese American family into two groups. The first is characterized by Lucy Huang (1981) and Evelyn Glenn (1983) as "dual worker family." The second is the middle class, white collar or professional Chinese American family. The dual working family is generally represented by the Chinese who came to the United States and settled in Chinatowns. Some of the characteristics of the dual working family, according to Huang (1981) and Glenn (1983), are as follows:

- Both husband and wife are employed as craftsmen, laborers or service workers;
- Both husband and wife are coequals as wage earners;
- Because both parents work, they and the children are frequently separated; in fact, the parents may work different shifts, thus having little time together.

The middle class or professional Chinese American family may be characterized as follows:

1. Having earned enough money to move away from Chinatown and live in suburbs;
2. View themselves as more American than Chinese, according to Lucy Huang (1981), Harry Kitano (1985), and Melford Weiss (1970);
3. Highly educated;
4. Semi extended family structure (family members such as parents and grandparents) do not live with them but live close.

Father's Role: Similar to the traditional Chinese family, the father is the primary authority figure. He may maintain respect and authority over the family in a manner that appears to be emotionally distant to persons who are acculturated to Western standards.

Mother's Role: As in most American families, the mother is responsible for the children. While according to Wong (1988) she decides what is best for the children, gives them commands, and the children are expected to obey.

CHILD-REARING PRACTICES

1. Public displays of affection is considered poor taste;
2. Independence and maturity are stressed early in the child's life;
3. Aggressive behavior is not condoned among siblings and young children, according to Richard Sollenberger (1968);
4. Older children are responsible for assisting young children in social activities and learning appropriate social behavior, according to Lucy Huang (1981);
5. Education is highly valued;
6. Control of children is often handled by the "sense of shame," as it is dishonorable to bring shame upon the family.

Japanese Americans

The various generations of Japanese Americans have been classified as Issei (first generation), Nisei (second generation), Sansei (third generation), and Yonsei (fourth generation).

Issei (First Generation): Issei constitute the first group of Japanese to immigrate to America. As stated earlier, most of this group was laborers contracted to work in the Hawaiian sugar cane fields and later migrated to the west coast of the contiguous United States to work on the railroads, canneries, and as farm laborers. Since the Issei represents the first group of Japanese immigrants, those who are alive are elderly. The purpose in mentioning them, other than to recognize them as the Japanese pioneers in America is to establish that they represent the beginning of the Japanese American family.

The majority of the first generation of Japanese Americans came as bachelors with the intent of making their fortune and returning to Japan to establish a family. Some did; however, many stayed in America. Because there were laws against Japanese marrying Euro-American women, many who remained in America selected their Japanese wives from pictures who became known as "picture brides."

Sylvia Yanagisako (1988) contributes to our understanding of the early Japanese family as she informs us that as a result of the way the Issei selected brides, the families of the bride and groom were closely associated with all stages of the marriage. Therefore, the traditional Japanese kinship bond reached into America.

The early research of Frank Miyamoto (1939) identified what he considered four aspects of the Japanese family system which, to a large extent, characterized Japanese life that has been passed down from the first generation (Issei) to succeeding generations:

1. The concept of the Japanese community as one large family in which family norms are reinforced by the community;
2. Patriarchal family organizational structure which emphasizes male dominance;
3. Primogeniture and adoption family system, which means the family property and other valuables as well as family power and control flows to the eldest son;
4. Family customs such as marriage, anniversaries, and holidays are celebrated, thus playing a significant role in the social and cultural life of the Japanese.

Another important fact to remember about the first generation is that they and their children were the group placed in the internment camps during World War II. Most, if not all, of the parents are deceased and the children are elderly or approaching that stage of life. Without doubt, this had an impact upon the emotional and psychological development of both generations and subsequent generations as the memories of the event is passed along to them.

Nisei (Second Generation): There is a wide age range among the Nisei group, some are elderly and others are in their middle-age years. Because of the age range, some Nisei spent time in the internment campus while others were born after the war ended. According to Leonard Broom and John Kitsuse (1956), one can easily recognize the difference between those who spent time in the campus versus those who had spent their adolescent years in a much freer environment.

One begins to see the beginning of the effects of acculturation on Japanese Americans in the second generation, which according to Kitano and his associates (1984) conflicts between the first and second generations were common. The Issei was of the opinion that the Nisei were too quickly becoming Americanized, thus turning their backs on Japanese traditions.

Nisei families represent a variety of cultural models. The wide age range and degree of the Issei's influence determined whether the second generation continued with the conservative Japanese family tradition or whether they gravitated toward the American family norms.

Sansei (Third Generation) and Yonsei (Fourth Generation): These generations have had more exposure to American life than the previous generations; therefore, it is understandable that each subsequent generation has become more acculturated. Harry Kitano (1988) provides the following excellent summarization of current Japanese American family characteristics. He concludes:

1. There is continuity from the first to the second and to succeeding generations.
2. Certain cultural styles have been retained including enryo (preference for ethnic peers), close family ties, ethnic celebrations, and high educational expectations. The retention of and changes in various cultural elements vary by family in terms of size, socialization, area of residence, influence of the ethnic community, and contact with the dominant community.
3. The most dramatic change in Japanese American families is that of out-of-group marriage. Sansei out-of-group marriage rates of over 60 percent may mean the eventual demise of a monolithic ethnic community.
4. Most Sansei families are similar to American models. However, there are some three-generation households, ensuring that the old ways are not completely forgotten.

Filipino Americans

Filipino Americans are excellent examples of why we should not aggregate Asian and Pacific Americans and generalize their cultures into one Asian Pacific culture. For example, traditional Filipino cultural values and beliefs not only encourage but expect women to work outside the home which is contrary to some other Asian Pacific subgroups. Also, the Filipino traditional marital relationship is rooted in egalitarian principles. Pido (1986) reminds us that Filipino women share most aspects of family responsibilities more equally with males than do most other Asian Pacific groups. Finally, the Filipino family is structured differently than some of the other Asian Pacific subgroups in that the power and authority flows differently. In many other Asian Pacific subgroups, the elders maintain considerable control over younger family members; whereas within Filipino tradition, the elderly are respected, but they do not continue to exert control.

Pauline Agbayani-Siewert and Linda Revilla (1995) increase our understanding of Filipino family characteristics with the following:

1. Open displays of anger or aggression are discouraged; whereas, displays of passive cooperative behavior are encouraged.
2. Family structure is more egalitarian than patriarchal.

3. Regardless of whether the relationship is by blood or fictive, kinship is highly regarded.
4. Fictive relations are incorporated into the family through the compadre (co-parent) system. Once accepted as a family member the individual is treated as blood kin.
5. Kinship takes precedence over persons outside the group. When a kinship member is threatened, the family will rally around the individual to provide protection and support.

Korean Americans

Noted scholars of Asian Pacific American cultures such as Min (1995), Hurh and Kim (1984), Reitz (1980), and Yinger (1980) contend that Korean Americans have a higher level of ethnic attachment than most other Asian Pacific American groups. In essence, this implies that Korean Americans maintain and practice a considerable portion of their traditional culture. Pyong Gap Min (1995) provides three reasons for this strong ethnic attachment:

1. South Korea is a small culturally homogeneous country which has only one racial group that speaks the same language. This homogeneity means cultural rituals are virtually practiced by everyone and is reinforced from generation to generation.
2. Most Koreans are affiliated with Korean ethnic churches. Therefore, religious beliefs and practices are transferred generationally. Additionally, the church serves as a center for social activities. Thus, more than religious principles are conveyed.
3. The propensity to own and operate small businesses creates the ability to hire persons from their cultural group and in a sense maintain a mini-community of persons with similar cultural beliefs and backgrounds.

Considering the very strong ethnic ties to the traditional Korean culture one may conclude that the Korean families are very conservative and tradition-bound. This is evident by the low divorce rate, low percentage of female-headed families, and in general a more stable family structure than Euro-American families as well as some of the other ethnic minority groups. Additionally, Korean families tend to be traditional in their approach to children showing respect to their elders. However, as Korean Americans become more acculturated, we begin to view some acceptance of American culture. More specifically, according to Min (1995), in Korea, the wife is expected to remain in the home and be a full-time homemaker; however, in America, more Korean females work outside the home. Again, referencing the work of Min, three factors contribute to this:

1. The economic reality of living in America often dictates that the family needs the income of both husband and wife.
2. The salaries in America are seven to eight times greater than in Korea, which makes the American work force very attractive to Korean women. It is obvious that both the husband and wife see an opportunity to "get ahead" financially with two incomes.
3. Living in America has caused a change in Korean's attitudes with regard to gender roles.

CHILD-REARING PRACTICES

1. Older Korean parents tend to be more authoritarian than Korean parents born and reared in America.
2. Korean parents place a high premium on education.
3. Punishment of children may appear to be harsher than Euro-American standards.
4. Respect for others, especially elderly, is strongly emphasized.

Intervention

Level of Acculturation

It cannot be overstated that because of the diversity of Asian and Pacific Americans (at least 32 distinct ethnic or cultural groups) one should not generalize Asian Pacific cultures into one culture. In analyzing these cultures, the helping professional must take into consideration whether the client was foreign-born or born in the United States. Additionally, she must be aware of the generation the client represents because, as was discussed earlier in this chapter, the acculturation level probably will be different depending upon how long the person has been in America and the cultural generation he represents. Moreover, if the client is third or fourth generation that was reared in America, the helper must be cognizant of the environment in which the person was reared. As an example, a fourth generation Korean American who was reared in a Korean ethnic community probably will be less acculturated to the dominant culture standards than fourth generation Korean reared in suburban America. Frederick Leong (1986) contends that the more Asian Pacific Americans are acculturated to Western standards, the better they respond to counseling.

When working with some Asian and Pacific Americans, it is helpful to also determine the level of acculturation of the parents, if applicable. As a result some groups, particularly Chinese, Japanese, and Korean, continue to respect the father's authority as the head of the family (regardless of whether the children are adults and married), therefore his level of acculturation will affect the client's actions.

Communication Style

Acculturation level also impacts communication style. The more an Asian or Pacific American identifies with Western culture, the greater the chance he will exhibit communication patterns that are similar to the dominant culture. Relatedly, the fact that Asian and Pacific Americans are such a diverse group and considering there can be tremendous variations within the group, the professional helper must put forth extra efforts to determine what, if any, influence cultural generation has on communication. As an example, a second-generation Chinese American, as Fong Chan et al. (1988) point out, may have been taught by his parents to show respect to authority figures by not speaking until being spoken to; therefore, he may appear to be quiet and shy. The reality is that it is not a matter of being non-communicative but a matter of how he has been reared. In addition to communication style from the standpoint of being verbal or non-verbal, the helper working with Asian and Pacific Americans has to be aware of language barriers, particularly if English is a second language for the client.

Expectation

Knowledgeable scholars of Asian Pacific American cultures, Chan et al. (1988), Sue and Sue (1990), Leung and Sakata (1988), and Ho (1987), inform us that with regard to mental health settings such as counseling, some Asian and Pacific Americans have quite a different expectation of the helping process than many Euro-American clients. To be more specific, first they may be very reluctant to see a counselor because in their minds emotional issues are symptoms of physical problems, thus they may have difficulty in understanding and accepting the idea that "talk therapy" will provide a solution to their problems. Second, when they are seen by a counselor, they view him as "the authority"; thus they may expect the professional helper to provide answers rather than pose questions. Given these concerns the professional helper would be wise to determine the client's perception of what is to occur between the two of them. An accurate understanding will allow the professional helper to explain what is to happen and also adjust his technique(s) to be more relevant to the client's understanding and expectations. This is not to say that the helper has to completely change his approach, but it may very well be necessary to make some adjustments.

Value Orientation

Gargi Sodowsky et al. (1995) identify what they consider as core values of U.S. Asian groups. These values emphasize personality traits such as silence, non-confrontation, moderation in behavior, self-control, patience, humility, modesty, and simplicity. Douglas Chung (1992) also adds to our understanding of Asian Pacific value orientation by identifying differences in Western culture which is pragmatic and individualistic in contrast to Eastern culture which is considered to be more idealistic and collective. Basically, this implies that some people influenced by Eastern cultures view group goals or the good of the group more important than individual accomplishments; therefore, working together is highly valued. These are important facts professional helpers would be well advised to remember when developing plans of action for some Asian Pacific Americans. As an example, a counselor working with a Chinese American client on vocational plans after his physical rehabilitation and/or education will probably be more successful if he includes the client's significant others and couch the vocational goals in terms of how his new occupation will be of benefit to both him and his family.

Social harmony, social control, and self-control appear to be the essence of Eastern cultures and they are anchored in family relationships. These points take us to the next area of assessment: situational controls.

Situational Controls

Sodowsky et al. (1995) provide us with information with respect to how social harmony, social control, and self-control are such an integral part of many Asian and Pacific American's lives. Social harmony is achieved through structured family relationships that have clearly defined codes of behavior, including language usage and hierarchical roles. Some of these formal relationships are those of father and son, husband and wife, older brother/sister and younger brother/sister, grandparent and grandchild, and uncle/aunt and nephew/niece.

Filial piety, especially that of the eldest son, is the cornerstone of morality in many Asian American families. Family identity is characterized by the interdependence of individual members, by individual members seeking the honor and good name of the family and protecting it from shame and by reciprocal duties and obligations that take precedence over individual desires. Social control is obtained through demands for obedience and fulfillment of obligations. If these behaviors are not observed, the principal techniques of punishment employed by the family are arousing moral guilt and making the morally reprehensible person lose face through social/public shame.

Considering these facts, the family serves as a major influence within the lives of many Asian or Pacific Americans. Helping professionals cannot ignore this fact and after assessing the person for controlling factors within her life, he determines that indeed the family influence is significant he as the professional helper must bring the family into the helping plan. In fact, the helping professional may have to exercise control on his part as the client takes time to discuss and perhaps receive the approval of the appropriate family members with regard to aspects of the plan. In counseling situations where issues of mental and/or emotional problems are at the heart of the therapy, the professional helper must keep in mind the issue of not bringing shame to the family. To discuss issues of mental or emotional problems outside of the family and especially without the permission of the appropriate family members may be difficult if not impossible for some clients to do. In situations such as this, the professional helper must encourage the client to discuss his feelings about disclosing sensitive information and ask him what would make him feel comfortable enough to engage in conversation. Offers to consult with the client's family (with his permission) may resolve the impasse. If the client refuses the offer and does not offer any solution, the professional helper has two choices: offer to refer the client, perhaps to someone with a similar cultural background, or explain to the client, given the circumstance; it appears no further progress can be made and the therapeutic relationship must be terminated. If this is to be done, the professional helper should provide the client with information on how to resume the therapy with him. Additionally, the client should be given the name of other helping professionals he can contact if he desires to again engage himself in therapy.

Conclusion

Most helping professionals know that Asian and Pacific Americans are a diverse group of people but often are treated as a homogeneous group. The fact that too often we think of Korean Americans as having the same cultural values as Filipino Americans causes helping professionals to react to them in a professional helping relationship similarly. This approach, coupled with the judgment made by using a Euro-American cultural yardstick, has caused a lack of return to the helping relationship after the first visit. As a result, the high rate of "no shows" clearly establishes that something is wrong with the helping professional system's approach to working with Asian or Pacific Americans.

An additional problem in working with Asian and Pacific Americans is created by the perception of them as the "model minority." While this title may be intended to be complimentary, it creates a false impression of Asian and Pacific Americans as a group of people who have no problems. They are considered to be above the United States averages for educational achievement and economic standards. Additionally, they are viewed as having a social network which takes care of its own, thus solving any problems that may confront them. These perceptions too frequently cause responsible agencies and organizations to overlook mental and emotional problems created by discrimination, poverty, and an unequal return on their educational investments.

Review Questions

1. Why have Asian and Pacific Americans been described as a "model minority?"
2. Identify some of the flaws in the concept of Asian and Pacific Americans as the model minority.
3. What do Issei, Nisei, Sansei and Yonsi mean?
4. Which of the Asian and Pacific American subgroups have the largest population in the United States?

Suggested Activities

1. Determine the number and/or percentage of Asian and Pacific Americans that live in your state.
2. If there are any Asian and Pacific American ethnic communities such as Chinatown in your area, visit at least one and observe the range of acculturation within the community.
3. Make a list of at least five agencies and/or organizations in your state that specialize in assisting Asian and Pacific Americans. Also, summarize the services provided.

References

Agbayani-Siewert, P., & Revilla, L. (1995). Filipino Americans. In P. G. Min (Ed.), *Asian Americans: Contemporary trends and issues.* Thousand Oaks, CA.

Cabezas, A., Shinagawa, L., & Kawaguchi, G. (1987). New inquiries into the socioeconomic status of Filipino Americans in California. *Amerasia Journal, 13,* 1–12.

Cordova, F. (1983). *Filipinos: Forgotten Asian Americans.* Dubuque, IA: Kendall Hunt.

Fong, R. (1992). A history of Asian Americans. In S. M. Furuto et al. (Eds.), *Social work practice with Asian Americans.* Newbury Park, CA: Sage.

Glenn, E. K. (1983). Split household, small producer and dual wage earner: An analysis of Chinese-American family strategies. In C. H. Mindel et al. (Eds.), *Ethnic families in America* (3rd ed.), Englewood Cliffs, NJ: Prentice-Hall.

Hasia, J. (1988). Asian Americans in higher education and at work. In M. J. Justiz et al. (Eds.), *Minorities in higher education.* American Council on Education. Phoenix, AZ: Oryx Press.

Hess, B. B., Markson, E. W., & Stein, P. J. (1995). Racial and ethnic minorities: An overview. In P. S. Rothenberg (Ed.), *Race, class and gender in the United States: An integrated study* (3rd ed.). New York: St. Martin's Press.

Ho, M. K. (1987). *Family therapy with ethnic minorities.* Newbury Park, CA: Sage.

Huang, L. J. (1981). The Chinese American family. In C. H. Mindel et al. (Eds.), *Ethnic families in America* (3rd ed.). Englewood Cliffs, NJ: Prentice-Hall.

Hurh, W. M., & Kim, K. C. (1995). Korean immigrants in America. In P. G. Min (Ed.), *Asian Americans: Contemporary trends and issues.* Thousand Oaks, CA: Sage.

Hurh, W. M., & Kim, K. C. (1995). Race relations paradigm and Korean-American research: A sociology of knowledge perspective. Quoted in In P. G. Min (Ed.), *Asian Americans: Contemporary trends and issues.* Thousand Oaks, CA: Sage.

Jensen, J. M. (1988). *Passage from India: Asian Indian immigrants in North America.* New Haven, CT: Yale University Press.

Kitano, H. H. L. (1969). *Japanese-Americans: The evaluation of a subculture.* Englewood Cliffs, NJ: Prentice-Hall.

Leong, F. T. L. (1986). Counseling and psychotherapy with Asian Americans: Review of the literature. *Journal of Counseling Psychology, 33,* 196–206.

Min, P. G. (1995). Korean Americans. In P. G. Min (Ed.), *Asian Americans contemporary trends and issues.* Thousand Oaks, CA: Sage.

Miyamoto, F. (1988). Social solidarity among the Japanese in Seattle. In C. H. Mindel et al. (Eds.), *Ethnic families in America* (3rd ed.). Englewood Cliffs, NJ: Prentice-Hall.

Pido, L. L. L. (1995). The Filipinos in America. In P. G. Min (Ed.), *Asian Americans: Contemporary trends and issues.* Thousand Oaks, CA: Sage.

Sandermeyer, E. C. (1973). *The anti-Chinese movement in California* (2nd ed.). Urbana, IL: University of Illinois Press.

Sollenberger, R. T. (1988). Chinese-American child rearing practices and juvenile delinquency. In C. H. Mindel et al. (Eds.), *Ethnic families in America* (3rd ed.). Englewood Cliffs, NJ: Prentice-Hall.

Sue, D. W., & Sue, D. (1990). *Counseling the culturally different* (2nd ed.). New York: John Wiley and Sons.

Suzuki, B. H. (1994). Higher education issues in the Asian American community. In Justiz et al. (Eds.), *Minorities in higher education.* American Council on Education. Phoenix, AZ: Oryx Press.

Tsukada, M. (1988). Income parity through different paths: Chinese Americans, Japanese Americans and Caucasians in Hawaii. *Amerasia Journal, 14*(2), 47–60.

Watanabe, C. (1973). Self-expression and the Asian-American experience. *Personnel and Guidance Journal, 51,* 390–396.

Wong, M. (1982). The cost of being Chinese, Japanese and Filipino in the United States, 1960, 1970, 1976. *Pacific Sociological Review, 5,* 59–78.

Yanagisako, S. J. (1988). Transforming the past. In C. H. Mindel et al. (Eds.), *Ethnic families in America* (3rd ed.). Englewood Cliffs, NJ: Prentice-Hall.

Suggested Readings

Ayndez-Sanchez, M. (1988). The Puerto Rican American family. In C. H. Mindel et al. (Eds.), *Ethnic families in America* (3rd ed.). Englewood Cliffs, NJ: Prentice-Hall.

Bastida, E. (1979). Family integration and adjustment to aging among Hispanic elders. In C. H. Mindel et al. (Eds.), *Ethnic families in America* (3rd ed.). Englewood Cliffs, NJ: Prentice-Hall.

Bean, F., & Tienda, M. (1988). *The Hispanic population of the United States.* New York: Russell Sage.

Becerra, R. M. (1988). The Mexican American family. In C. H. Mindel et al. (Eds.), *Ethnic families in America* (3rd ed.). Englewood Cliffs, NJ: Prentice-Hall.

Casas, J. M., & Vasquez, M. J. T. (1996). Counseling the Hispanic: A guiding framework for a diverse population. In P. B. Pedersen et al. (Eds.), *Counseling across cultures* (4th ed.). Thousand Oaks, CA: Sage.

Chilman, C. S. (1993). Hispanic families in the United States: Research perspectives In H. P. McAdoo (Ed.), *Family ethnicity* (pp. 141–163). Newbury Park, CA: Sage.

Fitzpatrick, J. P. (1971). *Puerto Rican Americans.* Englewood Cliffs, NJ: Prentice-Hall.

Latino Youth at a Crossroads. (1990). Washington, DC: Children's Defense Fund.

Murrillo, N. (1988). The Mexican American family. In C. H. Mindel et al. (Eds.), *Ethnic families in America* (3rd ed.). Englewood Cliffs, NJ: Prentice-Hall.

Padilla, A. O. (Ed.). (1995). *Hispanic psychology.* Thousand Oaks, CA: Sage.

Pedersen, P. B., Draguns, J. G., Lonner W. J., & Trimble, J. E. (Eds.). (1996). *Communicating across cultures* (4th ed.). Thousand Oaks, CA: Sage.

Rivera, O. A., & Cespedes, R. (1983). Rehabilitation counseling with disabled Hispanics. *Journal of Applied Rehabilitation Counseling, 14*(3), Fall.

Suarez, Z. E. (1993). Cuban Americans: From golden exiles to social undesirables. In H. P. McAdoo (Ed.), *Family ethnicity* (pp. 164–176). Newbury Park, CA: Sage.

Szapocznik, J., & Hernandez, R. (1988). The Cuban-American family: In C. H. Mindel et al. (Eds.), *Ethnic families in America* (pp. 160–172). Englewood Cliffs, NJ: Prentice-Hall.

Chapter 9

HISPANIC/LATINO AMERICANS

Chapter Outline
• Introduction
• Historical Backgrounds
• Social Issues
• Economic Issues
• Employment Issues
• Educational Issues
• Family Dynamics
• Intervention Strategies
• Conclusion

Chapter Objectives
• Identify specific historical events that have impacted the lives of Mexican Americans, Puerto Rican Americans, and Cuban Americans
• Identify the diversity of Hispanic/Latino Americans
• Identify social, educational and economic issues whic impact the lives of Hispanic/Latino Americans

Introduction

Terminology

As America has attempted to better attend to the needs of its ethnic and racial minorities, the federal government has attempted to classify the various groups. In the classification process, descriptive names have been attached. In most instances the groups being labeled have chosen to decide the name to which they feel most comfortable answering. In the case of African Americans, they have moved from colored to Negro to black to African American; likewise for Hispanics, there has been an evolution of names leading to the currently acceptable terminology of Hispanic/Latino. Terms that have been used are Chicano, Spanish-American, Spanish-Surname, Spanish-origin, and Spanish-speaking. Similar to the situation with the appropriate identity for African American, where not all persons of this group like to be called black or African American, there is not unanimity with regard to the most appropriate terminology to use in referring to Hispanic/Latino persons. The use of the terms Spanish-speaking or Spanish-Surname is misleading in that not all Hispanic/Latino persons have their origin as Spanish. This term tends to disregard the influence of Indian and African ancestry. The term Chicano, according to Marilyn and Carlos Molina (1994), "grew out of the ethnic and ideological movements of young political activists during the 1960s and 1970s, particularly in the Southwest." They continue by empha-sizing that these activists used the term Chicano to raise the awareness of the public to the depressed economic and political conditions that existed for persons of Mexican heritage. Since those activist days, the term has come to signify, for some, pride in their Mexican heritage. However, Munoz (1982) informs us that Chicano is used by some Mexican Americans to indicate ra-cial pride and consciousness while it is rejected by others, particularly older Mexican Americans, who consider the term to be an insulting reference.

The author acknowledges that the term Hispanic/Latino is not without limitation in describing this particular population of people. However, Hispanic and Latino currently appear to be the most widely accepted terms to use. Hispanic recognizes the Spanish influence and Latino recognizes the origin of those from the Caribbean and Latin America.

Diversity

Implied in the discussion with regard to terminology is the fact that per-sons of Hispanic/Latino origin are not a homogeneous group. Some of the Hispanic/Latino groups represented in the United States are: Mexican, Puerto Rican, Cuban, Dominican Republic, Costa Rican, Guatemalan, Honduran, Nicaraguan, Salvadoran, and Argentinean to mention a few. In this chapter, the three groups with the largest population, Mexican, Puerto Rican, and Cuban, will be discussed.

Historical Backgrounds

Mexicans

For approximately 200 years, Spain ruled Mexico, and during this period, a considerable portion of the United States, particularly the Southwest and

West (Texas, California, Arizona, and New Mexico) were part of Mexico. During the Spanish colonization of Mexico, missions were established in California, Texas, and Arizona. According to McWilliams (1968), the mission system helped establish the Catholic Church. The intermingling of the Spanish conquistadors, the Mexicans, and the indigenous Indians has created the racial mixture that we currently see among Mexican Americans. Additionally, the influence of African slaves can also be seen.

The Spanish colonization of Mexico ended in 1821 when Mexico achieved independence. Although their independence was gained, they continued to have conflicts with Euro-American settlers who wanted the land north of the Rio Grande River to be part of the United States. Perhaps the best known of these conflicts was when the Mexican General Santa Anna and his troops defeated a small group in a battle at the mission called the Alamo. Later that same year (1836), Sam Houston defeated Santa Anna at the battle of San Jacinto. As a result of this battle, Texas became independent of Mexico and later became part of the United States.

Battles between the U.S. and Mexico continued, culminating in the Mexican-American War, which ended with the Treaty of Guadalupe Hidalgo in which Mexico accepted the Rio Grande River as the Texas border. Additionally, Mexico sold parts of the Southwest and West to the United States. The acquisition of what is known as Texas, California, New Mexico and Arizona meant that a large number of persons of Mexican descent were living in the United States and it is from this foundation that many of the current Mexican American population originated.

Puerto Ricans

Puerto Rico became a territory of the United States as a result of the treaty signed ending the Spanish-American War in 1898. In 1900, the U.S. Congress passed the Foraker Act which gave Puerto Ricans U.S. national status but not citizenship. Seventeen years later Congress passed the Jones Act which granted citizenship to the Puerto Rican people. Because of their territorial status, and in 1917 citizenship status, Puerto Ricans have been able to enter and exit the United States with virtually no restrictions; however, the flow of Puerto Ricans into the United States appears to be tied closely to economic conditions on the Puerto Rican Islands. In other words, many have come to the States in search of a better life.

Cubans

The Spanish influence with regard to Cuba comes as a result of Spain's control of the island for over 300 years. Historians tell us that Spain's rule over Cuba, while in some cases economically beneficial to Cubans, was very domineering. The Spanish government maintained control over the government of Cuba, and made most of the important decisions by placing Spanish officials in most of the key Cuban governmental posts. This type of action on the part of the government of Spain is credited with developing within the Cuban people a mistrust of Colonial-type governments.

Jose Szapocznik and Roberto Hernandez' (1988) comments identify Africans and Chinese as also having a significant influence upon Cuban culture.

> In addition to the Spanish contributions to the formation of the Cuban national character, West Africa had a highly significant role in the molding of Cuban values and attitudes. The labor demands led to the massive importation of African slaves. It has been estimated that approximately one million slaves were transported to Cuba during the island's three and one-half centuries of slave trading. The vast majority, however, arrived during the last 100 years of this period to fulfill the increasing needs of the booming sugar industry. According to a census of Cuba's population conducted in 1846, the total slave population was 660,000 with an additional 220,000 free blacks and mulattoes. The white population, on the other hand, amounted to 565,000. After the decline of the slave trade following the enactment of the Emancipation Law of 1880, the demand for cheap labor was met by the importation of indentured servants from China, the arrival of a few thousand Indians from Mexico's Yucatan Peninsula and the continued Spanish immigration, largely from economically depressed Spain and the Canary Islands. After the blacks, the Chinese came to constitute Cuba's most important ethnic minority in the twentieth century.

The United States acquired Cuba after the Spanish-American War and occupied the country until 1902. Even after Cuba gained independence from the United States, the two countries maintained a close relationship until the Castro-led Cuban revolution took control of the government in 1959.

The immigration of Cubans to the United States has been in waves. McCoy and Gonzales (1985) inform us that the first wave came in the early 1900s resulting in approximately 79,000 Cubans of various economic and social backgrounds settling in the United States, with the majority locating in Florida. The second wave consisted of persons seeking exile from the Castro government. It is estimated that by 1973, there were 273,000 Cubans, primarily from the business and professional class, involved in this exodus. An estimate of 118,000 Cubans was part of the third wave of Cuban immigrants, many of whom left the island by boat. The majority of this group is considered unskilled. There continue to be groups of persons from Cuba seeking a home in the United States, most arrive in Florida having come on small and sometimes overcrowded boats. In working with persons who have come to the U.S. from Cuba, it is important to recognize the effect of arriving in waves or "wave effect." To be more precise, with regard to the first wave, those who are still alive obviously are elderly; however, a helping professional would be working with second, third, and fourth generations of descendants of those immigrants, thus various levels of acculturation come into play. There will be more discussion of this in the intervention strategies section of this chapter. An important matter to note with respect to the second wave is that these Cuban immigrants were generally well educated, had been high in the Cuban social society, had significant contacts within the United States, and probably had reasonable economic resources, certainly more than any of the wave of immigrants that were to come after them. The third and subsequent waves have consisted of the economically, educationally, and socially poorer groups. There have been contentions that some persons in these groups have been those who have mental disabilities and/or are criminals. In attaching labels to this group, one should remember that in a dictatorial government such as the Castro regime, mental disability and criminal status for some may be applied for reasons that are different than why the U.S. would make similar labels.

Demographics

According to Pew Research in 2011 there was 51.9 million Hispanic's living in the United States, giving them 17 percent of the United States population. A further breakdown of this population is 64% native born (American) and 36% foreign born. Additional demographic information of interest to helping professionals is that the Hispanic/Latino ethnic group is younger than the Euro-American group. Furthermore, the Hispanic/Latino group, in the 2000 U.S. Census, surpassed African Americans as the most populated ethnic/racial minority group in America. From a technical standpoint, Hispanic/Latino is not a racial minority; they are an ethnic minority group, since Hispanic/Latino persons can be of any racial background. This fact is simply a technicality and should not detract from the fact that they are a large minority group and will continue, in the twenty-first century, to increase in numbers.

Mexican Americans

As previously stated, Mexican Americans and persons of Mexican descent comprise the largest population of Hispanic/Latino's. The majority of the Mexican American population lives in California, Texas, Arizona, and New Mexico.

Puerto Rican Americans

Puerto Ricans are the second largest population of Hispanic/Latino in the United States. The majority of the population lives in New York with significant numbers in Illinois and New Jersey.

Cuban Americans

Of the three major Hispanic/Latino subgroups, Cubans have the smallest population. Florida's Cuban population is by far the largest in the United States with the states of New Jersey, New York, and California also having significant populations of Cubans.

Social Issues

Poverty and Discrimination

With the exception of Cubans, the migration of Hispanic/Latinos to the United States has been an ebb and flow conditioned by the United States' need for cheap labor. For decades, Mexicans have been welcomed and encouraged to come to the states to help meet the labor demands of the country, only to find that they were equally unwelcome when the demand for their labor diminished. Similarly, Puerto Ricans have been attracted to the United States to meet some of the labor needs, especially in times when the Puerto Rican economy has had problems providing work for its willing population. Thus, poverty and discrimination have been major social problems, at least for Mexicans and Puerto Ricans. According to the United States Commission on Civil Rights, "Both Mexicans and Puerto Ricans have been victims of economic and social discrimination and prejudice; it appears that Puerto Ricans have suffered even more intensely than any other group."

With regard to Cubans, since much of their entry into the United States has been in waves, there are considerable economic and social differences among the United States' Cuban population. The group of Cuban immigrants who came to America fleeing the Castro government was more affluent and well educated; therefore, they experienced fewer problems integrating into Euro-American society. Experiencing less discrimination and prejudice than many of the groups to follow has meant their social plight has been less traumatic.

As previously stated Hispanic/Latino is not a racial group but an ethnic group. In fact, their composition as a group of people consists of members from all racial groups, thus their skin pigmentation ranges from white to black. Consequently, some human rights observers indicate that in America, the darker the skin pigmentation of a Hispanic/Latino, the more he/she is subject to experience various kinds of discrimination.

The proximity of the Mexican/American border makes for relatively easy access to the United States, resulting in considerable friction between Mexicans who have wanted to enter the United States seeking increased opportunities for themselves and their families and the United States government. A variety of opinions among United States citizens exist with regard to the entry of undocumented Mexicans. Some feel that they are in the U.S. illegally taking jobs and resources that should be reserved for U.S. citizens and others believe the U.S. should be compassionate and offer opportunities to those seeking to improve their lives. Of considerable concern to social and health care workers is the access, or in some cases lack thereof, of health and welfare services. It appears that the debate will continue well into the twenty-first century as to how much and what type of services can be provided to non-U.S. citizens; however, one important aspect with regard to disability was settled as it has been determined that non-U.S. citizens are protected by the Americans with Disabilities Act (ADA) from discrimination based on their status as a person with a disability. As of the date of this writing the United States Congress is debating legislation with regard to immigration which will impact immigration for Mexicans. Also as of this writing the exact wording of the legislation is not known, nor whether the legislation will be passed by congress and enacted into law.

Language Barriers

A major contributing factor to the high rate of poverty among some Hispanic/Latino groups and the prejudice and various forms of discrimination they experience is based upon communication barriers. The inability on the part of some Hispanic/Latinos to speak English and/or communicate effectively in English tends to cause them to become isolated in groups of persons who have similar limitations. Being unable to effectively communicate in the language of the dominant culture makes them easy targets for both discrimination and exploitation. To be more specific, they can easily be placed into unsafe work conditions, underpaid and overworked, as well as being forced to live in unsafe and unhealthy living environments.

The limited English communication skills, along with being undocumented creates problems of accessing and maintaining good health. More discussion with regard to this will occur in health issues.

Teen Pregnancy

Teenagers between the ages of 15 to 19 account for a high rate of Hispanic/Latino births. While this rate is not as high as African Americans, it does, however, represent a high rate of teenage pregnancies. Based upon a National Center for Health Statistics report, among the Hispanic/Latino subgroups, Mexicans are the highest followed by Puerto Ricans, and Cubans have the lowest rate, of the three Hispanic/Latino groups.

HIV/AIDS

It is impossible to separate HIV/AIDS into either a social or health issue; it is in fact, both. It is a social issue because the sexual taboos about homosexuality and the barriers to communicating about sex between men and women thwart prevention efforts in Latino communities (Amaro, 1988). It is a health issue because Hispanic/Latinos are twice more likely to be affected by HIV than the general population.

Economic Issues

In 1982, Carillo made the observation that Hispanic/Latinos are overrepresented among the poor and he further observed that there is a significant discrepancy between the annual incomes of Hispanic/Latino and Euro-Americans; this observation remain true today. As Carlos and Marilyn Molina (1994) remind us, there is a danger in clustering all of the subgroups of Hispanic/Latinos into one category and with regard to review of economic conditions; the problem is that the overall or median family income for all Hispanic/Latino groups mask the depressed economic status of Puerto Ricans. Relatedly, it also does not adequately represent the higher level of family income representing the Cuban population.

The point to be made for the purpose of helping professionals, when evaluating the economic condition of Hispanic/Latinos is to pay closer attention to the subgroup, rather than relying totally on the overall Hispanic/Latino group statistics.

Employment Issues

Whether one is employed and, if employed, the type of employment help determine one's earning potential which, in turn, has an impact upon one's socioeconomic status. Some of the reasons for the high rate of poverty among some Hispanic/Latinos are, as the Molinas' describe, low wages, under education, increasing numbers of single heads of households, discrimination, and inadequate national attention being given to the socioeconomic conditions of Hispanic/Latinos.

Consistently, the unemployment rate for Hispanic/Latinos has been at least double the national unemployment rate. In 1980 the unemployment rate for Hispanic/Latinos was 10 percent, while it was 5 percent for non-Hispanic/Latinos. According to the Children's Defense Fund (1990) in 1987, more than one-fourth of all Hispanic/Latino families earned incomes below the poverty level as compared to less than 10 percent of all non-Hispanic/Latino families, and Hispanic/Latinos in the work force were 50 percent more likely to be unemployed than non-Hispanic/Latinos. This trend has continued into the first quarter of the twenty-first century. As indicated, some reasons for the type and rate of employment can be attributed to discrimination; however, a portion has to be related to level of educational attainment.

Educational Issues

Although dated, perhaps the American Council on Education (1994) continue to adequately summarizes the educational situation of many Hispanic/Latino youth with the following: "School statistics indicate that almost half of the Hispanic students drop out of high school, and those who do graduate are not prepared for higher education." Other researchers, such as Johnson (1994), Orum (1986), and Howe (1987), have tended to support the American Council's summarization. Dropping out of school too frequently mobilizes events that have lifelong consequences, such as inability to secure gainful employment, low self-esteem, marital discord, and underemployment or unemployment.

Valencia (1989) lists several possible reasons for the poor academic success of some Hispanic/Latinos and the following are a select few: (1) racial and ethnic segregation in the schools, (2) language and cultural bias in school practices, (3) poor or low quality student-teacher interaction, (4) special education practices, and (5) absence of Hispanics in the teaching force.

Family Dynamics

Historical Perspective of Hispanic/Latino Families

Melba Sanchez-Ayendez's (1988) following remarks alert us to be cautious in attempting to describe a typical ethnic minority family such as Puerto Ricans: "In speaking of the traditional Puerto Rican family, one must realize that cultural traits are subject to variation by socioeconomic status, area of residence and even racial or age group." She continues by asserting, "the notion of a traditional family is mostly an idealized version, although one that allows for a starting point from which to make comparisons." This is very good advice and, with this admonition in mind, a discussion of Hispanic/Latino families will occur. In an attempt to avoid overgeneralization, the three major subgroups (Puerto Rican, Cuban American, and Mexican American) will be discussed separately.

Similar to American Indians, many people think of Hispanic/Latinos as a homogeneous group and, as already discussed, the ethnic groups of which Hispanic/Latinos are comprised are varied, some having similar cultural traits, but in most instances, there are considerable cultural differences among the various groups as well as significant differences within groups.

Historically, when describing Hispanic/Latino families, various authors have lumped all of the subgroups into one category and promoted stereotypical attributes as representing the composition of a typical or traditional Hispanic/Latino family. To be more specific, Hispanic/Latino families have been described as (1) male dominated, (2) extended family-oriented, (3) strictly adhered to old-world age and sex roles, (4) and the wife as a submissive partner. While certain aspects of these stereotypes exist within some families, however, by no standards are these the universal family structure of all Hispanic/Latino families. By reviewing the three major subgroups, a more realistic view of Hispanic/Latino families will come into focus.

Mexican Americans

The previously mentioned stereotypes of the Hispanic/Latino family is perhaps attached to the Mexican American family at least as much, if not more, than any of the other subgroups. Rosina Becerra (1988) believes these stereotypes have a foundation in facts. According to Becerra, the structure of the male being dominant, family protector and the female as the child-rearer and nurturer began as Mexicans lived in rural and isolated areas. Consequently, when the father was away, the elder son was expected to provide protection for the family. Relatedly, if the mother was absent, the elder female was responsible for overseeing the children as well as providing the cooking and cleaning aspect of family life. Thus, the stereotypical Hispanic/Latino family structure began as a method of survival.

FATHER ROLE. While the concept of machismo or complete male dominance is no longer the standard for many Mexican American males, they have, however, maintained their role as head of the household providing guidance and protection for the family. The point is that the dominating male who rules with an iron fist without regard to the feelings and needs of his wife and children is not accurate. Respect is a valued concept among Mexican Americans and within the family structure, it is a "two-way street." The male expects respect from his wife and children; likewise, he is expected to give proper respect to the feelings and needs of his family. Since approximately 80 percent of Mexican Americans live in urban areas, they have considerable contact with mainstream American life; therefore, they are influenced by the dominant culture's views. One of the influences is the expanding role of the female which requires that the male share family nurturing responsibilities with the female.

MOTHER ROLE. The idea of the Mexican American female as a totally submissive individual, accepting the husband's dominance, is as inaccurate as many of the other stereotypes already discussed. In the past, the female's role may have been submissive; however, today, her role within the family has evolved to the point she is able to express herself as an equal, especially since a significant number of Hispanic/Latino mothers are in the work force providing their earnings as part of the family's economy.

FAMILY-ORIENTED. The Mexican American family, according to Murrillo (1971) offers emotional support and security to its members. The extended family concept is a major component of Mexican American family life. Extended family members provide valuable services such as financial support, babysitting, personal advice, and health care as well as emotional support. In summary, the extended family exists as an effective means of survival.

Today's Mexican American families, generally speaking, are larger than the other Hispanic/Latino subgroups. An important fact to remember is that members of large families are often supported by small incomes. Perhaps Becerra (1988) summarizes the modern Mexican American family best with these remarks:

Today's modern Mexican American family can be characterized as having a disproportionate percentage of members in low socioeconomic status. They have lower incomes that support larger families. In part, these lower incomes are a result of higher levels of unemployment and lower paying jobs, which are partially explained by low educational attainment, which in turn creates a high proportion of family poverty.

Despite the adversity, some Mexican American families encounter the strong kinship bonds which serve as a powerful force in helping the family overcome the adversities. This is a point to be remembered by helping professionals.

Cuban Americans

According to Jose Szapocznik and Roberto Hernandez (1988), Cuban families are examples of Hispanic/Latino families who have deviated from the stereotypical extended family concept often ascribed to minority families. They contend that Cuban families have in recent years moved more toward a nuclear family orientation; they further point out that this transition did not occur only after Cubans had migrated to the United States, but began before many of them left Cuba in the 1959 exodus.

HUSBAND AND WIFE RELATIONS. Continuing to use the works of Szapocznik as a reference to the evolving Cuban family structure, he convincingly argues that as Cuban women entered the labor market in America and their earnings became essential to the household budget, they began to gain an increasingly stronger voice in the family affairs. As a result of the women exercising their rights within the home, the traditionally patriarchal family structure changed. Similar to Mexican Americans, the male dominance has decreased where there is more sharing of responsibilities and decision-making. Consequently, the young Cuban American families of which are usually comprised of a husband and wife team which grew up in the United States, thus have fewer problems with the equality of males and females than perhaps their parents and grandparents.

Bicultural. The Cuban American families of this part of the twenty-first century are primarily bicultural, bicultural in the sense of being capable of adapting and successfully functioning within the dominant culture values of the United States as well as adhere to old country values. In older Cuban American families, bicultural adaptation occurs as the parents maintain Cuban mainland customs and values while the children who were born in the United States grow up interacting with the U.S. dominant cultural values. The ability of parents and children to successfully adjust to each other's viewpoints to a large degree determines how well the family functions as a unit. In most cases, these families become very skillful at communicating and negotiating in different cultural contexts which helps them to adjust to the larger American society.

Puerto Rican Americans

FAMILY STRUCTURE. A modified version of the extended family exists in many Puerto Rican families, according to Mintz (1966), Bonilla (1958), Steward (1956), and Safa (1974). In this setting, the child-rearing responsibility is primarily the responsibility of the nuclear family. Even so, extended family members play an important role in many aspects of family life, particularly providing emotional support, personal advice and if needed, financial support. Bastida (1979) describes the relationship as interdependence which views the individual as being unable to do everything or do everything well and, therefore, in need of other's assistance.

Intervention

Acculturation

As illustrated in the beginning of this chapter, Hispanic/Latino Americans are among the most diverse group of people in the United States. With regard to acculturation, J. Manuel Casas and Melba Vasquez (1996) correctly emphasize that "individual Hispanics can be found at different levels of the acculturation process." The social issues section of this chapter sheds light on this point as the fact was discussed that some Cubans have had fewer problems adjusting to American life than Puerto Ricans and Mexicans because of the educational and economic resources they possessed when they enter the country. Even so, today the acculturation level of individual Cuban Americans varies considerably when one considers that most of the latest Cuban immigrants do not have the same educational and economic background as the earlier immigrants. Similarly, within groups, differences occur in the Mexican American and other Hispanic/Latino American populations; however, in this case, acculturation variations generally revolve around educational level and one's abilities or lack thereof to speak English. Additionally, Casas and Vasquez (1996) inform us that proximity or availability of inexpensive means of travel to the native homeland also influences level of acculturation. To be more specific, the easier it is for a person to keep in touch, especially physically involved with his native culture, the greater the chances he will maintain significant parts of his native culture. This, however, does not mean that the person will not take on significant portions of the dominant culture. It may mean the rate of acquiring the dominant culture traits will be slower (utilization of English, for example) and that the person will attempt to live in two cultural worlds. These are important facts that the helping professional would be wise to consider as she attempts to assess the acculturation level of Hispanic/Latino American clients.

Returning to the sage advice of J. Manuel Casas and Melba Vasquez, these comments proved somewhat of a capstone on thinking with respect to reason why assessing levels of acculturation of Hispanic/Latino Americans is important for the success of helping plans. There is no way to understand and counsel a Hispanic client, or any client, without assessing cultural factors as well as the individual's experience of oppression.

- A Hispanic individual's culture, history, and experience with oppression cause variations in human behavior.
- As with all clients, counselors and other helping professionals must develop the ability to see individual Hispanic clients as products of their unique life experiences and maintain a valid and realistic perspective on the differences between the helper's and the client's cultural environments and the learning and conditioning that result from the cultural contexts.
- Acculturation is a major contributor to the dynamic, ever-changing aspect of the Hispanic population. The rate is faster for the younger generation and among Hispanics at the lower end of the socioeconomic spectrum; men who work outside the home acculturate more quickly than women who may find themselves working solely within the home.

Final comments with regard to assessment of levels of acculturation relate to the fact that the helping professional should as Olmedo (1979) remind us be aware of three major dimensions: (1) language, (2) socioeconomic status, and (3) culture-specific attitudes and value orientation. These factors can serve as a guide for the professional helper to begin her assessment.

Communication Style

Similar to Asian and Pacific Americans, Hispanic/Latino Americans' communication styles are a two-prong issue. One relates to style, verbal or nonverbal, quiet or aggressive in the approach to communicating and the second prong is type, English, non-English or bilingual.

With regard to the first prong style, the helping professional should not automatically interpret silence, or slowness to speak, as a sign of lack of intelligence, lack of understanding and/or lack of interest. Often silence denotes respect; respect shown to family, elders, and persons of authority is highly regarded. Being polite, letting others such as the helping professional speak before one begins to speak is a trait that is emphasized in many Hispanic/Latino families. This may be an unfamiliar communication style for a helping professional who is accustomed to the aggressive, get-your-point-in-first Euro-American style.

When a helping professional encounters a person who has a conservative communication style, rather than make the previously mentioned assumptions, he perhaps will obtain better results by asking questions. Rather than have gaps in needed information and classifying the client as uncooperative, simply be direct and attempt to obtain the needed information by asking the appropriate questions. In some cases, the questions may also go unanswered and often this is the result of the second prong of the communication fork that is language. The Hispanic/Latino person may not understand English well enough to respond and/or may not speak English well enough to adequately explain himself. This type situation may be best solved by either referring the client to someone who speaks his language or having an interpreter assist.

Orlando Rivera and Rosonito Cespedes (1983) astutely point out that in the helping setting language and cultural barriers present a particular problem with regard to psychological testing. If the helper is not sensitive to the level of English spoken and comprehension, having a Hispanic/Latino client take a test in English will in all probability provide inaccurate results and generally the errors of the results are to the detriment of the client. In most helping settings, many psychological and other tests are available in other languages such as Spanish; therefore, this problem will not occur if the helper is sensitive to the client's needs. Rivera and Cespedes point out that professional helpers' sensitivity is needed in understanding cultural impact of psychological tests. They emphasize that the Hispanic client, particularly male clients, may not see the relevance of the test and tests that require manipulation of objects such as blocks may be viewed as child's play. To avoid this situation, the helping professional must take the appropriate time to explain the relevance of the test and for what purpose the results will be used.

Expectations

Whenever there are communication differences between the helper and client, there are the increased chances of misunderstanding. Certainly no more important and potentially devastating misunderstanding can occur than in the area of the helping professions such as physical, psychological and physical rehabilitation when there is a difference in expectations of the rehabilitation plan and process. Clearly stated goals and objectives provided both verbally and in print are essential. The use of an interpreter and/or referring the client to someone with whom he is better able to communicate may be necessary.

In most cases, plans will have input from the client and perhaps significant others, thus dependent upon the degree of involvement of the client and/or his significant others will help determine his understanding of expectations. The more the client is involved, the less likely there are gaps between the client and helper's expectations. Conversely, less involvement increases the probability of incongruence in expectations. If there are concerns with regard to the lack of congruence in expectations, the helper can ask the client to explain what he expects to happen in the helping process and what the expected results from the process are. In questioning the client, the helping professional must phrase the questions in nonthreatening terms and tones as well as making sure they cannot be interpreted as questioning the client's intelligence.

Value Orientation

Orlando Rivera and Rosonito Cespedes (1983) list dignity, respect, personalism, a person's word (LaPalabra), and folk medicine as important values held by many persons of Hispanic/Latino backgrounds, of which helping professionals should be familiar.

Dignity, according to professors Rivera and Cespedes, is central to the person's self-respect; it must be guarded, honored, and cannot be compromised. The person not only expects to be able to maintain his dignity in situations but also he feels he must respect the other person's sense of dignity. A very important point is made by the professors that helping professionals must take into consideration when working with Hispanic/Latino persons, the helping professional cannot expect the client to ask for, beg, or seek services at the expense of his dignity.

Respect is accorded to everyone, elders, adults, children, as well as strangers. As previously stated, the dignity of others is honored. The lesson for helping professions is Hispanic/Latino American clients and/or significant others may refuse to answer sensitive questions, especially regarding someone else if the client and/or significant other feel the response will be disrespectful of others.

Personalism refers to the fact that many Hispanic/Latino persons prefer to work with agencies or organizations with which they are familiar. Likewise, they may be more comfortable working with someone with whom they are familiar. It is unrealistic to think that the helping professional is going to know every Hispanic/Latino person within his service area; however, familiarity does not always mean personal acquaintance. Familiarity can also mean reputation. By becoming acquainted with services, agencies, and organizations that have positive interaction with Hispanic/Latino individuals, the helping professional will establish a reputation of being a caring and trustworthy individual.

Rivera and Cespedes emphasize that many Hispanic/Latino persons do not negotiate with written contracts but through verbal contracts. In other words, their words are their bond. What a helping professional should gain from this is without carefully explaining the "why's" and "what for's," many of the written documents that the client is asked to read and sign may be viewed by the client as a lack of trust.

With regard to health issues the helping professional, when preparing to refer the client for medical evaluation should be aware that some Hispanic/ Latino persons prefer folk medicine. This does not mean that the client should be sent to the person who assists with folk medicine for an evaluation; however, it does mean the helping professional must be sensitive to the client's understanding of and involvement with modern medicine and the health care system. In other words, the process will not be as simple as referring the client to a physician. Persons whom the client trusts may need to be asked to help with conveying the need for the referral and resulting information.

With regard to the helping professions, J. Manuel Casas and Melba Vasquez (1996) offer the following advice in working with Hispanic/Latino American clients:

> Depending on level of acculturation, Hispanics often display a great concern for immediacy and the "here and now"; frequently attribute control to an external locus (causality replaced by luck, supernatural powers, and acts of God); favor an extended family support system (rather than a basic adherence to the nuclear family); often take a concrete, tangible approach to life (rather than an abstract, long-term outlook) may practice a unilateral communication pattern with authority figures that uses avoidance of eye contact, deference, and silence as signs of respect (as opposed to more self-assertive patterns); and may develop multilingual communication skills, using English, Spanish and "Spanglish" a hybrid of the two.

They conclude their comments with the following admonishment: "counselors must be aware of these culturally dictated traits just as they must avoid broad, all-encompassing generalizations." This is good advice that all helping professionals should use as part of their helping techniques.

Situational Control

To refresh, situational control refers to what influences, or exert control over the person's life. Previously, a reference was made to Casas and Vasquez' point that many Hispanic/Latino individuals attribute external controls such as luck, supernatural power, acts of God and family as having significant influences on their lives. The relevance of this information to the helping professional is that she may need to include family members, clergy, and even faith healers in the helping process. This may require the counselor/helper to rethink and adapt her theoretical approach to working with clients. However, if it aids the process and helps the client, the success will have justified the effort.

Conclusion

Helping professionals must consider that even though Mexican Americans, Puerto Rican Americans, and Cuban Americans are classified as Hispanic/Latino, they come from very different backgrounds. In many instances the Spanish language may be the only link. In some parts of the United States, Mexicans and Mexican Americans face considerable discrimination and have been relegated to low-paying, dead-end jobs. In contrast, many Cuban Americans, especially those who came to the United States prior to 1959, were well educated, economically secure, and politically connected. Therefore, they have experienced less discrimination and have done better in employment and educational areas than either Mexican Americans or Puerto Rican Americans.

Helping professionals must consider the length of time the Hispanic/Latino persons have been residing in the United States and their level of acculturation. Additionally, language may be of concern in that English may be a second language for many Hispanic/Latino clients.

Finally, in working with some Hispanic/Latino clients, the helping professional may be well advised to explore the client's environment by visiting his/her community and talking with significant persons in the community. By doing so, he establishes his desire to be helpful as well as obtaining a better understanding of the client's culture.

Review Questions

1. Of the three major Hispanic/Latino American groups, Cuban, Puerto Rican, and Mexican, which has the highest poverty rate and which has the lowest poverty rate?
2. Identify five reasons for poor academic success of some Hispanic/Latino Americans

Suggested Activities

1. Determine the number and/or percentage of Hispanic/Latino Americans living in your state.
2. Conduct an informal interview of at least ten (10) Hispanic/Latino persons to determine which name they prefer–Hispanic, Latino, Spanish American, etc.
3. Make a list of five agencies and/or organizations in your state that specialize in working with Hispanic/Latino persons. Summarize the services provided.

References

Ayndez-Sanchez, M. (1988). The Puerto Rican American family. In C. H. Mindel et al. (Eds.), *Ethnic families in America* (3rd ed.). Englewood Cliffs, NJ: Prentice-Hall.

Bastida, E. (1979). Family integration and adjustment to aging among Hispanic elders. In C. H. Mindel et al. (Eds.), *Ethnic families in America* (3rd ed.). Englewood Cliffs, NJ: Prentice-Hall.

Becerra, R. M. (1988). The Mexican American family. In C. H. Mindel et al. (Eds.), *Ethnic families in America* (3rd ed.). Englewood Cliffs, NJ: Prentice-Hall.

Children's Defense Fund. (1990). *Latino youth at a crossroads.* Washington, DC: Adolescent Pregnancy Prevention Clearinghouse, January/March.

McCoy, C. B., & Gonzales, D. H. (1994). Cuban immigration and immigrants in Florida and the United States. Quoted in *Latino health in the U.S.: A growing challenge.* Washington, DC: American Public Health Association.

McWilliams, C. (1968). *North from Mexico.* New York: Greenwood Press.

Munoz, R. F. (1990). The Spanish-speaking consumer and the community mental health center. In D. W. Sue & D. Sue (Eds.), *Counseling the culturally different.* New York: John Wiley and Sons.

Murrillo, N. (1988). The Mexican American family. In C. H. Mindel et al. (Eds.), *Ethnic families in America* (3rd ed.). Englewood Cliffs, NJ: Prentice-Hall.

Olmedo, E. L. (1996). Acculturation: A psychometric perspective. In P. B. Pedersen et al. (Eds.), *Counseling across cultures* (4th ed.). Thousand Oaks, CA: Sage.

Szapocznik, J., & Hernandez, R. (1988). The Cuban American family. In C. H. Mindel et al. (Eds.), *Ethnic families in America.* Englewood Cliffs, NJ: Prentice-Hall.

Valencia, R. R. (1994). For whom does the school bell toll? Chicano school failure and success: Research and policy agenda for the 1990s. In Justiz, M. J. et al. (Eds.), *Minorities in higher education.* Phoenix: American Council on Education.

Suggested Readings

Bean, F., & Tienda, M. (1988). *The Hispanic population of the United States.* New York: Russell Sage.

Becerra, R. M. (1988). The Mexican-American family. In C. H. Mindel et al. (Eds.), *Ethnic families in America* (pp. 141-159). Englewood Cliffs, NJ: Prentice-Hall.

Carillo, C. (1982). Changing norms of Hispanic families. In E. E. Jones & S. J. Korchin (Eds.), *Minority mental health.* New York: Praeger.

Casas, J. M., & Vasquez, M. J. T. (1996). Counseling the Hispanic: A guiding framework for a diverse population. In P. B. Pedersen et al. (Eds.), *Counseling across cultures* (4th ed.). Thousand Oaks, CA: Sage.

Chilman, C. S. (1993). Hispanic families in the United States: Research perspectives In H. P. McAdoo (Ed.), *Family ethnicity* (pp. 141-163). Newbury Park, CA: Sage.

Fitzpatrick, J. P. (1971). *Puerto Rican Americans.* Englewood Cliffs, NJ: Prentice-Hall.

Latino Youth at a Crossroads. (1990). Washington, DC: Children's Defense Fund.

Giachello, A. L. M. (1994). Issues of access and use. In M. Molina & C. Molina (Eds.), *Latino health in the U.S.: A growing challenge.* Washington DC: American Public Health Association.

Marin, G., Marin, B. V., Pérez-Stable, E. J., Sabogal, F., & Sabogal-Otero, R. (1995). Cultural differences in attitudes and expectancies between Hispanic and Non-Hispanic white smokers. In A. M. Padilla (Ed.), *Hispanic psychology: Critical issues in theory and research.* Thousand Oaks, CA: Sage.

McWilliams, C. (1968). North from Mexico. New York: Greenwood Press.

Molina-Aguirre, M., & Molina, C. (1994). Latino populations: Who are they? In M. Molina & C. Molina (Eds.), *Latino health in the U.S.: A growing challenge.*

Munoz, R. F. (1990). The Spanish-speaking consumer and the community mental health center. In D. W. Sue & D. Sue (Eds.), *Counseling the culturally different.* New York: John Wiley and Sons.

Murrillo, N. (1988). The Mexican American family. In C. H. Mindel et al. (Eds.), *Ethnic families in America* (3rd ed.). Englewood Cliffs, NJ: Prentice-Hall.

National Center for Health Statistics. (1994). In M. Molina & C. Molina (Eds.), *Latino health in the U.S.: A growing challenge.* Washington DC: American Public Health Association.

Olmedo, E. L. (1996). Acculturation: A psychometric perspective. In P. B. Pedersen et al. (Eds.), *Counseling across cultures* (4th ed.). Thousand Oaks, CA: Sage.

Padilla, A. O. (Ed.). (1995). *Hispanic psychology.* Thousand Oaks, CA: Sage.

Pedersen et al. (Eds.), *Counseling across cultures* (4th ed.). Thousand Oaks, CA: Sage.

Pedersen, P. B., Draguns, J. G., Lonner W. J., & Trimble, J. E. (Eds.). (1996). *Communicating across cultures* (4th ed.). Thousand Oaks, CA: Sage.

Rivera, O. A., & Cespedes, R. (1983). Rehabilitation counseling with disabled Hispanics. *Journal of Applied Rehabilitation Counseling, 14*(3), Fall.

Suarez, Z. E. (1993). Cuban Americans: From golden exiles to social undesirables. In H. P. McAdoo (Ed.), *Family ethnicity* (pp. 164-176). Newbury Park, CA: Sage.

Szapocznik, J., & Hernandez, R. (1988). The Cuban-American family. In C. H. Mindel et al. (Eds.), *Ethnic families in America* (pp. 160–172). Englewood Cliffs, NJ: Prentice-Hall.

Chapter 10

WOMEN

Chapter Outline

Chapter Objectives
• To identify some of the ways in which women are discriminated
• To identify the prevalence of disabilities among women with disabilities
• To identify some of the impacts a disability has on women

Introduction

Women since recorded history, and undoubtedly before, have made considerable contribution to the societies in which they were inhabitants; however, the manners in which they have been treated often have left the impression that they were second class human beings or stated in other terms lesser than males. The truth is women's contributions at least equaled males' contributions to society and given the roles society has bestowed upon them often exceeded males' contributions. Stated in other terms, given the roles of child rearing and providing various supports to males, to mention only two, in this author's opinion women's contribution to the development of various societies has been exceptional.

Despite the roles some women have experienced they have accomplished much. These accomplishments often have not come easily; as an example we will take a look at a major struggle women in the United States of America has experienced, namely Women's Rights Movements.

Women's Rights Movements

Right to Vote

This author views women's rights movements in the United States, as of relatively recent history, containing two major events. The first being acquisition of the right to vote. The second major women's rights movement event is the unresolved Equal Rights Amendment to the United States Constitution.

The demand of women's right to vote in the United States drew significant strength from the abolitionist's anti-slavery movement. Both of these social movements had the goal of promoting the expansion of liberty and equality to all humans in the United States. To accomplish their goal a group of women led by Elizabeth Cady Stanton and Lucretia Mott formed a Women's Right's Convention and on July 19, 1848 held their first convention in Seneca Falls New York, in attendance was Susan B. Anthony who was a dedicated and strong supporter of women's rights. Crucial to the development of the convention were the following families: Mott, Wright, Stanton, M'Clintock and Hunt all of which were active in the abolitionist movement. Jessica Houston (2013) informs us that at this historic convention Elizabeth Cady Stanton drafted and presented to the participants a Declaration of Sentiments. This declaration was based upon the United States' Declaration of Independence and among other issues the declaration demanded that women be given the right to vote. The declaration was signed by 68 women and 32 men. The following is the Declaration of Sentiments.

> When in the course of human events, it becomes necessary for one portion of the family of man to assume among the people of the earth a position different from that which they have hitherto occupied, but one to which the laws of nature and of nature's God entitle them, a decent respect to the opinions of mankind requires that they should declare the causes that impel them to such a course.

> We hold these truths to be self-evident: that all men and women are created equal; that they are endowed by their Creator with certain inalienable rights; that among these are life, liberty, and the pursuit of happiness; that to secure these rights governments are instituted, deriving their just powers from the

consent of the governed. Whenever any form of government becomes destructive of these ends, it is the right of those who suffer from it to refuse allegiance to it, and to insist upon the institution of a new government, laying its foundation on such principles, and organizing its powers in such form, as to them shall seem most likely to effect their safety and happiness.

Prudence, indeed, will dictate that governments long established should not be changed for light and transient causes; and accordingly all experience have shown that mankind are more disposed to suffer, while evils are accustomed. But when a long train of abuses and usurpations, pursuing invariably the same object, evinces a design to reduce them under absolute despotism, it is their duty to throw off such government, and to provide new guards for their future security. Such has been the patient sufferance of the women under this government, and such is now the necessity which constrains them to demand the equal station to which they are entitled.

The Declaration continues with a list of how the American male dominated society basically enslaved women. (Only a portion is listed here).

The history of mankind is a history of repeated injuries and usurpations on the part of man toward woman, having in direct object the establishment of an absolute tyranny over her. To prove this let facts be submitted to a candid world.
He has never permitted her to exercise her inalienable right to the elective franchise.
He has compelled her to submit to laws, in the formation of which she had no voice.
He has withheld from her rights which are given to the most ignorant and degraded men–both natives and foreigners.
Having deprived her of this first right of a citizen, the elective franchise, thereby leaving without representation in the halls of legislation, he has oppressed her on all sides.
He has made her, if married, in the eye of the law, civilly dead.
He has taken from her all right in property, even to the wages she earns.
(Extracted from Rothenberg, P. S., 995)

As indicated from the portion of the Declaration of Sentiments during the early years of the United States women's rights were determined by males and whatever legal rights they had were associated to males primarily if they were married the rights were derived from being the spouse of a male. Stated in other terms, women had only a few, if any, legal rights that were not associated with being the spouse and/or dependent of a male person. In an attempt to bring this injustice to the attention to the United States Congress Elizabeth Cady Stanton, in 1892, addressed two United States congressional committees and presented what has been called "Solitude of Self" presentation. In this presentation Ms. Stanton advocated for women being legally treated as independent individuals, not as dependent to their spouses.

Ms. Stanton died in 1902 without realizing her and other's dream of voting rights for women being accomplished; there is no question that her efforts along with the efforts of other women and some men led to the passage of the 19th. Amendment to the United States Constitution and became effective in 1920. While the 19th. Amendment gave women the right to vote in national election, the fact should be noted that several states or territories such as Wyoming in 1893 gave women the right to vote in territorial or state elections. Also others such as Colorado, Utah, Idaho, Washington State, California, Oregon, Kansas, Arizona, Alaska, Illinois, Montana, Nevada, New York, Michigan, South Dakota, and Oklahoma provided voting rights to women prior to 1920. These allowed women to vote in state or territorial elections and in some instances in federal elections.

Equal Rights Effort

The Equal Rights Amendment was written in 1923 by Alice Paul. Ms. Paul was a very well educated Quaker woman with doctoral degrees in both the Arts and Sciences and Law. She was considered by some to be a feminist, suffragist and political strategist and her work which became the initial version of the Equal Rights Amendment occurred in 1923, three years after the passage by the United States Congress of the 19th. Amendment to the United States Constitution giving women the right to vote. The Amendment was debated by the United States Congress until its passage by both houses of the Congress in 1972; however to become law the bill had to be ratified by three-fourth of the States. There was a time limit for state ratification which expired and Congress voted an extension. There has been debate with regard to whether the extension was legal. Legal or not legal as of this publication the required number of states for ratification has not occurred. The proposed amendment reads as follows: "Equality of rights under the law shall not be denied or abridged by the United States or by any state on account of sex." While this proposal's wording seems clear and straight forward, there have been objection to this becoming law. The following are a sample of some of the objections to the Equal Rights Amendment becoming law in the United States. Protective laws such as sexual assault and alimony would be nullified. Mothers receiving child support in divorce cases would be negatively affected. The law would abolish the presumption that the husband should support his wife and the law would take away Social Security benefits from wives and widows. The law would create a unisex society.

Although, as of this publication the Equal Rights Amendment has not been ratified by the required number of states there have been significant, perhaps not enough, changes in American societal attitudes with regard to the rights of women. The United States has not become a unisex society; however, women's rights in the United States have become more equal to their male counter parts than ever before in the history of the country. However this does not mean equality of treatment of women should not continue to be a priority in the United States.

The Efforts Continues

Despite the lack of equal rights amendment to the United States Constitution many women continue to advocate for equal rights. For some time women have been permitted to enter the military; however, their roles in the military has had some restriction such as limited roles in military combat areas. Some military personnel, both females and males have pointed out that some of the restrictions cause women in the military not to be able to move up in the military ranks and receive the rewards and benefits of such promotions. One may argue that military officials were not implementing prejudice against women military personnel rather they were attempting to protect female military personnel from being involved in extreme danger zones or activities. Regardless of the reasons the result has been unequal opportunities for some females in the United States' military. An encouraging note to this situation is the fact that recent action by military leaders is now allowing female military personnel to be part of areas which before now have been restricted to male military personnel. This change in direction should allow women in the military greater opportunities with regard to advancement in the military.

Societal Attitudes Toward Women

Past

The fact that women in the United States only gained the right to vote in 1920 speaks volumes to the past treatment of women in America. The fact that they were not allowed to vote is sufficient proof that women have been victims of discrimination; however, this is only one example of the oppression women have experienced. Giving consideration to the fact that for many years, married women were treated as property of their husbands-in many cases they could not make debts or conclude business transactions without the approval of the spouse.

Despite the subjugated treatment of women, history is replete with examples of women working with their spouses to accomplish remarkable things such as building homes in the wilderness, and establishing communities, schools, hospitals and other facilities that added to the community structure. Regardless of their accomplishments and contributions to the building of America as it currently exists, women were considered the "weaker sex," and in this context, early American society (as well as most other nations) treated women as not being equal to men. In addition to the perceived inherent weakness, women were considered fragile, unable not only to match the physical prowess of men, but also overly sensitive and unable to withstand the pressures of leadership. Given the fact women are the child bearers, it was felt that their natural role in life was nurturing. Nurturing not only consisted of caring for the children; additionally, it included caring for the home and the husband. Therefore, the "pedestal" upon which many women, particularly Euro-American women, were placed, some social scientists as well as feminists have described as being built to help the males maintain their dominance over women. In other words, by characterizing women as the ones who must have the protection of males and by describing the nurturing role as one that could only be done by or at least best be accomplished by females, women were kept in an inferior and dependent condition in relationship to males.

Present

At approximately 51 percent of the United States population, women numerically are not a minority; however, because of continued discrimination by males, women are considered in the same classification as ethnic minorities. Considerable progress with regard to civil rights has been made, particularly in the past thirty years. Women have increasingly moved from being unpaid laborers in the home to being paid employees in businesses and industries. Currently, women constitute over 45 percent of all U.S. workers. In previous years, if Euro-American women worked outside the home it was considered a reflection on her spouse's inability to adequately provide for the family. However today the previously mentioned attitude has been softened considerably because over 60 percent of Euro-American women are employed outside the home. Likewise, over 57 percent of African American women and over 50 percent of Hispanic/Latino women also work outside the home.

Part of the reason for changing attitudes with respect to the role of women is the changes in the U.S. economic situation. Today, in the majority of families, two wage earners are necessary to provide the standard of living many

Americans demand. Additionally and perhaps more important has been that many women have demanded equal treatment.

Employment Status

While women have made gains with regard to equality there remain vestiges of the male dominance. This may be best seen in the U.S. labor force with regard to how women are clustered in certain jobs, particularly the lower paying jobs, while males enjoy better access to higher paying jobs, particularly executive positions.

In addition to not being paid at the same rate as men for the same or similar jobs, women also indicate that they are discriminated when competing with men for promotions. Many women believe that they are not given an equal chance at higher paying and more prestigious jobs as their male counterparts. This glass ceiling effect is the same complaint that ethnic and racial minorities lodge as they compete with Euro-American males for promotions.

Sexism

Henderson (1994) defines sexism as the process of assigning life roles according to gender. As previously demonstrated, women in the labor force have been traditionally assigned specific roles and in many instances these roles are subordinate to males. As sexism is a reality in America, one must ask, "How and why does it exist?" George Henderson (1994) argues that sexism begins in the family and is perpetuated and supported by the manner in which males and females are socialized. He further believes that the behaviors associated with sexism are so deeply ingrained into our minds that sexist behaviors are generally unconscious. Sexism is a two-way street; both sexes practice the behaviors that lend itself to sexism. Similar to racism, sexism is motivated by power, prejudice, and prestige. The use of one's gender to gain an advantage is just as unfair as the use of one's race to place oneself in a more advantageous position. Perhaps the ultimate discrimination occurs when one combines one's race and gender to afford him/her a position of privilege.

Women are not immune from discriminating within their own gender. To be more specific, there appears to be a pecking order with Euro-American females at the top, next women of color, and at the lowest are women with disabilities, regardless of racial background. Since women with disabilities occupy a declined position within the female hierarchy, this is an indication that they perhaps experience some unique problems related to the fact they have a disability. Next we will look at the impact of disabilities on women.

The Other Sister–Impact of Disabilities on Women

It is a stated and proven fact that women experience disabilities at a greater rate than men. Also, with the exception of American Indian women, females of the other major U.S. racial and ethnic groups have a higher percentage of disabilities than males.

The following provides a brief example of the magnitude of disabilities among women:

- Of those with work-related disabilities in the 16-64 age groups, 50 percent are women.
- Of the work-related disabilities which are classified as severe, 55 percent are women.
- Of the severely disabled women, 34 percent are African Americans or of Hispanic/Latino origin.

These facts related to work-related disabilities. Adrienne Asch and Michelle Fine (1988) estimate that approximately one-sixth of the U.S. female population has a disability. Regardless of the source, in almost all accounting of rate of disability among Americans, women have the highest rate. Knowing this certainly has value-perhaps of greater value is the impact disabilities have on women.

Feminine Role

The degree to which a disability impacts one's ability to meet society's prescribed female role often plays a major role in the development and maintenance of a healthy self-esteem. Since the early 1970s, physical fitness has been emphasized. No doubt this emphasis has been good for most citizens in that healthier lifestyles have been promoted, i.e., better diets, no smoking, and regular exercise as well as reduction of emotional stress. Various types of diets appear almost monthly, new exercise devices appear at about the same rate as diets and a variety of "experts" write books and articles all with the expressed purpose of developing the ideal American man or woman. With regard to women, the image goes beyond the perfect body but also includes an unrealistic view of facial beauty. The multitude of beauty products as well as the increased use of plastic surgery is sufficient proof as to the extent some will go in attempting to attain the all-American girl or woman image.

Women with disabilities and other women who may not be financially able to avail themselves of the expensive beauty treatments glean facts and images from the media and realize that to a great extent society's judgment of them as attractive or unattractive persons depends upon how close they can approximate the previously mentioned image of the American female. With regard to disabilities the more severe the disability, generally the more the person deviates from the societal norm of beauty. Thus, a female who has a missing limb, cerebral palsy, or some type of facial disfigurement generally will find it difficult to be accepted as a beautiful person. Deborah Kent (1988), a female with a visual impairment, provides an excellent summarization of the impact of being a female with a disability:

> I can't remember a time when I wasn't aware that I was different from most other people, and that my differentness was a judgment against me. By the dawn of adolescence I had absorbed enough innuendoes to suspect that, no matter what social graces I managed to cultivate, no matter how I dressed or wore my hair, I would never be the kind of girl boys wanted to flirt with or ask on dates. My reading heightened my apprehensions about the future. In books, it seemed the only way a woman could be fulfilled was through the love of a man and the only women worthy of that love were lithe and lovely, unblemished, and physically perfect. The smallest flaw-an uneven gait, a malformed hand, a squint was enough to disqualify a woman from romance, and from all hope of happiness. If even a trifling imperfection could loom as such an insurmountable obstacle to fulfillment, what chance was there for a girl who was totally blind and I was?

Deborah Kent's self-disclosure reflects the difficulties often experienced by females with a disability as they are maturing into adults and the difficulties associated with fulfilling the adult role.

Violence Against Women with Disabilities

A growing concern among rehabilitation helping professionals is violent acts committed against women who have disabilities. Experts in the areas of disabilities and women studies point out that women with disabilities are vulnerable to violence because they are often isolated by society—unable to access needed services. Too frequently, they live in poverty and their disabilities may create mobility and communication problems. Additionally, if a woman has a mental, emotional, and/or severe disability such as cerebral palsy, society tends to discredit her feelings and even disbelieves her when she reports acts of violence, particularly rape.

Because of the nature of some disabilities, women are often unable to escape or defend themselves. Mobility and communication problems place them in extremely difficult situations to provide effective resistance.

Frequently, attackers are persons whom the woman with a disability knows, such as parents, siblings, caregivers, and even husbands. These persons know how easily it is to violate the woman with a disability. They also know that in most cases the violence is never reported because the attacker has either threatened to discontinue assistance or she is made to believe officials are unlikely to believe her. Unfortunately, because of feelings of shame, guilt, and/or fear of further isolation or abandonment, women with disabilities endure abusive situations. Sadly, in some instances, their only escape is either death or psychologically retreating into a world in which they feel safe.

Marriage and Family

In some instances, parents overprotect a child who has a disability. This is particularly true of female children. The result of the overprotection quite often is that the child with a disability has difficulty establishing reasonable interaction with members of the opposite sex. It is a proven fact that prejudice and stereotyping gain a foothold as a result of lack of interaction between individuals and groups of individuals. As one adds these misperceptions of females with disabilities with the males evaluating their attractiveness with the aforementioned societal standards, females with disabilities too frequently experience difficulties in establishing meaningful and lasting romantic relationships. To add to the problems of females establishing relationships with the opposite sex that may lead to marriage, frequently nondisabled persons view females with disabilities, particularly those who are visible and/or severe, as asexual, devoid of the normal sexual feelings and urges that most humans experience. While this perception is generally not intended to be malicious it nevertheless has the effect of being a devastating blow to one's self-esteem. When a woman with a disability marries, some people think it is unrealistic for her to have children. The general thought pattern is that persons with disabilities cannot produce a nondisabled child. One only has to remember that in the not-too-distant past, males and females with intellectual disabilities were sterilized to "keep them from reproducing persons similar to themselves."

In addition to the feeling of producing a defective child, there also is the belief that women with disabilities will be unable to adequately care for their offspring. Of course, many of these fears are unfounded and based upon ignorance of what persons with disabilities are capable of doing. Adrienne Asch and Michelle Fine (1988) convincingly argue that women with disabilities have been ignored in studies and research which if conducted would shed light and be very revealing with regard to the needs of women with disabilities and their abilities as well. They explain their position with these comments.

Women with disabilities traditionally have been ignored not only by those concerned about disabilities but also by those examining women's experiences. The popular view of women with disabilities has been one mixed with repugnance. Perceiving disabled women as childlike, helpless and victimized, nondisabled feminists have severed them from the sisterhood in an effort to advance more powerful, competent and appealing female icons.

According to Asch and Fine, not only have social scientists been negligent in researching and discussing women with disabilities' needs but also women's rights groups have backed away from including them in their manifestoes. The exclusion of women with disabilities, according to Asch and Fine, is deliberate because some of the feminist groups believe women with disabilities not only do not add anything to their cause but in fact detract from their efforts. The following statement, which the authors indicate was made by a feminist academician, speaks clearly to this question, "Why study women with disabilities? They reinforce traditional stereotypes of women being dependent, passive and needy."

Economic Status of Women

Women are in general paid less than men for similar work. Additionally, women have been stereotyped and cluster in certain types of jobs and, in general, these jobs are at the lower end of the pay scale, while males, particular Euro-American males, enjoy open access to the higher paying jobs. This information provides a vivid reminder how women, particularly minority women, are discriminated with regard to their incomes when compared to Euro-American males with similar or even less education and/or training. As deplorable as these facts are, they are even more shocking when a disability is added to the status of a woman. Asch and Fine (1988) state that "disabled men and women are poorer than those without disabilities. Again, disabled women are at the bottom of the ladder, with black disabled women having less income than any other race/gender/disability category."

It is reasonable to expect that a person with a disability who is unable to work will not have a monthly income equal to those who are employed full time; therefore, the fact that women unable to work have a median monthly family income that is 40 percent less than nondisabled females who work full time is not shocking. However, according to Mitchell LaPlante and his associates (1996), the fact that 36 percent of women with disabilities who are unable to work live in poverty does produce waves of shock.

Intervention Strategies

It appears clear, at least to this author, that in addition to providing basic rehabilitation services that will assist women with disabilities to engage in a productive life, there is a tremendous need for rehabilitation helping professionals, social workers, psychologists, and educators to advocate with and for women with disabilities.

Conclusion

It is shameful that women with disabilities are forced into positions where they are isolated and totally dependent on others, thus making them easy targets for uncaring and demented family members, friends, and caregivers. The helping professional must not allow himself/herself to continue to see women with disabilities as the ward of their family. As a nation, America has made considerable progress in accepting women as equal to men. No longer do we view wives as the property of their husbands and no longer are men free to treat wives in any manner they desire. Even though these changes have been made with regard to our view of nondisabled women, some women with disabilities continue to be at best indentured servants to their husbands and family. We continue to think that the woman with a disability is incapable of taking care of her needs or express her needs and perhaps know what her needs are; therefore, our society is willing to place women with disabilities in positions that require them to be subservient to their families.

As one considers that women experience disabilities at a greater rate than men, the issue of women with disabilities' rights are of significant importance. These women should not be separated from their families unless it is an abusive setting; however, needed resources should be made accessible and available. Their income should be equal to their male counterparts and economic assistance programs should provide enough so that they are not totally dependent upon their families for needs.

Finally, as helping professionals work with women with disabilities they must remember the ethnic/racial background will impact how women view the world as well as the opportunities that are available to them. The helping professional must keep in mind that for some women with disabilities, society views them as having three strikes against them, gender, disability, and race.

Review Questions

1. Define sexism.
2. Who has the highest rate of disabilities, men or women?
3. Why are women with disabilities vulnerable to violence?
4. Who are the most frequent abusers of women with disabilities?

Suggested Activities

1. Visit a battered women's center and determine how accessible it is for women with a mobility disability.
2. If your college or university has a women's study program, see if they have a course or courses with regard to women with disabilities.
3. Check with the most available social work and/or counseling programs to determine if they have any courses relevant to women with disabilities.
4. Check with your state vocational rehabilitation agency to determine the percentage or number of women with disabilities in your state. If available, obtain the types of disabilities.
5. Interview at least five women with disabilities and obtain their perspectives on being a woman with a disability. Make sure that you pick persons who represent a variety of disabilities.

References

Fine, M., & Asch, A. (Eds.). (1988). *Women with disabilities.* Philadelphia: Temple University Press.

Henderson, G. (1994). *Cultural diversity in the workplace: Issues and strategies.* Westport, CT: Praeger Press.

Houston, J. (2013) *Women's rights movement.* Unpublished paper, University of Oklahoma.

Kent, D. (1988). In search of a heroine: Images of women with disabilities in fiction and drama. In M. Fine & A. Asch (Eds.), *Women with disabilities.* Philadelphia: Temple University Press.

National Committee on Pay Equity. (1995). The wage gap: Myths and facts. In P. S. Rothenberg (Ed.), *Race, class and gender in the United States* (3rd ed.). New York: St. Martin's Press.

Rothenberg, P. S. (Ed.). (1995). *Race, class and gender in the United States: An integrated study* (3rd ed.). New York: St. Martin's Press.

Suggested Readings

Asch, A. (1984). The experience of disability: A challenge for psychology. *American Psychologist, 39*(5), 529–536.

Goffman, E. (1963). *Stigma: Notes on the management of spoiled identity.* Englewood Cliffs, NJ: Prentice-Hall.

Rothenberg, P. S. (1995) *Race, Class, and Gender in the United States* (3rd. ed.). New York: St. Martin's Press.

Stone, D. A. (1984). *The disabled state.* Philadelphia: Temple University Press.

Chapter 11

ELDERLY

Chapter Outline

Chapter Objectives
• To identify significant facts with regard to African American elderly and the implications for the helping professional
• To identify significant facts with regard to Asian and Pacific American elderly and the implications for the helping professional
• To identify significant facts with regard to Hispanic/Latino American elderly and the implications for the helping professional
• To identify significant facts with regard to American Indian elderly and the implications for the helping professional

Introduction

D efining what is considered elderly in America appears to be difficult. Some suggest that "old age" begins at age 50 while the majority of experts in the field of aging view age 65 as the defining point for the elderly. The lack of agreement with regard to what constitutes an elderly person emphasizes that in many instances aging is a state of mind. There is no question that aging involves physiological and psychological changes; however, there are persons who have been alive for over 60 years and have fewer physiological deficits than someone half their age. Relatedly, it would not be difficult to identify persons who are 60 years of age who have been rendered by the aging process physically and/or mentally incapable of carrying out normal activities of daily living. In general terms, it is true that as one grows older he or she experiences decreased abilities to function at previous levels of activity and often experiences pain and soreness from performing activities that were formerly done with little effort and no side effects. However, the rate at which one ages varies from person to person which accounts for the 60-year-old man being able to function at a higher level than his 30-year old junior.

The elderly population is one of the fastest growing groups in America. The following narrative of aging in America, provided by Deborah L. Best and John E. Williams (1996), gives us a glimpse of how the elderly population has grown in America.

> In 1790 when the USA was just 14 years old, the official census began and has been conducted every 10 years ever since. At the time of the first census, barely 2% of the population of the USA was over the age 65, and that number had grown to only 4 percent by 1900 (Kalish, 1982). As of 1990 more than 35 million persons, or almost 16% of the population of the USA was 65 years of age or older. (Hoffman, 1991)

According to the U.S. Census Bureau's projections the elderly population will double between 2010 and the year 2050, to approximately 80 million. If this project is correct one in five persons will be sixty-five and older.

Those persons born in the late 1940s and early 1950s if they have not retired are thinking seriously about retirement. Consequently, America is experiencing increasing numbers of persons reaching the senior citizen status. This will undoubtedly influence many facets of American life. As one analyzes the population aging in America, we realize that with a large number of Americans approaching senior citizen status, tremendous political influence will be seen with this population base. Therefore, more laws and policies favorable to the needs of this population will be placed at or near the top of the American agenda. A second factor to consider is that the majority of the economic wealth will be concentrated within this group; therefore, business will begin to pay more attention to the wants, desires, and needs of this group. In summary, this group will exert considerable influence in America during the twenty-first century.

As stated before, even though aging can be a state of mind for some, the reality exists that as we grow older, our bodies begin to show the effects of years of use and, in some cases, abuse. By virtue of the increase of persons reaching age 65, and considering the normal aging process, it is within reason to state that helping professionals will encounter an increased number of persons who are considered elderly. The helping professional must purge from his or her mind many of the stereotypes of elderly persons, such as unproductive, fragile, uncooperative, and desiring to be young again. Instead, she must see them as a diverse group to be viewed also from their cultural base. Because they are now considered "old" does not mean they shed their skin and suddenly become a member of a neutral ethnic/racial group–the elderly.

Changing Times

As mentioned in the introduction to this chapter there are numerous aspects that are occurring in American society which are impacting the lives of persons who are considered seniors or age sixty-five and older and these aspects are causing cultural shifts in thinking and reaction to persons whom we have in the past considered as elderly. According to the United States Census Bureau the United States' population sixty-five years and older is over forty million and is projected to increase to over 72 million by the year 2030. It is further projected by senior citizens research groups that by the year 2030 the number of citizens over the age of 85 will experience a dramatic increase and forty percent of the United States population will be over the age of 50. An obvious conclusion that can be extracted from the previously mentioned statistics is that Americans are living longer and this trend will continue for a significant period of time.

One of the cultural impacts of Americans living longer and hopefully productive lives is the desire and quite likely the need to be employed longer. Stated in other terms senior persons in the United States will want to and expect to continue to be employed beyond the age of sixty-five. This need of senior citizens and quite likely demands of the same group will have a double edge impact upon the American society. The first impact will be the United States workforce will benefit from the years of experience that the seniors have developed as productive members of the workforce. The second impact will be because the seniors are working several and/or many more years than past generation of workers, perhaps fewer higher paying jobs will not be available to younger workers, employees under the age of forty, and an additional impact is possibly fewer higher level management positions will be available to younger workers. This last fact could be considered **reverse ageism**.

Reverse ageism could add an extra dimension to attitudes toward the elderly. One method of lessening of the impact of seniors being employed more years, primarily beyond the age of sixty-five, is for employers to, whenever possible, develop a mentorship arrangement where older workers take younger workers metaphorically under their wings and provide them with the benefits of their years of experience. This hopefully will develop a bond between the younger workers and the more seasoned older workers. This approach can be accomplished at virtually all levels of the workforce. This approach will have the best chance of succeeding if the management introduce and promote this approach as a worker's partnership, where both the younger worker and the seasoned worker assisting each other and emphasize that this process benefits all personnel in the workforce. This approach also can have the effect of lessening the competitive tendency of the younger worker where he/she attempts to be more successful than the seasoned worker at the expense of cooperation and overall productivity. Additionally, this approach encourages the seasoned worker to share his/her experience with the younger worker by the fact that the seasoned worker will develop pride in the employment success of his protégé.

Another cultural shift is changing attitudes toward person who are considered elderly. Whereas in past years persons who were considered elderly were often treated as though they were no longer significant contributors to American society; in some instances they were considered as takers from society rather than significant contributors to American society. Takers in the sense, as previously mentioned, occupying jobs that younger workers could have to rear their families. Additionally takers from society because they, the elderly, utilized national economic resources as a result of medical and insurance costs, which some persons believed, increased the cost of these resources for younger and healthier persons.

The cultural shift with regard to attitudes toward older persons has occurred for at least two major reasons. The first reason is the fact that older persons are living longer and healthier lives; this means that older persons are have more positive contacts with their younger counterparts. Stated in other terms, older Americans as they live longer are living as healthier individuals and are seen by the younger population as active and vibrant members of their communities. Additionally, as older persons live longer they are having extended contact with their family member and this contact is as contributors rather than persons for whom the family members have to spend considerable time and other resources administering helping services. A second reason for the cultural shift is as older persons live a longer and productive life they are accumulating significant economic resources. It is estimated that the senior population in the United States have over nine hundred billion (and growing) in money available to be spent. There can be no doubt that there are many American seniors who are not economically affluent therefore the previously mention economic resource figure should not be interpreted as the American senior population is wealthy. However, what is being stated is that the American senior population cannot and should not be considered as taking away from the economic strengths of the United

States and this reality is beginning to change some attitudes with regard to the American senior population. The change of attitudes is from takers to significant contributors.

As Americans we are categories; for very good reasons we categorize persons by ethnicity, gender, social status, economic status and age to mention only a few areas. A category such as gender is very straight forward and there is very little debate with regard to this categorization. However, categorizations of age present a different situation; the dissecting of age is problematic and subjective. To be more specific, answers to the following questions hopefully illustrate this point; at what age does youth end and adulthood begin? At what age does youth end and middle age begin? At what age does elderly begin? In past years and to some extent presently many considered and continue to consider the age of sixty-five to be the beginning of the elderly category. As the population of American begins to live longer and productive lives the concepts of elderly are beginning to change. There are persons within the forty to fifty year age range that are less physically and mentally productive than some who are in the sixty to seventy age ranges. Likewise there are persons in the twenty to thirty age ranges that are less mentally astute than some in the seventy to eighty age ranges. Thus the question is at what age does elderly begin?

The American population has begun to realize to a certain extent the identification of a person by his/her age may have some good points however, to classify persons with regard to what they can do and how long they can continue to do certain things has considerable faults. One of the faults relate to the fact that as a society we are too often losing the benefits of experience and wisdom of older persons.

Even though some if not many things attitudinal wise has improved, with regard to persons who are considered seniors or elderly this improvement has to be tempered with the knowledge that some groups, especially ethnic minorities have not received full benefits of this improvement. Helping professions and others who are working with or plan to work with seniors or elderly persons must view the needs of this group both from the standpoint of being a senior or elderly person as well as a senior or elderly ethnic/racial minority person. Therefore the remainder of this chapter will discuss elderly from the standpoint of race and ethnicity. As one reads the remainder of this chapter one should be aware that some of the information provided for ethnic/racial groups can also be applied to lower socioeconomic Caucasian persons.

African American Elderly

Although dated, however, the following remains true today. In 1971, the Committee on Aging in the Group for the Advancement of Psychiatry issued the following statement that summarizes what it means to be an elderly African American:

> Being black and aged frequently means the piling up of life problems associated with each characteristic. The black aged often have less education, less income, smaller or no social security income, less adequate medical service, and fewer family supports than the aged in general. . . . Racism and "ageism" may be combined to prevent the black aged from getting needed services of all types.

It is often from this background that helping professionals must begin their work with elderly African American clients. Additional information of which a helper must be aware is that while many groups reach retirement age, they either retire, semi-retire, or begin a second career. Many African American elderly persons must continue working far beyond the initial time they could retire. In many cases, due to economic reasons, they must continue working even though their health care provider(s) advise against them continuing to work. Rose Gibson (1987) identifies the employment patterns of elderly African Americans and provides the answer to why the elderly black person must work even though working may react negatively to his/her health status.

> The level and source of income for blacks in old age have also been affected by their lifetime work experiences. Restriction to jobs characterized by instability, low earnings, and few benefits are directly related to low levels of retirement pensions and Social Security benefits. Therefore, the income packages of older blacks, compared to other groups, contain a greater proportion of money from their own work and non-retirement sources.

In addition to inadequate retirement incomes, some African American elderly must continue to work to support grandchildren. An unfortunate result of violence, teen pregnancy and substance abuse has resulted in an increasing number of elderly rearing their second and sometimes third set of children. Many African American families have a strong philosophical viewpoint that there are no unwanted children in the family; therefore, children who become "parentless" are frequently informally adopted by grandparents or other close relatives or family friends.

Implication for the helping professional: the previously mentioned factors have been pointed out because the helping professional must be aware that in many cases his elderly African American client may have few skills, poor educational background, minimum income, and maximum needs. Many times these needs require immediate attention; therefore, long-term planning should not be of immediate concern to the helper. The professional helper should become aware of the immediate needs of his client. The helper can be of tremendous benefit to the African American client by identifying resources and assisting the client to access the resources by helping cut through some of the red tape that too frequently is associated with various agencies and organizations. The helping professional can assist the client by linking them with support groups which may help by being a social outlet. Additionally, the professional helper can assist by counseling the client(s) to recognize that there is nothing wrong with needing and receiving help. Often African American clients feel guilt about requesting help; they sometimes feel it displays their weakness and failures. In most instances, they are embarrassed about having to ask for help. Despite the stereotype of African Americans as "dole hogs," most would prefer not to receive help; however, circumstances often dictate otherwise.

The helping professional must become aware of the environment in which the person lives. Becoming acquainted with the client's religious beliefs, family support, formal and informal social activities, and the client's crisis-meeting resources will be invaluable information.

Asian and Pacific American Elderly

Kenneth Sakauye (1990) reminds us that unlike African American elderly, "For most Asian Pacific subgroups the culture of poverty is not the primary factor underlying differences. The impact of ethnicity and culture may be more important." Therefore, we will look at Asian Pacific American elderly from the vantage of Chinese Americans, Japanese Americans, Korean Americans, and Filipino Americans.

Chinese American Elderly

As discussed in Chapter 8, Chinese values promote the concept of family power flowing through the father to the eldest son. Likewise, it is the responsibility of the son to provide for the elderly parents. As more and more generations of Chinese Americans are born and reared in the United States, the more acculturated they have become; therefore, according to Huang (1981), there has been a lessening of this responsibility concept. This is not to imply that the Chinese elderly are abandoned by their children, but there is not the strict adherence to the old tradition. It is not uncommon for the Chinese elderly to continue to live in their ethnic community, whereas their offspring have moved to the suburbs.

Implications for the helping professional: It is important for the helper to be aware of the generation to which the Chinese elderly belong as well as how much he/she follows the old traditions. It is also helpful to determine the kind of social, emotional, and economical support the person has.

Japanese American Elderly

Because of the experience of the internment campus, it is important to understand the generation of the Japanese American. Scholars have pointed out that many Japanese who were placed in these camps refuse to talk about their experiences. Holding in feelings and emotions of this magnitude that would be generated by such an experience has to have an effect on the helping process. While it may be difficult, if not impossible, to get them to express their thoughts and feelings with regard to the incident, it is imperative that the professional helper be cognizant that feelings and emotions exist and they are having an impact. It is noted that many of the Japanese who experience internment camps are deceased, thus the previously mentioned impact may not have as much relevance as it did several year ago; however as is discussed in the following paragraphs information passed on by the elders to their children and possibly grandchildren will have some impact upon those groups.

The helper should be aware that the Japanese elderly have experienced situations that were hurtful, embarrassing, and cruel. On the other hand, the younger generation did not experience the event but may have been told stories of the camps by their elders. The younger generation will be more acculturated, having moved away from some of the old Japanese traditions. A combination of the emotions associated with the indignities suffered in the camps, plus a feeling of stepping away from traditions can cause emotional stress in the Japanese elderly. The helper must be prepared to deal with this stress, regardless of whether it is verbalized by the Japanese elderly client.

Filipino American Elderly

Paul Kim (1990) speaks of three cultural characteristics cherished among Filipino American elderly of which the helping professional should be aware: respect, social structure, and shame. Respect is extended to everyone, including children, parents, and the elderly. According to Kim, those who are to be respected receive special treatment in Filipino society. Social structure refers to good relationships, or avoidance of disagreements or conflict.

Shame relates to an inner fear of being left exposed, unprotected, and unaccepted.

Implication for the helping professional: The helping professional would be well advised to keep these guiding principles in mind, particularly respect and shame, as he works with Filipino elderly clients. First, respect is a two-way street. The Filipino culture has considerable respect for authority, and the helping professional will be viewed as an authority figure. Therefore, this client may expect direct advice and answers rather than the exploratory, "How do you feel about this," or "How does that make you feel." On the other side, the helper must show respect to all clients; however, he must be aware of the importance this culture places upon respect and may view expressions of disapproval on the part of the professional helper as disrespecting him as a person. Consequently, the professional helper must make sure that when disagreeing with the client, he does it in a manner that does not invoke feelings of disrespect. The professional helper must not exclude the elderly Filipino client when executing the helping plan. One might ask how a plan can be executed without including the client? While not recommended it is not uncommon when working with a person who has a disability, especially an older person, to talk to his family or caregiver rather than address questions and comments directly to the client.

Korean American Elderly

> Paul Kim offers the following: Unlike the Japanese elderly who maintain a strong informal support network among their cohort group members, the Korean elderly appears to be independent, too proud to ask for help from others outside their immediate family. They seem most concerned about their traditional values, (face saving) and tend to internalize their problems. They are highly competitive even among their family members, and thus the mutual support system is much weaker than that of other Asian groups.

Implications for the helping professional: The professional helper, similar to working with Filipino Americans, must make sure that he does not do anything that will shame the elderly Korean client. Additionally, the helper must not force the client into a "corner," he should always be allowed to "save face." To be more specific, sometimes when a counselor encounters a client who has difficulty committing to things and/or making a decision, the counselor will set the situation where he has to make a commitment. To a Korean American elderly person, this may be viewed as a situation that is embarrassing.

Hispanic/Latino American Elderly

The best estimates indicate a population of over 50 million Hispanic/ Latinos residing in the United States. The Hispanic/Latino population is relatively young; however, it also indicates that in the next 20 to 30 years there will be increasing numbers of persons who are of Hispanic/Latino decent becoming elderly.

Mexican American Elderly

With the current generation of elderly and those about to numerically become elderly, several issues are of paramount concern to helping professionals working with Mexican American elderly. One in particular is the language barrier. Additional isolation becomes a problem for many Hispanic/Latinos as they are unable to communicate as their circle of friends will begin to decrease due to death, moving, etc.

Implication for the helping professional: The language barrier presents an obvious communication problem for a helping professional who is unable to effectively communicate in the client's primary language, and likewise the client has difficulties expressing himself/herself in English. In such cases, referral to a Spanish-speaking helping professional is appropriate or services sought from an interpreter. In some instances either one of these solutions may not be available. At this point, the use of family members as interpreters would be advised. The professional helper may be surprised to see a young child who speaks English assisting an elder, because the elderly client's older children may not speak English well or their employment keeps them from attending their parent's appointment. The professional helper may need to consider contacting the elderly client after hours when English-speaking family or friends are available. Additionally, the helper should become aware of community resources such as clubs, churches, and other civic organizations that are willing to assist.

Puerto Rican American Elderly

Jose Cuellar (1990) discusses the importance of the family in Hispanic/Latino persons' lives. This is particularly relevant to a helping professional who plans to work with Puerto Rican Americans in that many families remain very close to their parents—especially as they age.

> Most Mexicans, Cubans, Puerto Ricans and other Hispanics place a great deal of value on their family relations. Attempts to instill a sense of family pride and obligation begin early in a person's life and are nurtured throughout. Most Hispanics are socialized to believe that the needs or welfare of the family, as a

whole or other individual family members, particularly the very young or very old, should take precedence over one's own needs. These children and older adults alike are often reminded that during good times or bad, la familia comes first.

Implications for the helping professional: The professional helper should be able to use the very strong commitment to the family as an advantage to the elderly in the helping process. Therefore, keeping family members involved and informed is of major importance. This does not mean the family should make decisions for the client when he/she is capable of making decisions, but it implies that both the professional helper and the client should probably consult frequently with family members.

Cuban American Elderly

As discussed in the "Cuban American" section of Chapter 9, Cubans came to the United States in waves. The second group represented a better educated and more economically affluent group than the later groups. This implies that many of the elderly from the second group will have fewer problems with English and will have the economic resources to access appropriate services when needed. The reverse is likely for later groups coming to America.

Implications for the helping professional: Since the second group of Cuban elderly have possessed adequate resources, they will be a group that is easier to work with, especially if the helping professional will remember cultural values. The subsequent groups of Cuban American elderly may present more of a challenge because of language barriers and inadequate resources. Since many of this latter group will be cut off from their family and other support networks in Cuba, many of this group will rely on their Cuban community support system. The professional helper must work to keep them connected to this system. This means the professional helper must be knowledgeable of the system(s).

American Indian Elderly

With the magnitude of the health problems American Indians face throughout their lives, it is conceivable that those who reach an advanced age may have considerable health and physical difficulties. Alcoholism, accidents, emotional stress, and diabetes are some of the health factors that contribute toward their quality of life, or perhaps better stated–decrease their quality of life. Also influencing quality of life are educational levels and language barriers, in that some elders speak their tribal language and use English secondary.

There are over 500 American Indian tribes; many have their own language which creates considerable cultural diversity within this group. E. Daniel Edwards and Margie Egbert-Edwards (1990) list the following values they believe can be generalized to the majority of American Indian groups:

1. Appreciation of individuality with emphasis upon the individual's right to freedom, autonomy and respect.
2. Group consensus in tribal/village decision making.
3. Respect for all living things.
4. Appreciation, respect and reverence for the land.
5. Feelings of hospitality toward friends, family, clans people, tribe men, and respectful visitors.
6. An expectation that tribal/village members will bring honor and respect to families, clans, and tribes. Bringing shame or dishonor to self or tribe is negatively reinforced.
7. A belief in a Supreme Being and life after death. Indian religion is the dominant influence for traditional Indian people.

Implications for the helping professional: The professional helper should be aware that many American Indian elders believe in all or some of the previously mentioned concepts and these concepts have guided their lives to some extent. Therefore, the helper should work within and respect these values as he/she works with the elderly. Additionally, the professional helper must be aware that in most American Indian tribes, the elders are very highly respected. They may no longer be involved in day-to-day decision making with regard to issues affecting the tribe, but their wisdom and counsel is respected by tribal leaders.

Finally, the professional helper must be cognizant that the tribe has considerable influence on the members' lives; therefore, the helper should become familiar with tribal customs and beliefs, particularly as they relate to treatment of the elderly.

Conclusion

Speaking of the elderly in general, there are many concerns facing them. Diminishing physical ability and slowing of mental function are often the major changes that are associated with growing older. However, things such as isolation, abuse by family members and caregivers, loss of life-long friends, or decreasing freedoms such as driving a car or taking vacations are situations that elderly persons encounter.

When we are very young, we feel that time passes too slowly, it seems like an eternity from one major holiday to the next; when we become an adult, we think we do not have enough time to do all things we need to do; then, when we become elderly, we realize that we truly are running out of time. The reality of life is about time and how we use same. As helping professionals, the most important accomplishment in working with elderly, or aged clients, is to help them make the best use of their time.

Review Questions

1. Why will "baby boomers" (persons born in the late 1940s and early 1950s) have a major impact upon American society as they reach retirement age?
2. What are some of the stereotypes of older persons?
3. What are some issues faced by African American elderly?
4. Is the culture of poverty a major issue facing most Asian and Pacific American elderly?
5. What are some issues faced by Hispanic/Latino elderly?
6. What are some of the health problems often encountered by American Indian elderly?
7. Name five cultural traits believed to be common among American Indians.
8. How will understanding the importance of cultural traits impact the helper-helpee relationship?

Suggested Activities

1. Visit a nursing home, a senior citizens center, and a retirement center. Observe the services of each. Compare the goals and objectives among the three.
2. Discuss with a vocational rehabilitation counselor the types of services rehabilitation agencies provide for the elderly.
3. Contact the American Association of Retired Persons to determine the benefits of joining this association.
4. Interview at least five persons 10–14 years of age and ask them their perceptions of being an elderly person. Ask at what age one becomes elderly?
5. Interview at least five persons 21–26 years of age to determine their views of aging and what they think life will be like for them when they become elderly. Ask at what age one becomes elderly.
6. Interview at least five persons over 64 years of age to determine if they view themselves as elderly. Ask their views on growing older.

References

Best, D. L. & Williams, J. E. (1996). Anticipation of aging: A cross-cultural examination of young adults' view of growing old. In J. Pandey et al. (Eds.), *Asian contributions to cross-cultural psychology*. New Delhi: Sage.

Committee on Aging of the Group for the Advancement of Psychiatry. (1971). Quoted in *Minority aging*. Washington, DC: U.S. Department of Health and Human Services.

Cuellar, J. B. (1990). Hispanic American aging: Geriatric education curriculum development for selected health professionals. In *Minority aging*. Washington, D.C.: U.S. Department of Health and Human Services.

Edwards, E. D., & Egbert-Edwards, M. (1990). Family care and the Native American elderly. In *Minority aging*. Washington, DC: U.S. Department of Health and Human Services.

Gibson, R. (1987). Reconceptualizating retirement for black Americans. Quoted in *Minority aging*. Washington, DC: U.S. Department of Health and Human Services.

Huang, I. J. (1981). The Chinese American family. Quoted in *Minority aging*. Washington, DC: U.S. Department of Health and Human Services.

Kim, P. K. H. (1990). Asian-American families and the elderly. In *Minority aging*. Washington, DC: U.S. Department of Health and Human Services.

Sakauye, K. (1990). Differential diagnosis, medication, treatment and outcomes: Asian American elderly. In *Minority aging*. Washington, DC: U.S. Department of Health and Human Services.

Suggested Readings

Brody, E. (1985). *Mental and physical health practices of older people*. New York: Springer.

Folstein, M. S., Anthony, J. C., & Parhad, I. The meaning of cognitive impairment in the elderly. *Journal of the American Geriatric Society, 33,* 228–235.

Ho, M. K. (1987). *Family therapy with ethnic minorities*. Newbury Park, CA: Sage.

Jackson, J. S., Newton, P., Ostfield, A., Savage, D., & Schneider, E. L. (1988). *The black American elderly*. New York: Springer.

Chapter 12

CULTURAL EVOLUTION

Chapter Outline
• Introduction
• Lesbian, Gay, Bisexual and Transgender
• Elderly
• Immigration
• Interracial Marriage
• Disability
• Race Relations
• Conclusion

Chapter Objectives
• To identify some of the ways American culture has and is continuing to evolve

Introduction

Societies are composed of among other things human beings and this society of humans succeed or fail based upon, among other things; the ability to adjust and except new ideas as well as ability to reject ideas which are not congruent with its beliefs and views with regard to the growth and stability of its inhabitants and institutions which they have established. The United States of America has developed one of the most powerful and successful societies in human history and it have not become this successful without evolving its thinking and approach to human interaction and human relations. This evolution has been highlighted with mistakes and some serious inhumane interaction with some of its inhabitants. As have been discussed in previous chapters of this book, enslaving fellow human being, removing original inhabitants from their homeland and replacing this loss with less than ideal living conditions; denying women basic rights such as the right to vote in national elections, denying some ethnic/racial groups the

239

right to marry outside of their racial group and denying some racial groups quality education. Despite these past societal failures the United States has made corrections to these and many other injustices to human dignity. No doubt not to the satisfaction of all but corrected enough to maintain a reasonable degree of servility and balance.

No society has ever been perfect nor will there ever be a perfect society. This statement is true if for no other reason than perfection is in the eyes of the beholders and humans have free will and the ability to be independent thinkers. Because societies are composed of humans and these humans have opinions, ideas and beliefs there will always be some level of disagreement with regard to the rights of other individuals and disagreement as how a society is supposed to be conducted. Despite the truth of these statements most progressive societies should and do attempt to right wrongs and open its society to various view points as well as provide opportunities for expression of these rights, taking into consideration how the expression of these rights will impact society as a whole.

The United States of America is, in this author's opinion, working its way through the evolution of several cultural issues that can be equated to the racial civil rights evolution of the 1950s and 1960s, and the results of this current deliberation and decision formation will impact the social and cultural fabric of American societies for many years into the future. Some of the cultural evolution issues that will be discussed in this chapter are: lesbian, gay, bisexual, and transgender rights, rights of the elderly, and immigration rights. These are only a few of the issues that are currently or will in the not too distant future be entering the realm of evolutionary cultural issues facing the American public.

Lesbian, Gay, Bisexual and Transgender

Definition

The author would like to acknowledge the King County Public Health department of Seattle and King County Washington as a major source for the following definitions of lesbian, gay, bisexual and transgender persons. [www .kingcounty.gov/healthservices/health/personal/glbt/definitions.aspx 2013].

A lesbian is a woman whose primary sexual and romantic attractions are to other women.

Gay may be used as an inclusive term encompassing gay men, lesbians, bisexual people and sometimes transgender persons.

Bisexual men and women have sexual and romantic attractions to both men and women.

Transgender persons are people who identify more strongly with the other gender than the one to which he or she was born.

Lesbian, Gay, Bisexual and Transgender (LGBT) Persons' Rights

Some have identified the rights of lesbian, gay, bisexual and transgender persons as the civil rights struggle of the 21st century. Dayna Lovett (2013) in the following comments succulently frames this rights issue as a civil rights struggle.

> Throughout history in the United States there have been many struggles of individual's rights who are by someone's definition not as equal. The struggles have been tragic in so many ways and in all ways they were unnecessary because these struggles were for each individual living here in the United States to have the basic human rights that should be given to all; the right of life, liberty and the pursuit of happiness. This sentence does not have a "but" or "only" if you believe like the majority or act like the majority. It is a right that should be given to all. It seems that over the many years of struggles and horrible tragedies as a nation we still have not learned anything.

There are two major issues at stake in this civil rights struggle with regard to the LGBT community? (1) The right to be romantically associated with anyone that both parties choose and not be harassed and/or discriminated for that choice. (2) The right to legally marry someone of the same gender. Continuing with the impact of this civil rights struggle what is to be gained if same sex marriage becomes a legal right in the United States? (1) Same sex couples can gain the right to immunity with regard to testify against their spouse in court. (2) Same sex couples will be able to transfer property ownership from one spouse to another without paying taxes on the value of the property as is the case with regard to the sale of land. (3) Same sex couples will gain the right of next of kin.

Objections to Gay Rights

Much of the objections are based on religious/moral grounds. Some objections are based upon beliefs that having sexual relations with someone of the same gender is simply immoral and many of those that make this proclamation use the Holy Bible as their main source as documentation of the inappropriateness of this behavior. Whether one subscribes to this type of objection is a personal belief and those that disagree with using the Holy Bible as justification for their belief can point to the fact that in years past persons justified enslaving and separating persons based upon their racial classification on words in the Bible. Additionally, some may point out the fact that the Holy Bible speaks against strong drink, commonly referred to as intake of alcohol beverages; however, the sell and consumption of alcohol is legal in the United States. Others justify objection to some gay rights based upon what they believe is nature never intended for persons of the same gender to marry and/or have intimate sexual relations.

To illustrate the evolution the United States is experiencing with regard to gay rights I will briefly present two important decisions which impacts gay persons. First is the repeal of the military "Don't Ask, Don't Tell" policy. It had been a long-standing policy that gay persons were not supposed to serve in the United States military; however the fact was there were gay persons in the military. If a person was found to be gay the likelihood was he or she would be dismissed from the military. President candidate William Jefferson Clinton campaigned for allowing gay persons to serve in the military and presumably if elected president would end the ban on the previously mentioned position of the military with regard to persons who were gay. After being elected president of the United States, President Clinton experienced considerable congressional opposition to his proposed ban of the military policy with regard to gays in the military. The result of the executive branch and the congressional branch's differences of opinions was a compromise that became known as Don't Ask Don't Tell policy. In simplistic terminology this meant the military was not supposed to inquire about a person's sexual preference and the person was not to identify his or her sexual preference. This policy lasted from December 21, 1993 to September 20, 2011 when President Baraka Obama signed into law a repeal of the policy.

The second act that is signally an evolution in policy and thinking is the United States Supreme Court ruling of the Defense of Marriage Act unconstitutional. A divided U.S. Supreme Court, five to four decision, overturned the federal law that defines marriage as a heterosexual union, saying it violates the rights of married gay couples by denying them government benefits.

The 104th United States Congress (1995–1996) had passed the Defense of Marriage Act (DOMA) with the following wording.

> No state, territory, or possession of the United States, or Indian tribe, shall be required to give effect to any public act, record, or judicial proceeding of any other state, territory, possession, or tribe respecting a relationship between persons of the same sex that is treated as a marriage under the laws of such other state, territory, possession, or tribe, or a right or claim arising from such relationship.

In essence what this law is stating is that if State X allows same sex marriages this does not mean that states which do not allow same sex marriages have to accept persons married in State X as legally married in their state. As previously stated, the United States Supreme Court in 2013 ruled this law unconstitutional.

In this author's opinion this is just the beginning of more evolution with regard to improved laws and attitudes toward the rights of LGBT persons.

Elderly

Before I discuss what I consider the evolution I consider will occur with regard to older persons, within the next twenty-five years in the United States I must set the stage by identifying where we currently are with regard to the perceptions and treatment of older person. To set the stage I will discuss ageism, age discrimination, and laws which protect older persons. These subjects represent the current status of persons who are identified as older individuals.

In today's American and many other industrialized societies the definition of what is old age or who is considered elderly has become a difficult definition to succinctly define. A major reason is one has difficulty identifying when old age begins. The author has asked students in several of his classes to identify at which age they consider elderly begin and he has found that there is no consistent numerical identification put forth by this relatively large sample. Some students say old age or elderly began at age 50 and for others the number goes as high as 70. Not many years ago many persons considered old age or elderly began at either age 60 or no later than 65. In today's society, even though some may consider age 50 as elderly the vast majority of persons believe elderly begins at a much older age. The question becomes, why has, in the minds of many, the line for declaring someone as old age so dramatically moved? An answer is that people in many industrialized societies have better and advanced medical care than existed twenty-five or thirty years ago. Additionally, the work environment has also improved over the previously mentioned time frame. Work which, in past years, required considerable physical labor has been replaced by technology, thus allowing persons whose physical strengths may have decreased to continue to be productive in the workplace.

Unfortunately, despite the improving view of age and aging persons as well as the improvements in working condition that have allowed older persons to continue to be productive, age discrimination continues to be prevalent in today's society. One of the areas where age discrimination tends to remain a stumbling block for persons considered to be old or elderly is in the area of employment. The Association of American Retired Persons (AARP) has mapped the general position of older workers over many years, revealing that older workers continue to be, proportionately speaking, underrepresented in the labor market, although their participation rate has slowly increased. Harcourt, Wood, and Wilkinson (2008) reminds us that age discrimination is a particularly prevalent form of discrimination and older individuals often face an unenviable position between poverty and workplace discrimination.

Branch, Harris, and Palmore (2005) describe age discrimination as a combination of beliefs, norms, attitudes and values which people consistently use to justify their discrimination and prejudice against people of a particular age. To be fair in our assessment of age discrimination, this type of discrimination is not restricted to older persons and can and is seen with regard to discrimination of younger adult persons. Branch et al. (2005) identified two forms of age discrimination and they identify them as adultism, which discriminate in favor of the adult age group. The second type of age discrimination identified by Branch et al. is jeunism, which is discrimination directed in favor of younger persons in order to give advantage to the younger members of society. Richardson, Smith, Webb, and Webber agree with Branch that age discrimination can be favorable to or against older persons; however, they point out age discrimination is more often found to affect the elderly. They further postulate that age discrimination is perhaps the single most important issue facing older people in the labor market (Harcourt, Wilkinson, and Wood, 2008).

Richardson et al. (2008) makes us aware of a study that tends to support the assertion that potential older workers experience discrimination more than potential younger workers. They inform us that participants of a study rated a job applicant whose age was manipulated across three conditions which were 25 years, 40 years, and 55 years. The result showed that the 25-year-old applicants were more likely to be hired compared with the 40- and 55-year-old applicants. An additional point that Richardson and associates made was their figures showed that older workers, between the ages of 45 and 64, experience a higher rate of unemployment and tend to remain unemployed for longer periods of time compared with younger workers. Harcourt, Wood, and Wilkinson (2008) point out that before reaching the interview or application process, older workers are often discriminated subtly, by being discouraged from following job leads and told there are no suitable vacancies or that they are overqualified or overexperienced. The good news in this discussion is there are efforts to eliminate age discrimination, in and out of the workplace. These laws as well as other actions represent an evolution in the thinking and actions with regard to persons consider older or elderly.

Laws Which Protect Older Persons

The Age Discrimination Act of 1975 is a national law that prohibits discrimination on the basis of age in programs or activities receiving federal financial assistance. The Age Discrimination Act applies to persons of all ages.

The Age Discrimination in Employment Act of 1967 (ADEA) protects individuals who are forty years of age or older from employment discrimination based upon age. The ADEA's protection applies to both employees and job applicants. Mary Moore (2013) informs us that the ADEA makes it unlawful to discriminate against a person because of his or her age with respect to any term, condition, or privilege of employment, including hiring, firing, promotion, layoff, compensation, benefits, job assignments, and training.

The Older Workers Benefit Protection Act of 1990, which is an amendment to the ADEA, prohibits employers from denying benefits to older employees. As the title indicates, this law helps avoid discrimination to older Americans with regard to benefits.

The Age Discrimination in Employment Act (ADEA) promotes the employment of older persons based on their ability and not their age, prohibits arbitrary age discrimination in employment, and assists employers and employees in finding ways to meet the problems arising from the impact of age on employment. According to Cavico and Mujtaba (2011) laws such as the Age Discrimination in Employment Act make it illegal for an employer to refuse or fail to hire a person, or to discharge an employee, or to otherwise discriminate against any person with respect to compensation, terms, conditions, or privileges of employment, including hiring, firing, promotion, layoff, compensation, benefits, job assignments, and training, due to the person's age. The ADEA also makes it illegal for an employer to limit, segregate, or classify its employees in any way that would deprive a person of employment opportunities or otherwise adversely affect a person's status as an employee because of age.

The United States federal government has given the Equal Employment Opportunity Commission (EEOC) the authority to enforce anti-discrimination laws, including cases related to age discrimination. Cavico and Mujtaba (2011) remind us that the EEOC may bring lawsuits on behalf of an aggrieved employee, or the aggrieved employee may bring a suit for legal or equitable relief him or herself. However, before the EEOC files a lawsuit on behalf of one who is alleging discrimination the EEOC must follow several guidelines including sending a 'right-to-sue' letter and present evidence that, if left unexplained or not contradicted, would support the discrimination allegations.

Cavico and Mujtaba (2011) point out that while the Age Discrimination in Employment Act and other laws are designed to protect against age discrimination, employers especially large corporations are able to produce defenses against charges of age discrimination. An employer may be able to prove that there is a reasonable cause for what may appear to be age discrimination. The authors provide the following explanation.

> There are many factors–age related but arguably sufficiently distinct–that an employer could cite reasonable ones, such as the following: recruiting concerns, such as attracting or keeping technically knowledgeable and capable employees; reputation concerns, such as honoring commitments to hire recent graduates or to recruit and hire a particular schools; budgeting concerns, such as reducing payroll costs by eliminating higher-salary positions or offshoring and outsourcing; performance concerns, such as making decisions based on performance or review ratings, evaluations, or needed skills; and dealing with the ramifications of mergers and other fundamental change and restructuring, such as workforce reductions, layoffs, reduction in force and downsizing.

In order to help eliminate age discrimination, these types of loopholes must be eliminated or at the very least made more difficult for employers to enact. Ideally, employers should and hopefully will develop a corporate conscious that values the contributions older workers can and do provide to a company, business and/or agency or as Harcourt, Wilkinson, and Wood (2008) stated, "curtailing age discrimination will take entrepreneurs willing to raise awareness about age discrimination."

Again, Mary Moore (2013) helps us better understand past laws that have provided assistance to older individuals such as the Social Security Act of 1935 which was one of the first laws designed to assist older worker and remains very much relevant to financially assisting today's older workers and retirees. This law when enacted provided a federally administered system of social insurance for the aged through payroll taxes paid by employees and their employers. Ms. Moore further points out that Social Security (SSA), Social Security Disability (SSDI) and SSI, Social Security State Supplemental and Medicare are all programs within the Social Security family. SSA is social security that when a person works, he or she makes a contribution through his/her job or self-employment taxes, and the person collects when he/she reaches the appropriate age of receiving. SSDI, as previously stated, is Social Security Disability, and persons who receive this part of Social Security are those persons who are approved for Social Security and have a disability. SSI is the state supplemented portion of Social Security, and the funding is through the Social Security Administration. As previously pointed out, states administer and monitor this program as well as being a contributing source.

As discussed in the chapter on the elderly, in the United States, Americans, as a result of improved health care, healthier eating habits and overall improved physical fitness, are living longer and productive lives. This means older people in the United States are more active and seen in society as healthy and vibrant persons. The attitudes of younger persons and people in general with regard to the usefulness of older persons is changing. Because of the improvements in life for older persons, as previously mentioned, they are living longer and more productive lives; the result is more active older persons in society purchasing goods and services with increased economic power. As a result, many industries are developing services specifically for older persons and many older persons have sufficient financial resources that make them attractive prospects for financial investments.

In many other industrialized nations, there is a significant evolution in thinking with regard to the value and usefulness of older persons in society. This evolution in thinking is exploding many of the previously held myths about the elderly and older persons. In America, the "baby boomers" are reaching the age of "extra maturity," and many of the younger generation are recognizing and marveling at the technological, educational and economical advancements this group of people has bestowed upon America. The younger generation additionally recognizes that their lives have been made better because the now older generation helped pave the road to success for them.

Immigration

Very few if any will disagree that the United States of America has one of the best if not the best standard of livings of any country in the history of world civilization. This remarkable standard of living has developed as a result of intellectual ingenuity, hard work, and scientific innorvation. A significant number of these remarkable traits have been displayed by persons from numerous backgrounds; among them are immigrants who have viewed the United States as the land of freedom by which they are able to improve their lives and the lives of their loved ones. Immigrants have come to the United States to build a life for themselves and their loved ones or to earn and develop the resources to improve the lives of themselves and loved ones in their native countries.

With the exception of American Indians, all other Americans are the product of some form of immigration—some of which was planned, other immigration was forced. The point is that immigration certainly is not a new concept to the United States. With regard to culture, immigration has been a positive force in the United States. Numerous inventions and intellectual ideas can be attributed to contributions from persons not born within the United

States and its territories. Perhaps one of the most recognized aspects of immigration is workers who are non-citizens of the United States who come to earn money either to send to their home country to provide for a better life in that country or they come to the United States to work and earn resources to qualify for citizenship.

In the first quarter of the twenty-first century a major discussion within the United States with regard to immigration revolves around immigration from Mexico to the United States and to a lesser degree immigration from Cuba and other countries to the United States. The discussions and the result of these discussions will undoubtedly cause the evolution of American's thinking with regard to how immigration into the United States will be handled and how these immigrants will be treated when they enter the United States. However, before we engage ourselves in this discussion let us take a look at how past immigration has been handled by the United States.

Author Pyong Gap Min (1995) provides us with summary type review of the impact of immigration with regard to some Asian persons entering the United States.

> After the California Gold Rush in 1848, a large number of Chinese Workers were brought to California to be used as cheap labor for mining and railroad construction. The Chinese Exclusion Act of 1882 and the ensuing rampant racial violence against Chinese workers pushed most Chinese workers away from California. After the Chinese were legally barred from entry in the United States, plantation and farm owners in Hawaii and California began to bring in Japanese, Filipino, Korean and Indian workers. But laws passed in the early 1920s barred Asian nationals from entering the United States for about 40 years. Many Japanese and Korean women came to the United States as wives of American servicemen after World War II and the Korean War. Nevertheless, until 1970, the Asian American population had been kept to a relatively small number.

Pyong Gap Min points out the United States has a long history on immigration issues; whereas some immigration issues can be traced to some of the Asian immigrates–namely, Chinese, Japanese and Korean. Young-Shi OU and Harriette Pipes McAdoo (1999) inform us with regard to how Chinese immigration occurred in the United States.

> Most Chinese Americans migrated to America in two main streams of decidedly different characters. The first stream started in 1820. Most of these early Chinese immigrants came to the United States to work on the nation's railroads or in the mines. They were regarded and exploited as an abundant source of cheap labor.

The second stream of Chinese immigrants, which began in 1847, came largely from the upper or middle classes. Unlike their predecessors, who had limited occupational aspirations, these Chinese came to seek higher education or to join their relative, who already possessed advanced degrees in the fields of physical science, art and medicine. Most of them spoke fluent Mandarin and could read and write in their native language. As a result, they were able to finish school and often received advanced degrees.

Regardless of their socioeconomic status, most of the Chinese immigrants were discriminated against by their employers, classmates, and the American public in general. This discrimination took a variety of forms, from differential wage and salary scales to lack of equal protection under the law, to the development of local, state, and federal legislation controlling the movement of Chinese immigrants and limiting their integration into the larger society. An example of federal legislation was the Chinese Exclusion Act of 1882. The act not only limited Chinese immigration to the United States but also led to a decline of about 31,000 in the country's Chinese American population.

As a result of the lack of local protection, many Chinese were forced to band together in small towns for their own safety. These enclaves developed into large ethnic communities in New York, San Francisco, and other large cities which came to be known as Chinatowns. Chinatowns may be described as ethnic communities in which the Chinese inhabitants have developed and maintained their cultural economic and social/psychological independence from the larger society. (pp. 253–254)

As time has passed, non-Chinese Americans have begun to recognize the contribution Chinese immigrants have made to American society; thus hostility and some discrimination toward them has decreased. As Young-Shi OU and McAdoo have informed us, the United States Congress in 1942 repealed the Chinese Exclusion Act. Other discriminatory federal legislation was eliminated in 1965.

As Chinese immigration was effectively stopped by the Chinese Exclusion Act, efforts of immigration by the Japanese began to occur. Around 1869 a small number of Japanese persons were brought to Hawaii to work in the agricultural fields; however because of poor treatment the Japanese government encouraged some of them to return to their native land and discontinued this attempt at immigration. Immigration of Japanese persons reoccurred at different times between 1884 and the early 1900s, until what has been called "Gentlemen's Agreements" between the United States and the Japanese governments prohibited passports to laborers intended for Hawaii and the United States.

Setsuko Matsunaga Nishi in the following comments further provides a historical trail of Japanese immigration into the United States.

The 1924 Oriental Exclusion Act effectively halted immigration from Japan for nearly 30 years. Japanese immigration resumed in 1952 with the passage of the McCarran-Walter immigration Act. In addition to a tiny annual quota of 185 immigrants assigned to Japan, relatives of U.S. citizens could come as non-quota immigrants under the family reunification provisions of the act. (p. 98)

The Oriental Exclusion Act, prohibited entry to "aliens ineligible for citizen-ship." This policy effectively barred any significant Asian Immigration, except for tiny quotas, until the 1952 McCarran-Walter Act, in which one provision removed the racial basis of eligibility for citizenship. (p. 103)

Pyong Gap Min (1995) summaries the early Korean immigration to the United States with the following comments:

Like other Asian immigrants to Hawaii and California, the pioneering Korean immigrants were admitted mainly to serve the economic interests of plantation owners. In this connection, it is important to note that the immigrants in Hawaii were admitted through the contract labor system, a practice outlawed in the United States at that time; recruiting agencies made it look like they were free immigrants so they would not violate the law. Contract labor was a system in which an immigrant was indentured to an employer for period of (usually seven) years at wages lower than those paid to American citizens. As contract laborers, Korean immigrants were forced to accept low wages and working conditions set by plantation owners. (p. 200)

Melanie Norris (2013) informs us that a shortage of available labor work-ers in the United States lead Congress to pass the Immigration and Na-tionality Act of 1917, which interestingly imported tens of thousands of Mexi-can workers. Later, after the Great Depression, which had disastrous impact upon the nation's economy, thousands of Mexicans were deported. This up and down cycle of migrant workers continued with the passage of the Bracero Agreement in 1943 which allowed Mexican workers to enter the United States. In more recent times some improvement with regard protecting the health and welfare of migrant workers has been made through the United States legislative process with the passage of the Migrant Health Act in 1962, the Migrant and Seasonal Agricultural Workers Protection Act in 1983 and the Immigration Reform and Control Act in 1986.

As can be seen, the United States has had a mixed human relationship with its use of immigrants as well as its immigration policies. The United States is not the only nation that has had a somewhat dubious reaction to and use of immigrants. On one side of the immigration issues is the undeniable fact that all nations have the right and responsibility to secure and protect its national interests, and on the other side is the fact that all nations should be humane and respectful of human rights and human needs, as it protects and promotes its national interests.

In this first quarter of the twenty-first century considerable emphasis has been directed toward Mexican people entering or attempting to enter into the United States. For the most part the majority of the persons entering is for legitimate reasons–namely to obtain work and secure a better life for their loved ones. It has been documented, therefore, that there can be no doubt that some have entered the United States for less than honorable reasons; however, it appears that these are in the minority and as previously stated the majority are entering for humane personal reasons. Because the nations of Mexico and the United States adjoin each other or separated by easily crossable water entering into the United States can be accomplished without going through the formal process of immigration.

In some cases, perhaps many cases, Mexican individuals and families enter into the United States, both legally and illegally, to become part of the American culture. They secure work, establish a home, birth and rear children, send their children to school and in many ways become like average American citizens without becoming an American citizen. Many Mexicans fall into this scenario. Given the fact that Mexican children born in the United States or enter into the country at a very young age, the United States is their home and the only life and culture they know. Therefore, a major question becomes, in situations where the parents do not plan to leave the United States, should the children be punished for their parents' mistake of not making their stay legal by forcing them to return to Mexico? If the answer to that question is no, then what should the United States do to help and encourage the parents to correct their mistakes? If the response is to develop a legal way for Mexican parents and their children to remain in the United States and also develop a way for Mexican immigration to be easily understood by Mexicans, this will cause a paradigm shift in Mexican and American relationships with regard to immigration. Additionally, this will constitute an evolution in our immigration policies and procedures with regard to Mexican and American relationships.

Interracial Marriage

To develop the point with regard to interracial marriage or miscegenation, I must reiterate my definition of culture, which is commonly held characteristics such as attitudes, beliefs, values, customs and patterns of behavior possessed by a group of people that have been learned and reinforced through a socialization process. We humans develop our attitudes, beliefs and tolerance, or lack thereof, of our fellow humans to a large extent from our immediate and extended families, friends and associates. What our family, close friends, persons with whom we have significant respect and admiration believe and promote as truth and appropriate beliefs and behaviors quite often is what we adapt to and include in our attitudes and beliefs system.

For many years in the United States there were taboos with regard to what was called "race mixing." This meant interracial dating and marriage primarily between African Americans and Caucasians, and to a lesser degree American Indians and Caucasians was viewed with disdain. In fact, it was not until 1967 that the United States Supreme Court ruled in *Loving v. Virginia* that state's bans on interracial marriage violated the Fourteenth Amendment of the U.S. Constitution. The following is a brief background with regard to actions which precipitated the *Loving v. Virginia* case. Richard Loving, a Caucasian male, and Mildred Jeter, an African American female, were reared in the state of Virginia, they fell in love and went to Washington DC and married. After their marriage, they returned to Virginia to carry forward their lives as husband and wife; however, the state of Virginia had different plans and arrested them for breaking the state's law against interracial marriage. They were found guilty and were given a jail sentence, but the sentence was suspended upon the condition that they leave the state of Virginia for twenty-five years. These conditions were accepted by Mr. and Mrs. Loving and they moved to Washington DC. At some point in their exile from the state of Virginia they returned to the state for a visit and they were again arrested. This led to a lawsuit against the state of Virginia which eventually resulted in the previously mentioned Supreme Court decision that declared the ban on interracial marriage violated the United States' Constitution's Fourteenth Amendment. This ruling overturned an 1883 Supreme Court ruling, *Pace v. Alabama,* which stated that state's bans on interracial marriages did not violate the Fourteenth Amendment.

Although not all states had bans on interracial marriages, the reality is until the late 1960s, and through most, if not all, of the 1980s, there were considerable resentment toward what was called race mixing, which is evident in the civil rights struggles of the 1970s and 1980s where considerable resentment occurred with regard to African American students attending school with Caucasian students as well as African Americans eating in and resting in establishments that were considered for "whites only." It is this author's contention that much of the opposition to public school integration as well as integration of other public facilities can be directly associated with the attitudes generated to the so-called race mixing. To further elaborate on attitudes regarding race mixing, one must ask the question, where did the adults who opposed integration obtain their negative attitudes and how did their attitudes impact and influence their children? The most plausible answer is from family, friends and persons with whom one had considerable respect for their opinions. One may disagree with this statement and say that his/her attitudes and beliefs were developed from firsthand experience. To respond to this line of thinking one should ask the questions, what is the sampling upon which you are basing your opinion and were your beliefs already formed from parents, friends, etc. and this incident(s) simply cemented in your mind what you already believed?

Separation of ethnicities and races occur to some extent because of ignorance. This ignorance occurs because of feelings of racial/ethnic superiority passed down from generation to generation. With regard to the belief of inferiority of African Americans has to do with how a significant number of Africans were brought to the Americas. As is discussed in Chapter 6 most Africans were brought to North America as slaves. In order to justify the treatment of the black slaves one had to view them as lessor humans than their owners and other Caucasians. To justify the inhumane treatment, the owners and those who subscribed to human ownership had to convince themselves and others that slaves were a lower form of human being. With regard to American Indians a similar justification occurred for their removal from their homeland to poorer quality living conditions. With respect to some Asian populations, many were encouraged and allowed to immigrate to the United States to work as cheap laborers; thus this also had the effect of casting them as lessor human beings.

Fortunately, the racial struggles of past years, to change attitudes and secure humane if not always equal treatment, have not been in vain. The fact that today persons of different racial backgrounds work together, learn together, eat together, love together and most importantly communicate on a relatively equal level has resulted in the collapse of opposition and segregation. The integration of races has to a great extent dismantled many past prejudices that have separated Americans and others around the world. Persons of different races in many, and hopefully most, areas of the United States are free to communicate, live and love whomever they feel represent compatibility. This change in societal attitudes has brought about a cultural shift with regard to interracial dating and marriage. A significant result of this cultural shift means the offspring of these relationships will not be related to outdated racial attitudes, stereotypes and thinking. Loving relatives, especially most grandparents, will find it difficult to maintain negative racial attitudes and discriminate against their grandchildren. These attitude changes are bringing about new and positive attitudes in racial relations and hopefully these negative attitudes will be eliminated in the near future.

Disability

As discussed in Chapter 5, "Disability," the cultural beliefs about disabilities has been varied; however, in most instances it has been negative. To be more specific too often persons with disabilities have been viewed from a negative perspective as persons who are in need of charity and at best protection. In worst-case scenarios, these were persons to be eliminated because they extracted resources from the overall community. The United States has not had some of the more extreme views of persons with disabilities. However, in the not too distant past, persons with disabilities were treated as second-class citizens.

Fortunately, through a variety of actions such as federal legislation, laws have been passed that have initiated evolutionary changes in thinking and action toward persons with disabilities. Laws such as the Americans with Disabilities Act and its amendments, deinstitutionalization and independent living acts, civil rights and advocacy acts and employment acts, to mention only a few have help initiate an improved way of thinking and interacting with persons with disabilities. With persons with disabilities, while continuing to be a distance away from being totally treated as equals and first-class citizens as the so identified non-disabled persons are treated, there can be no question that attitudes and treatment have significantly improved over the past fifty years. Institutionalization of persons with mental and emotional disabilities is no longer the first option considered when attempting to devise rehabilitation plans. While the unemployment rate for persons with disabilities continues to remain high, the improvement side of this equation is that more persons with disabilities are being employed as a result of improved attitudes of employers and the public in general regarding the capabilities of persons with disabilities. Unemployment of persons with severe disabilities continues to be a major problem, and this is something as a society we must continue to work toward finding ways to employ persons in this category.

Persons with disabilities are becoming more integrated into American society. Because of laws and attitudinal changes in America, persons with disabilities, including persons with severe disabilities, are being seen shopping in stores, at recreational cites and events, eating in restaurants, and driving cars, to mention only a few changes. To the credit of American society many of these changes have occurred because of improvements in facilities such as public transportation, access to facilities for wheelchairs and other mobility-helping devices, all of which have begun to change attitudes toward persons with disabilities.

All of these things are a true sign of evolving attitudes in the United States about persons with disabilities and their place in American society. Additionally, this evolution has been a motivating factor for persons with disabilities to develop more positive attitudes about themselves and their place in American society.

Race Relations

As has been discussed in various chapters of this book the relationship between Euro-Americans and various ethnic/racial groups in the United States has not always been one that is deserving of placement in cultural human relationship halls of fame. Despite this less than stellar human relations record the United States has to be given credit for recognizing wrongs and making efforts to correct this. Some have said that laws may force people to do certain things, however, they do not change people's opinions and attitudes. In this particular situation of race relationships this belief and assumption, in my opinion, is wrong. Laws that required Americans and others of all ethnicities and races to attend public schools together may not have changed the minds and attitudes of the most diehard bigots; however, over time sons and daughters and grandchildren of those opposed to integration of public schools and eating establishments, to mention only two, learned that persons of different ethnic and/or racial backgrounds were not what their parents had portrayed them to be; they were more like themselves than they were different.

A result of this forced integration we are seeing more civil interactions and relationships than has occurred in past years. Children, as they played and learned together, realized that regardless of racial/ethnic identity they were more alike than they were different and that friendship did not have to had color boundaries. This learning experience has carried over to employment, religious services and marriage, to mention only three evolutionary changes in American society.

Conclusion

The greatness of the United States, and any country, depends upon its population continually evaluating its policies, attitudes, views and ways of treating its people as well as others, both human and otherwise, and changing discriminatory and oppressive thinking and behaviors. This author recognizes that this is often not an easy process, but it is a necessary process. Just as we thought certain types of thinking, attitudes, and behavior fifty years ago were appropriate and acceptable, which have proven to be inappropriate, discriminatory and repressive to our current ways of thinking, fifty years from now we will find some of our current thinking and actions are repressive and inappropriate. In summary, the greatness of any country is its willingness to think through its problems and issues and to evolve its thinking and actions to be more humane and in this way become a more whole and just culture.

References

Branch, L., Harris, D., & Palmore, E. B. (2005). *Encyclopedia of ageism.* Philadelphia: Haworth Press

Cavico, F. J., & Mujtaba, B. G. (2011). Discrimination and the aging American workforce: Recommendations and strategies for management. *SAM Advanced Management Journal,* 76(4), 15–26.

Dayna, L. (2013). *Gay marriage: It matters.* Unpublished paper, University of Oklahoma.

Harcourt, M., Wood, G., & Wilkinson, A. (2008). Age discrimination in the evaluation of job applicants. *Journal of Applied Social Psychology, 43*(1), 35–44.

Harcourt, M., Wood, G., & Wilkinson, A. (2008). Age discrimination and work life: Perspectives and contestations–A review of the contemporary literature. *International Journal of management Reviews, 10*(4), 425–442.

McAdoo, H. P. (1999). *The ethnic socialization of Chinese American children. In family ethnicity strengths in diversity* (2nd ed.). Thousand Oaks, CA: Sage.

Moore, M. (2013). *Ageism in America.* Unpublished student paper, University of Oklahoma.

Norris, M. (2013). *The migrant worker.* Unpublished student paper, University of Oklahoma.

Pyong G. M. (1995). *Asian Americans: Contemporary trends and issues.* Thousand Oaks, CA: Sage.

Richardson, B., Smith, K., Webb, J., & Webber, L. (2013). Age discrimination in the evaluation of job applicants. *Journal of Applied Social Psychology, 43*(1), 35–44.

NAME INDEX

SUBJECT INDEX